                                    continued inside back cover

ADAPTATION IN SCHIZOPHRENIA

The Theory of Segmental Set

ADAPTATION IN SCHIZOPHRENIA

The Theory of Segmental Set

DAVID SHAKOW
National Institute of Mental Health

A WILEY–INTERSCIENCE PUBLICATION

JOHN WILEY & SONS, New York • Chichester • Brisbane • Toronto

Library of Congress Cataloging in Publication Data:

Shakow, David, 1901-
    Adaptation in schizophrenia.

    (Wiley series on personality processes)
    "A Wiley-Interscience publication."
    Includes index.
    1. Schizophrenia.   2. Set (Psychology)   I. Title.
[DNLM: 1. Adaptation, Psychological.
2. Schizophrenic psychology.   3. Set (Psychology)
WM203.3 S527a]
RC514.S44   616.8'982   79-14979
ISBN 0-471-05756-8

Printed in the United States of America

10 9 8 7 6 5 4 3 2 1

To Sophie

Series Preface

This series of books is addressed to behavioral scientists interested in the nature of human personality. Its scope should prove pertinent to personality theorists and researchers as well as to clinicians concerned with applying an understanding of personality processes to the amelioration of emotional difficulties in living. To this end, the series provides a scholarly integration of theoretical formulations, empirical data, and practical recommendations.

Six major aspects of studying and learning about human personality can be designated: personality theory, personality structure and dynamics, personality development, personality assessment, personality change, and personality adjustment. In exploring these aspects of personality, the books in the series discuss a number of distinct but related subject areas: the nature and implications of various theories of personality; personality characteristics that account for consistencies and variations in human behavior; the emergence of personality processes in children and adolescents; the use of interviewing and testing procedures to evaluate individual differences in personality; efforts to modify personality styles through psychotherapy, counseling, behavior therapy, and other methods of influence; and patterns of abnormal personality functioning that impair individual competence.

IRVING B. WEINER

University of Denver
Denver, Colo

David Shakow: An Appreciation

It is my impression that David Shakow comes as close as anyone to being psychology's equivalent of the renaissance man. Perhaps the best way to substantiate this is to note some of the titles of his articles that span 50 years:

The Psychological Department in a State Hospital (1930)

Psychological Avenues of Approach to Schizophrenia (1934)

Psychology: Its Contribution to Psychiatry and Mental Hygiene (1942)

Some Aspects of the Problem of Unsuccessful Personality Screening (1943)

The Carbohydrate Tolerance of Mentally Disturbed Soldiers (1944)

Some Hypotheses Concerning Psychology and Learning (1949)

Psychology and its Relations with Other Professions (1952)

Some Aspects of Mid-century Psychiatry: Experimental Psychology (1953)

The Psychological System (1956)

Comparison of Psychological and Group Foci (1956)

Artificial Limbs: Their Human Owners (1956)

Psychotherapy Research and the Problem of Intrusions on Privacy (1958)

How Phylogenetically Older Parts of the Brain Relate to Behavior (1958)

Sound Motion Picture Facilities for Research in Communication (1966)

On the Rewards (and, alas, Frustrations) of Public Service (1968)

Clinical Psychology as Science and Profession: A Forty-Year Odyssey (1969)

Psychoanalysis and American Psychology (1969)

Patterns of Institutional Sponsorship (1971)

The Education of the Mental Health Researcher: Encouraging Potential Development in Man (1972)

These, and more than a hundred other of his books and articles, do not represent a mere patchwork quilt of isolated studies and opinions, but are all part of an attempt to achieve an integrated view of psychology, especially of the human condition, in states of normality and disequilibrium. He has concentrated his research efforts on schizophrenia, not only because it is such a seriously unbalancing disorder but also because he could see normality in schizophrenia, and because from a deeper understanding of this disorder one might hope to shed light on the condition we call normality.

Shakow began his professional career as Chief Psychologist and Director of Psychological Research at the Worcester State Hospital. There he initiated two lifelong commitments: he introduced one of the nation's first internship programs in clinical psychology, and he pioneered in the systematic application of experimental methods to the study of psychopathology. Later, directing his energies and leadership to national affairs, he served with distinction as President of the Clinical Division of the American Psychological Association, and as consultant to the Veterans Administration, the National Research Council, and the National Institutes of Health. Following World War II, he headed a task force to set national standards for training clinical psychologists. The recommendations of that task force guided the development of training programs in clinical psychology in most American universities during the next two decades. Standards established by the group are still recognized by licensing agencies as a basis for admitting psychologists to clinical practice.

Shakow was one of the foremost pioneers to apply the techniques of the psychological laboratory to the experimental analysis of schizophrenic disorder. Because of his lead, in good part, literally thousands of studies in a similar vein have since been carried out in the past four decades, contributing greatly to our understanding of the psychological aspects of schizophrenia.

Whereas many scientists have lost faith in the value or meaning of classical subtypes in schizophrenia, Shakow has stressed their importance, veridicality, and diagnostic assessment, and has discovered differences between them in many test situations. His finding of numerous significant differences between paranoids and hebephrenics has inspired much current research that supports his findings and contributes importantly to our understanding of the different forms of schizophrenic illness.

He made the most detailed and thorough experimental analysis ever done of the nature of *deterioration* in schizophrenia, the original hallmark of the disease, and evaluated this concept in terms of capacity, capability, ability, and achievement, to reveal the particular nature of the performance deficits found.

He developed the concept of *normalizing trends* in schizophrenia, in which initial performance deficits disappear with repetition, a finding that seems to have relevance to the discovery, in recent clinical studies, of normalizing trends in schizophrenics as they grow older.

He was among the first scientists to document experimentally that schizophrenics manifest no deficit in simple sensory or physiological functioning, and indicated for the rest of us that the deficit would have to be found at a more complex level of integrative functioning.

He pointed out how research on schizophrenia has contributed so importantly to our understanding of normal psychological functioning.

In a broader sense, especially in his capacity as President of the American Psychological Association's Division of Clinical Psychology and as Chairman of the Committee on Training in Clinical Psychology during the Post World War II period, Shakow more than any other person has shaped the course, mode, style, and direction of research on psychological aspects of mental health and illness for at least one full generation. Similarly, as Chief Psychologist and Director of Psychological Research at the Worcester State Hospital in its heyday, as Chief Psychologist at the Illinois Neuropsychiatric Institute, and as the first Chief of the Laboratory of Psychology, NIMH, for 12 years, he was a major influence on the training of mental health researchers and on the directions of mental health research.

The major theme of Shakow's research has been the psychological aspects of schizophrenic behavior, a theme he pioneered and has continued to focus on to this day. This theme has instigated and stimulated a major role for psychologists in carrying out research on all forms of psychopathology, and in the process has provided psychology with a sound basis for studying and understanding *normal* behavior.

DAVID ROSENTHAL

Bethesda, Maryland
March 1979

Preface

One of the most troublesome dilemmas faced by the investigator of schizophrenia is the reconciliation of the contrasts between the complexities presented by an inscrutable and multifaceted clinical patient before him, and the patent simplicities and poverty of the data that his experimental or even his more molar clinical approach provides (to say nothing of what the mere process of "observing" or "studying" does to introduce distortions in the normal as well as in the pathological material!—cf. Wheeler [1974]). Unless he is willing to abandon his customary methods of attack, he cannot but accept such limitations in his data and endeavor to make his approach as comprehensive as possible, while being mindful always of Hamlet's admonition. As for the deductions to be made from his data, he must be even more sensitive about the inherent limits enjoined by his methodological approach. The combination of experimental and clinical procedures is a partially tolerable solution to this dilemma that has been cogently supported by Romano (1976).

It is in the context of this quandary that I approach the discussion of the generalizations involved in formulating the principles of set, which I consider central to a psychological understanding of schizophrenia. By presenting a detailed exposition of the set concept, I hope to provide a systematic framework for examining the multifarious symptoms and characteristics of schizophrenia.

I believe that the study of set pathology in schizophrenia may further elucidate the psychology of the normal set process (Shakow, 1968), just as the study of neurological disorders has contributed to our knowledge of normal central nervous system functioning. In this monograph I examine the normal and particularly the pathological processes of perception and response that constitute generalized and segmental set, which requires a close analysis of the stimulus/response process. The pathological stimulus/response process in schizophrenia is described, particularly with regard to the bipolarity of responses, and is then explained in terms of the theory of segmental set. I believe that segmental set may be considered the fundamental determinant of the clinical symptoms and experimental aberrancies exhibited by the schizophrenic. Whereas it may be true that the principles of segmental set are applicable to other types of psychopathology (some of which I mention), I believe that their application to the understanding of schizophrenia is far more significant. Although this theory is developed more thoroughly here than ever before, it is still in hypothetical form, having many unexplored areas needing refinement, elaboration, and analysis.

The theory of set in schizophrenia presented here has been developed through decades of research by multidisciplinary teams of investigators, including myself at Worcester State Hospital and the National Institutes of Health, as described in Chapter 2. In explicating the theory of segmental set, I draw primarily on data from this research at Worcester and at NIMH. Ideally, the vast body of experimental and clinical literature (integrated with this theory) would be explicitly garnered for support in these pages. This enormously complex task is not undertaken, although I believe that a good part of the pertinent data supports the theory.

The preparation of this volume was in part aided by a grant from the Benevolent Foundation of Scottish Rite Freemasonry, Northern Jurisdiction, U.S.A. The people who have contributed to the theory of segmental set are many, but I must make special mention of Paul Huston and Eliot Rodnick, from the days at the Worcester State Hospital, and David Rosenthal and Theodore Zahn at NIMH, who have contributed considerably to its development. John Romano has contributed in other ways. Above all, I wish to acknowledge Ann Masten, who has conscientiously worked and reworked this manuscript. Not only has she tackled stylistic and syntactical idiosyncracies, but she has asked the searching questions that led to considerable clarification of the application and the implications of the theory. To her I owe more than I can repay.

David Shakow

Bethesda, Maryland
April 1979

Contents

CHAPTER 1

Introduction

Quite early in my association with psychology, the problem of attention and the ubiquity of its expression began to intrigue me.[1] Indeed, this interest was initially aroused over half a century ago by the first psychology text I used at Harvard, Pillsbury's *Essentials of Psychology* (1921), in a course I had during freshman year with Langfeld. Somewhat later, between undergraduate and graduate study, when I spent 15 months as assistant to Grace Kent at the Worcester State Hospital, I was further struck by the aberrations in attending, both involuntary and voluntary, revealed by the psychotic, particularly schizophrenic, patients with whom I was in daily contact.[2]

After graduate study,[3] I returned to the Worcester State Hospital to begin an extended period of intensive involvement in a research program on schizophrenia (Shakow, 1972). Early in this Worcester period (1928–1931), attention and the related but broader concept of "set" began to take on even greater importance. Here, it seemed to me, was an activity central to all of the other psychological functions that were markedly affected in these patients.

An important, though indirect, influence on the developing interest of our Worcester group in the topic of set came from William J. Crozier, the general physiologist. As a graduate student, I had taken his Zoology course, "The Analysis of Conduct," the first time it was offered. Crozier's preference for studying the organism as a whole (intact and undisturbed), rather than following the pattern then standard in physiology of studying segments of the organism, impressed me greatly. Shortly after my return to Worcester, the *Foundations of Experimental Psychology* (Murchison, 1929) appeared, with a notable contribution by Crozier on "The Study of Living Organisms." A major emphasis of this chapter, which was similar to his course, was its discussion of variability, particularly the distinction between intrinsic and extrinsic variability. Since variability, so strikingly present in schizophrenia (and, for us, obviously related to set), had already become one of our special concerns, we were deeply influenced by his discussion.

By then, one of the psychological areas we had decided to investigate was reaction time. We chose this technique because it allowed for the study of an individual under simple conditions subject to fairly rigorous measurement, as well as provided an excellent vehicle for the study of variability. The study of reaction time involved us directly in the problems of attention and alertness and led naturally to more extended considerations of set.

[1] William James, " . . . consciousness is at all times primarily a selecting agency." (*Principles of Psychology*, Vol. I, 1890, p. 139).

[2] What a difference the 50 or so years since then have made! This was brought home to me by the Rochester/Scottish Rite Conference on Attention and Information Processing held at the end of the Second Rochester International Conference on Schizophrenia in 1976 (Wynne, Cromwell, and Matthysse, *The Nature of Schizophrenia*, 1978).

[3] I did not, however, obtain the Ph.D. at this time. It may interest the historically oriented student that the topic I had selected and worked on during the 1926–1928 period for my doctoral dissertation, under Edwin G. Boring, was intrinsically related to attention. I was investigating the hypothesis that peripheral stimuli of borderline intensity ("subliminal") could distort the psychometric function in the areas of lifted weights and brightness discrimination. Unfortunately, 2 years of experimentation yielded inconclusive results. Because family considerations had become paramount, I abandoned further efforts to obtain the degree at that time and accepted the Worcester appointment then being offered. It was some 14 years later, at the urgings of Gordon Allport and Boring, that I returned to Cambridge for the degree, with a dissertation on schizophrenia (Shakow, 1946).

Our study of reaction time was part of a carefully organized multidisciplinary experimental program at Worcester to study schizophrenic behavior, ranging from the biological through the sociological. We started with the assumption, arrogant perhaps, that there was little definitive experimental knowledge available about schizophrenia. In this context, our psychological program deliberately sampled behavior at different levels of complexity, from the simplest impersonal level, as exemplified by patellar tendon reflex latent time, to behavior in group situations, such as competition and cooperation, as well as in personal, affective situations, such as behavior under stress.

Our first published mention of set appeared in a paper by Huston on direct current threshold (1934, p. 592). It happened to be the first paper accepted for publication of the many deriving from the large number of tests and experiments (including several reaction time experiments) that we were engaged in during this early period. The concept of set was already involved in our formulations, having played a considerable role in the planning of our research program. In my thinking about the schizophrenia problem over the years, the concept of set has continued to serve as a significant theoretical construct in conceptualizing the process of schizophrenia.

The fundamental conceptualization of set by my colleagues at Worcester and myself thus developed gradually from an extended series of studies collected over several decades of a wide range of psychological functions. Concentrated clinical observation of patients over long periods provided us with relatively detailed records of their development. Because practically all of our investigations in schizophrenia involved repeated studies on the *same* patients, patients belonging to carefully defined and selected samples of various types of schizophrenia (frequently with controls from other disorders, and almost always from normal groups), we had the unique opportunity to make comparative and differential studies of set over time.

The diagnostic process we used at Worcester is followed explicitly and implicitly in all my writings on schizophrenia, because to my knowledge it was the most carefully carried out group examination and analysis of the diagnostic process in large scale research on schizophrenia that had ever been attempted (and in some respects, that has been attempted since). At Worcester great care was taken to arrive at adequate classifications of both schizophrenia and subtype in each of the three different stages in the process of diagnosis: a) the accurate description of the phenomena exhibited by the patient, b) the syndromization of these collected descriptions, and c) the process of assigning patients to different categories. Because of the care, repeated diagnoses, and particularly, the competence of the group making the diagnoses, I believe the classifications were unusually reliable. In addition, the classifications were made when the patients were free of drugs, which I believe added to the "authenticity" of diagnosis. Appendix A describes in detail the process of diagnosis at Worcester.[4]

It is of interest that the proposed DSM-III operational criteria for a schizophrenic disorder (Spitzer et al., 1975; Strauss, 1975), still in the process of being developed, do not differ essentially from the Worcester criteria (given in the Appendix) developed during the thirties. If consideration is given to the fact that our criteria were developed on a population that was largely chronic, the proposed DSM-III phenomenological subtypes and ours correspond quite well:

DSM-III	*Worcester State Hospital*
Disorganized (hebephrenic)	Hebephrenic
Catatonic	Catatonic

---

[4] The International Pilot Study on Schizophrenia (Strauss, Carpenter, and Bartko, 1976) is also of interest in this context, as is the monograph on the topic by Frank (1975), which brings the classification/diagnostic problem up to that date. The spectrum diagnosis of schizophrenia reflects a radical and distinct advance in the diagnostic problem in that it recognizes the continuum that exists in schizophrenia and schizophreniclike psychosis (Rosenthal, 1975). See also *Psychiatirc Diagnosis* (Rakoff, Stancer, and Kedward, Eds., 1977), which is relevant in this respect.

Paranoid	Paranoid
subtypes	not specified
Confusional—turmoil	Acute
(Schizo-affective, depressed)	Not used by us, except on rare occasion, because we
(Schizo-affective, manic)	tried to keep our schizophrenic group "pure."
Mixed	Mixed
	Unclassified
Residual	Late indeterminate[5]

But it is particularly the paranoid/hebephrenic distinction that I wish to emphasize. In recent years a great deal of stress has been placed on the distinction between the paranoid and nonparanoid "other subtypes" of schizophrenia. Actually, this distinction originated over 40 years ago with the long-neglected (unpublished) study by C. E. Hall (1933), which was perhaps the earliest experimental analysis of these differences. Nevertheless, I believe that it is the hebephrenic that must be isolated from "other types" and contrasted with the paranoid, for the hebephrenic has a distinctive profile, and combining other subtypes with it dilutes the differences from the paranoid subtype.

[5] At Worcester, where we recognized the existence of such a condition, we instituted an additional subtype classification for marked presence of this characteristic state. When the florid symptoms were not apparent, we called the patients "late indeterminate." In such states the patients assumed a passivity that made for "good" adjustment in the hospital vocations and general behavior although largely limiting total responsiveness.

CHAPTER 2

History of
Set Concept

The discussion of set that follows is based primarily on my own background in psychopathology, since the concept has rarely been approached outside both its normal manifestations and observed behavior. One of the few exceptions to be considered is the work of the Georgian school of Uznadze. Otherwise the historical discussion is limited to a selective review of a few sources that have particularly influenced my conceptualization of set. For further detail and references, I recommend the essay on the theoretical history of set in the British and American literature by Ann Masten Appendix C (unpublished, 1976).

The concept of set, as I have indicated, is inextricably woven into that of attention. In recent decades, not only has attention acquired a new lease on life, but "set" has also regained prominence. The resurgence of set is exemplified in America particularly in the publications of Floyd Allport (1955), his predecessors Davis (1940, 1946) and G. L. Freeman (1939, 1940b, 1948), and in those of Bruner and Postman, who proposed the directive-state and hypothesis theories of perception (Bruner, 1951; Bruner and Goodman, 1947; Bruner and Postman, 1949; Postman, 1951).[1]

---

[1] There may be a second resurgence of set in the information processing movement in cognitive psychology. (See Neisser, 1967 and Kahneman, 1973.)

Extending Head's (1920) concept of the schema, Bartlett (1932), the major figure in the British revival, generated a number of investigations in this area. In France, Piaget's work resulted in numerous studies, especially in the area of developmental psychology. In Russia, the early studies of the Georgian school of Uznadze (1966) are prominent. This revival has occurred despite the many ambiguities in the concept pointed out in the searching review of set by Gibson (1941).

Although one could certainly find earlier statements relevant to set in the history of psychological literature, I shall not attempt to go back before Lewes and James. The literature on the Wurzburg school's concepts of *Einstellung, determinierende tendenz* and *Bewusstseinslage* is well known and covered fully in Titchener (1909), Boring (1950), and Murphy and Kovach (1972).

G. H. Lewes, in his *Problems of Life and Mind* (1880, Vol. III), discusses "preperception," a term that appears to have appealed greatly to William James. By this term Lewes means the "revival of many past experiences . . . *the escort of nascent states* which accompanies a sensation . . ." (emphasis added, p. 107). By including the "pre" in preperception, Lewes suggests that the "escort" precedes the perception, which must be "prepared for, *pre*conceived, and . . . by its congruity . . . may become the ground of its acceptance" (p. 108). James interpreted this process as a kind of "lying in wait" for impressions (1890, Vol. I, p. 439), a "premonitory imagination."

For James, "the intimate nature of the attentive process" involved: "1.) the accommodation or adjustment of the sensory organs; and 2.) the anticipatory preparation from within of the ideational centres concerned with the object to which the attention is paid" (1890, Vol. I, p. 434). Following his consideration of these two factors, James adds, some pages later: "So much for adjustment and preperception. The only third process I can think of as always present is the *inhibition* of irrelevant movements and ideas" (emphasis added, p. 445). This last is an important element of attention, one that Freud, as we shall shortly see, developed more fully in his concept of

Reizschutz (1920). For James, then, the important aspects of the attentive process are adjustment of sensory organs, pre-perception, and inhibition of the irrelevant. James remarks further, by paraphrasing Helmholtz' law of inattention:

We leave all impressions unnoticed which are valueless to us as signs by which to discriminate things . . . And all this is due to an inveterate habit we have contracted of passing from them immediately to their import and letting their substantive nature alone. (p. 456)

This "law of inattention" and James' concept of "ignoring" are important when dealing with schizophrenics. But, where Helmholtz says "unnoticed," the schizophrenic would require the substitution of *noticed;* the irrelevant takes on major importance.[2] Sullivan, in his concept of "selective inattention" (1953) comes close to this idea. I shall come back to this issue in more detail in a later section.

Having directed attention to this early background of principles related to set in Lewes and James, let me merely add some points about Freud and the Russian school of Uznadze. I mention them because they are likely to be neglected in the consideration of set. For the detailed discussion of British authors Head and Bartlett, and American authors Dashiell, Davis, Freeman, Bruner, Postman, Werner, Kaplan, and F. Allport, I again refer the reader to Masten's essay (unpublished, 1976). (A brief resume of the essay is provided in Appendix C.)

Despite the fact that I am not considering the traditional German literature, I want at least to discuss briefly a contribution from Freud, who is neither in the academic tradition nor in any formal way associated with the topic of set *per se,* but

---

[2] In his studies of Average Evoked Response (AER) (1975), M. Buchsbaum attempts to deal quantitatively with the intensity of sensory activity. He observes that the "averaging technique is adequate for general purposes and for partialling out the random effects of background noise." The danger in the case of the schizophrenic is that "deliberate" choices of irrelevant stimuli (which define the conduct of the schizophrenic) will *also* be eliminated. A technique must be found to distinguish between background noise, which is irrelevant, and such "deliberate" choices, which are relevant.

who nevertheless made a major contribution to this area. What James labels as the third constituent of the attention process, Freud, in the course of his speculations in *Beyond the Pleasure Principle* (1920, pp. 27 ff.) refers to as *Reizschutz*, the protective shield against stimuli. In this article, Freud points out that "Protection *against* stimuli is an almost more important function of the living organism than *reception of* stimuli" (emphasis added). As we shall see, the concept of inhibition is essential for understanding the process of set formation.

In the Soviet Union, the Georgian school of Uznadze (1966) is preeminent for its systematic experimental studies of set in both normal and pathological groups.[3] This school has been almost entirely disregarded by American (and British) authors. Gibson (1941) does not mention them; neither do Freeman (1939) and Davis (1946). Even Allport (1955), despite his otherwise comprehensive consideration of the topic of set, does not. Such oversight is perhaps not to be wondered at, because as Cole and Maltzman (1969, p. 603) indicate, there has been a similar neglect of this Tbilisi school by other Russian psychologists. It might be pointed out that the obverse is also true—the Georgians have paid no attention to the American and British literature on set.

Uznadze defines set as an integral state of readiness of the organism that is the precursor of *all* activity. His basic experimental technique is to present to a subject (who has been instructed to discriminate between pairs of discrepant stimuli) a series of stimuli clearly different in the amount they possess

---

[3] With respect to this school, I should note that in September 1929, I attended the Ninth International Congress of Psychology in New Haven. A paper by Usnadze, "*Einstellungsumschlag als Grundlage der Kontrasttauschungen*," was listed for the September 8th session. It was, however, read by title only; apparently Uznadze did not participate personally. In any event, I did not attend the session for which it was scheduled. When the abstracts of the Congress appeared approximately one year later, the opportunity was afforded me to become acquainted with Uznadze's abstract, which apparently represented one of his early publications on the topic of set. I have no recollection of having read it at the time. If I had, my attention might have been turned to the topic somewhat earlier than was actually the case.

of a particular dimension (e.g., size, brightness, etc.) in order to habituate him. Then, without warning, the experimenter changes the situation by presenting the subject with identical stimuli. Despite the altered stimulus situation, some 75% of the subjects apparently continue to make the original judgment.[4] This method has been applied widely to different modalities and to different types of subjects of various ages with the same general results. Uznadze suggests that the setting "creates" a need for solution (a "quasi-need," in Lewinian terms) and that the subject, when presented with the new situation, attempts to meet the need under the influence of an "illusion" created by the previously established *fixated set*. What follows is a continuation of the original judgmental attitude. A set fixated in one sensory modality may be transferred to other modalities; it is then a set of the subject as a whole.

In theorizing about set from this original experimental setting, Uznadze stresses, as a basic proposition, the causal role of set's unitary, central, and dynamic nature in behavior. As Herzog and Hritzuk (1968) phrase it: "set is a psychological phenomenon *sui generis;* it forms the basis for the emergence of consciousness; and it is the dynamic structural unit of the integral personality into which all activity of the organism is incorporated" (p. 452).[5] As Uznadze himself says at the end of his "Essay on Basic Principles of the Theory of Set" (1966):

Thus, human psychology is built on the principles of the activity of man as a whole—on the principle of his set. The so-called "mental functions" of man—observation, imagination, and attention—like his thought and his will, are only differentiated mental properties modifying his set.[6] (p. 247).

[4] The reader will recognize in this technique the old childhood game of "MacFarland, MacNamara . . . MacHine."
[5] In the context of this Russian contribution, it is useful to keep in mind another, that of the "functional barrier" about which Luria hypothesized (1932) over four decades ago. This appears to provide, on the motor side of human activity, a structure that *Reizschutz* provides on the sensory side.
[6] It might be pointed out that Uznadze and Bassin's (1969) tendency to consider the unconscious set a *negative* concept does not stand up (pp. 98 ff.). However, it is a minor consideration in the context of the whole, and I shall not pursue it.

CHAPTER 3

The Problems of Defining Set

As dictionaries attest, definitions have been bountifully be-
stowed upon the term "set". In fact, the *Guinness Book of
Records* considers it "the most overworked word in English."
(McWhirter and McWhirter, 1977, p. 201). Webster's *Unabridged* (1944) devotes six columns to one form or another of
the word, whereas the *Oxford English Dictionary* (1933) provides over 10 times as many—75 columns! [1] It is true that the
word "set" in these dictionaries covers a range far beyond
the psychological denotations, but there is still a sufficiency of
psychologically related definitions. Warren's *Dictionary of
Psychology* (1934) provides five definitions (about one third of
a column), and English and English (1958) provides approximately three columns of definitions. It is understandable why

[1] In a review of K. M. Elizabeth Murray's *Caught in the Web of Words*
(Yale, 1977), Steiner comments:

> The longest entry of all turns out to be "set," and here the treatment by
> Henry Bradley, who was to succeed Murray as the editor, amounts to lit-
> tle less than a miniature treatise on crucial social, philosophical, and
> scientific aspects of the Western imagination. (*The New Yorker*, Nov. 21,
> 1977)

Mark Van Doren, in describing his relationship with James Thurber, writes:

> Sometimes we would go upstairs to the room where he worked, just the
> two of us, and go through his O. E. D. together. He was proud of that
> handsome set . . . ."set"—that word has one of the longest entries in the
> O. E. D., fifty-four columns of nouns, verbs, adjectives, I think. That
> was what fascinated Thurber. I would read him the "set" definitions for
> hours on end. He depended on words for entertainment. Jim constantly
> had words dancing before him . . . (Bernstein, 1975, p. 376)

Werner and Kaplan (1963) retreat into suggesting another term for set. Despite the specificity of their term, "dynamic schematization," I must say that I am more inclined to go along with Dashiell, who argues for sticking with "just the simple but accurate Anglo-Saxon word 'set' " (1940, p. 300). For me, at least, there is an appealing nostalgic quality in the word.

No discussion of set can neglect the classic paper by Gibson (1941).[2] In this lucid and cogent analysis, Gibson points out that there are at least eight different meanings of set in the experimental literature, involving many ambiguities and contradictions. My attitude toward this criticism has been to take cognizance of it and to try to clarify the issues in my own utilization of the term. If, as I believe, we cannot get along without the concept because it contributes significantly to the understanding of normal and pathological behavior, it is incumbent upon me to (a) define what it is, (b) specify what it is not, and (c) describe what it subsumes at different levels of psychological response. For example, with respect to what Gibson considers the "most crucial ambiguities" (1941, p. 811)—the relation of set to past experiences or habits and its voluntary or involuntary character—my thinking has led me to believe that set is undoubtedly determined by both past experience and present exigencies, and is a system in which voluntary and involuntary classes of conduct both have a place. I shall attempt to meet some of Gibson's strictures by specifying what I include in the concept of set.

Another aspect of the difficulties of defining set derives from the use of such an all-encompassing term as set, when it is proposed to account for a broad range of psychological phenomena. A concept pervading so much of the behavioral spectrum appears at first glance to be not only pretentious but, by its very compass, doomed to failure as an explanatory principle. Any concept applied so widely to the complexities of human behavior should be held suspect at first and be forced to run the gauntlet of double scrutiny. The problem of

[2]Although he acknowledges his debt to Gibson's article, Floyd Allport (1955) does not examine Gibson critically in his insightful and otherwise thorough development of the concept of set.

the comprehensive explanatory usage of set will be implicitly considered in the discussion to follow.

The origins of set lie in its integral relationship to attention. Attending, the ongoing awareness of the outer or inner environment leading to active choice and emphasis on selected aspects of the range or qualities of stimuli to which the individual is responding or will respond, is basic to cognitive functioning.[3] Because of its indispensability, attending must be considered a fundamental biological characteristic on the order of "irritability" and "responsivity." It is difficult to conceive of any organism sustaining itself in its surroundings if it does not have an apparatus for developing awareness of both the presence of life-supporting and life-destroying stimuli. Such a potentiality is built into the organism on a constitutional genetic basis and then, with further development by maturation, conditioning, learning, and experience, becomes a fundamental device for dealing with both its outer and inner worlds. Biologically, it would seem that natural selection must favor organisms that attend most effectively. "Set" appears to be the mechanism nature has provided to make attending more efficient, enabling the organism to adapt more effectively to the increasing complexities of its expanding and changing environment. Set presumes the existence of *structures* that obviate the necessity of a new act of attending with each change in sensation or response, but nevertheless allows for continuing change. These structures are inferred from the organized disposition of attention, a quality of information processing that is being explored at length in cognitive psychology in general and in the study of schizophrenic processes. Two conferences evidence the interest in information processing with regard to schizophrenia: the Donders Centenary Symposium on Reaction Time held at Eindhoven, The Netherlands (July 29 through Aug. 2, 1968; reported in *Acta Psychologica*, Vol. 30, 1969) and the Scottish Rite Conference at the Second Rochester International Conference on Schizophrenia (May 3–6, 1976), including the session on Attention and Information Processing (May 6th) (Wynne, Cromwell, and Matthysse, 1978).

---

[3]See James' chapter on Attention in *The Principles of Psychology* (1890)

CHAPTER 4

Theory of Segmental Set

INTRODUCTION

Bipolarity has been described as an outstanding characteristic of schizophrenic behavior that results in extraordinary variability. Bleuler (1950) emphasizes the prominent swings and oscillations in schizophrenic behavior, and includes ambivalence (including ambitendency) as one of the fundamental symptoms. Indeed, if there is any notion prominent in Bleuler's work, it is of this swinging, which reaches its apex in the excited and mute states of catatonia. Two subtypes I have emphasized, the paranoid and the hebephrenic, represent psychosis at either end of this spectrum. Whereas the hebephrenic tends to process and respond to information in a superficial, simplified, overcontentual, confused, and loose way, the paranoid processes information in an overly specified, complex, overorganized and rigid way.[1]

[1]The process of ambivalence (and ambitendency) must be considered when the normal movement is toward the center of the distribution of the trait. When the normal response is over on either end, as in such traits as planfulness, level of organization, and logical sequence, the schizophrenic responses will fall on one side of the distribution.

A case in point is found in our play technique experiment. The experiment was carried out in a specially designed playroom by Shakow and Rosenzweig (1937) at the Worcester State Hospital. The room had one-way mirrors through which subjects were observed. The following instructions were given (pointing to the dolls, furniture, and blocks):

14

The source of bipolarity lies in the loss of central control, the failure of the basic integrating and balancing function. Bipolarity may occur in either the separable and identifiable aspects of the personality or in their "integrated" functioning. This characteristic of schizophrenic response supports the theory that a basic modulating mechanism in the schizophrenic system is not working properly. My hypothesis is that *generalized set* is not available to him. During schizophrenic episodes it has been replaced by *segmental set*, a pathological state of set functioning.

I am making a study of imagination and want you to help me out by constructing (putting together, building) on the table here (E. points to construction table) a scene showing something dramatic, exciting, or important happening in the life of a child. Go about doing this in any way you like. Use as many or as few of the things as you wish but try to show in the scene that you construct how something exciting or important is happening in the life of a child. I am going to leave you alone while you are building the scene so that you may work in any way you like. I will come back later to see whether you have finished. Take all the time that you need. (Pause.) Are there any questions that you wish to ask?

The instructions were amplified or repeated when necessary in order to assure optimum comprehension, the subject was left alone, and his behavior was observed.

The results showed that in characteristics such as planfulness, level of organization, and logical sequence, and, to a somewhat lesser extent in the sparing use of material and articulation, the normal's responses were at one extreme, the paranoid's were in between, and the hebephrenic's responses were at the other end. In fussiness and spontaneous personal reference the hebephrenic was in the middle, with the normal and paranoid at either end (the paranoid displaying a greater degree of both characteristics). The hebephrenic had the highest score in exploring, touching, and incidental activity and, to a somewhat lesser extent, in palpating, with the paranoid second. The exception was in incidental activity, where the paranoid was third. The one area where the paranoids distinguished themselves was in rigidity in interpretation of objects. There was a fundamental distinction between the three groups—the paranoids were most extreme at one end and the hebephrenics most extreme at the other. And, in another respect, only the paranoids showed a concern about disposal of the construction when the experiment was over. Thus the experiment shows the ways in which normals and schizophrenics distinguish themselves along a continuum and at the same time shows how paranoids and hebephrenics display other traits that are extremes of the normal.

GENERALIZED SET

I have come to think of generalized set as the kind of adjustment (conscious, preconscious, and unconscious) that disposes a person to perceive a situation objectively and to respond equally objectively, in an autonomous fashion. Underlying it, to paraphrase Floyd Allport, is a set of overwhelming strength to perceive accurately and to respond effectively (Allport, 1955, p. 417). "Generalized" or "major" sets are called such because the minor or irrelevant individual aspects of the stimulus/response process, the ones that first come to the fore in all situations, have been partialled out to leave only the principal aspects, those relevant to accurate perceptions and to effective responses. A conceptual process has taken place in which various degrees of schematizing and hierarchical structuring of sets and schemata are involved (See Appendix C or Masten, unpublished, 1976).

Bound into the very fiber of generalized set are the varied features of specific, appropriately *adaptive* responses. These derive from both the transient and persistent integrative structures of the cognitive/conative/affective components basic to information processing, motor control, and personality functioning. The level of generality achieved is the one needed for the most effective response to the task.

For example, in the typical clinical interview we might ask a specific question: "Where were you yesterday evening?" The subject defines "yesterday evening," reviews what he did on the particular day and time so defined, and then responds relevantly to the question. Or, in a typical reaction time experiment, the subject is instructed to respond to a certain stimulus, a yellow light, but not a red light, as quickly as possible. This results in a readiness to respond which, when triggered by the appearance of the yellow stimulus, results in the necessary movement for response—the removal of the finger from the telegraph key. If a red signal appears, the subject is prepared to inhibit the response. In either case we have a generalized set; the subject forms a correct "hypothesis" and acts upon it promptly.

Broadly viewed, the *cognitive* aspects of major set include a general receptivity to input, receptivity to specific stimuli following the appropriate attentional processes of sensory adjustment, perception and inhibition of the irrelevant, and a receptivity to hypothetical situations. Openness to a wide range of input includes alertness to, curiosity about, and active seeking out of new stimuli provided by the environment. This preparatory state is oriented as well to the inner world. Receptivity to specific stimuli requires discrimination between the focal and the irrelevant, and between the abstract and the concrete, following appropriate scanning and articulation of the figure from the ground.

Affectively, the major set includes appropriate types and degrees of emotional involvement with general stimulation and specific stimuli. Whether the stimuli have personal or impersonal connotations, suitable degrees of affect color the response.

Conatively, response is properly modulated in nature and strength for individual stimuli and for consecutive stimuli. There is freedom from perseveration and appropriate automatization (habituation). These constituents must be considered in the context of the total personality organization, both of the moment and over time.

When generalized set prevails, the transient integrative organization of the personality is reflected in realistic and conceptual responses to stimuli; its persistent integrative nature is manifested in an obvious central control, based on structure, reflected in a present valid behavior clearly grounded on a relevant past and oriented to a realistic future. The person performs with stability and flexibility at relatively close to capacity level; he is able to deal with the probable as well as the actual, and to maintain a proper balance between egocentric, allocentric, and alteregocentric interests. *The core of maturity is epitomized by the consistent ability to maintain generalized set.*

Segmental Set

Segmental set, on the contrary, is disclosed by an inconsistency within an aspect of the response (as in cognitive dispersion) or in the incongruous combination of the cognitive, affective, and conative aspects into a spontaneous unit. It is revealed by aberrancies in the level, the speed, and the consistency of preparation achieved. There is a dependency on a part, rather than on the whole self, and/or on others rather than on oneself. Segmental set involves a preparatory adjustment that is particularly directed to partial or minor aspects of the total stimulus/response situations, or, in the extreme case, to aspects entirely unrelated to the stimulus situation. A preponderance of successive (unintegrated) rather than consecutive stimulus/responses results.

In the clinical situation mentioned earlier where the question is asked, "Where were you yesterday evening?", processing results in segmentalization rather than in generalization. For instance, the *eve* of "evening" in the question may be given a different and overwhelming meaning based on personal and idiosyncratic associations—for instance, to Adam and Eve, and other remote diversions. When a response is made, it is irrelevant to the question from the viewpoint of the observer, regardless of its relevance in the schizophrenic's interpretation of the stimulus. In the experimental reaction time setting, where the instructions are to respond as quickly as possible to the yellow stimulus of the two possible stimuli, the patient may take longer to respond to the simple task than a normal subject because of preoccupations from within or distractions from without which complicate the situation for him. In the case of segmental set, intrinsic or extrinsic interferences occur in a situation that should be fairly straightforward.

Above all, the responses in segmental set appear to hark back to previously experienced but inadequate responses. Novelty is anathema, so there is a reversion to earlier modes of response. This may consist of a "schizokinesis" (Gantt, 1953), where old autonomic responses that were satisfactory in the past are called upon to serve in situations where they are no longer adaptive. Or it may be skeletal responses that were adaptive in the past but which are no longer adaptive (such as in the case of the match that "lit alright a minute ago"). Skeletal or autonomic responses that were never adaptive in the past ("string too short to be saved"—See this book, p. 95) may be tried again in the current situation, despite their persistent inadequacy. The response is, in any case, of the same general character; it is nonadaptive *now* because the response is inappropriate to the essential aspects of the present stimulus situation. It may involve a strong focus on the irrelevant and a weak focus on the relevant, or it may fall at either end of the bipolar extremes that so characteristically occur in schizophrenia. There may be a strong trend toward perseveration or its contrary, flightiness of behavior in which no two successive responses are alike. In any case, there is nonhabituation. In fact, the response may be actively segmental because of a *positive* need to segmentalize.[2]

Set is ultimately based on need, on motivation. As Rapaport has said, "all psychological happening is motivated",—directly or indirectly, consciously or unconsciously, voluntarily or nonvoluntarily, or automatically, I might add. The schizophrenic's need is frustrated, temporarily, or more often relatively permanently, because integration, the essential tool for reconciling situations and needs, has not been developed and maintained. Conflict or other interference ensues, and the discharge resulting in satisfaction does not take place. At the very least, the discharge is delayed. The inevitable detour is first evidenced by the appearance of anxiety and of a motor response that is part of this detour. Fundamentally, the response is an attempt to *change* the external environment to establish safe conditions for gratification. The reaction may take the form of an "hallucinatory" image, a nonveridical perception that is segmental rather than generalized. This is a private perception belonging only to the perceiver; it is not even an illusion that is common to all persons, such as those created for our entertainment by the mime (Simmel, 1972).

Segmental acts characterize the schizophrenic. Some are

---

[2]Cf. Sullivan's "selective inattention": "But in many cases, there is an unfortunate use of selective inattention, in which one ignores things that do matter." (1953, p. 233). See also Sullivan (1962, p. 85).

actually deliberate, "chosen," conscious acts (with their inevitable partial content of pre- and unconscious elements). But when habituation is finally established, the schizophrenic may be acting on preconscious, unconscious, or automatic considerations, depending on the degree of unawareness and recoverability of the consciousness of the act. This may be based on the unconscious in the other sense, which the Freudian theory postulates as well; it may arise from the *repressed* unconscious, which gains access to consciousness only if it undergoes distortion through defense. Thus, although segmental acts may give the appearance of passivity—appear to be unconscious, or automatic—they may be due to the process of habituation or repression that has occurred. They are not to be construed as passive any more than are the habituated form of generalized sets. Whatever the case, the result is segmentalization, the substitution of a part or some bipolar aspect of the situation for the whole, veridical perception and response. In the extreme case, entirely irrelevant and irrational material may be substituted.

The *cognitive* side of segmental set is reflected in a limitation of general receptivity to input as well as a distortion of reactivity to specific hyperreceptivity to input coming from both inner and outer sources. The cognitive discrimination associated with receptivity to specific stimuli may also be faulty, because the necessary preparatory scanning and articulation of figure from ground, or the focal from the irrelevant, is not appropriately carried out.

An illustration of cognitive segmentalization in schizophrenia is demonstrated by Renee (Sechehaye, 1970):

For I saw the individual features of her face, separated from each other; the teeth, then the nose, then the cheeks, then one eye and the other. Perhaps it was this *independence* of each part that inspired fear and prevented my recognizing her even though I knew who she was. (p. 37, emphasis added)

The *affective* disturbance lies in the degree and nature of emotional involvement with general and specific stimuli. Instead of a properly measured degree of affect, there is an extreme, pervasive affect that is excessive or inadequate, too personalized or too impersonalized.

On its *conative* side, the response is not properly modulated, considering the nature and strengths of the specific input. Quantitatively, it is too strong or too weak, and its quality is inappropriate. It is in the disharmony of these phases—cognition, affect, and conation, that the major aspects of segmental set occur.

In successive stimuli, there may be considerable evidence of both perseveration and insufficient automatization, even to the extent of increased reactive inhibition with repetition.

"Splitting," the primary characteristic from which schizophrenia derives its name, has two forms, only one of which describes schizophrenia. In *multiple personality* (hysteroid), there is a "longitudinal" but systematic split of the personality, so that the subsystems of cognitive-conative-affective functioning remain intact and work together, but they are limited in comprehensiveness to the separate personalities, whether it be A, B, or C. (See Figure 1.) Within each, the personality is more or less integrated, and there is practically no communication between the personalities (Prince, 1917 and several cases presented by McDougall, 1926). There is at least a partial amnesia from one personality to another, whether they are alternating or co-conscious personalities. In *schizo-*

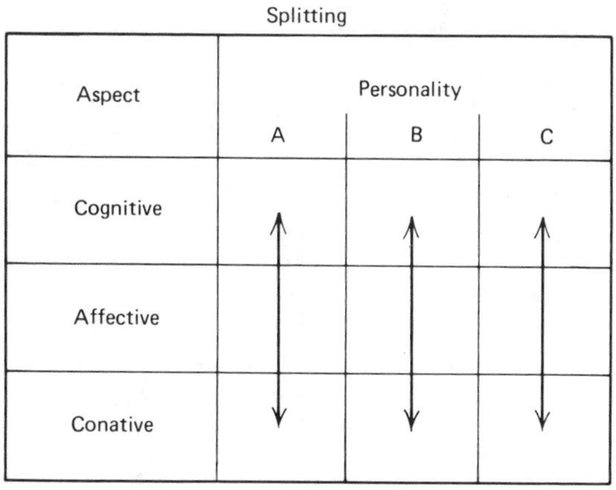

Figure 1   Multiple personality.

phrenia, however, the split is unsystematically horizontal. There is disintegration of the units of stimulus/response, in that each of the cognitive, affective, and conative elements may generally go their own way, without amnesia, as illustrated in Figure 2. It is a more profound disorder, and the units of the stimulus/response system disintegrate. Bleuler (1950) describes it as follows:

systematic splitting . . . may be found in many other psychotic conditions (e.g. hysterical) . . . Definite splitting, however, in the sense that various personality fragments exist side by side in a state of clear orientation as to the environment, will only be found in our disease [schizophrenia] (Bleuler, 1950, pp. 298–299) . . . .*The splitting is the prerequisite condition of most of the complicated phenomena of the disease.* (p. 362)

There has been a trend for many commentators on the social scene to characterize certain behaviors of individuals or groups, who didn't know what the right hand was doing while working with the left, as *schizophrenic*. These acts are more correctly termed -'dissociated''— a characteristic of multiple personalities.

When segmental set prevails, the transient integrative disorganization of the personality is reflected in unrealistic and concrete reactions to stimuli. Its persistent disorganized na-

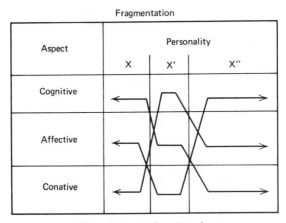

Figure 2   Schizophrenia.

ture at the level of schemata or schematization is manifested by a general lack of central control, presumably structural in character. The "rudderless" nature of the control is revealed by present behavior that is unrealistic. It appears to derive from a past that is largely irrelevant for adaptation, because its traumatic qualities are overemphasized and are too little oriented to the immediate future. Performance is unstable and either markedly loose or extremely rigid. The person seems to be working at a level considerably below true capacity. So involved is he in his problems that he finds it difficult to maintain a proper balance between egocentric and alteregocentric interests.

All sets involve some degree of conceptualization, or at least some aspect of thinking, which may be associative rather than conceptual. Unless a person is automatically responding to each individual stimulus separately, and then acting in a kind of specious present, he must make comparisons with the previous stimuli—which involves some degree of associative or conceptual thinking. In generalizing, the normal person uses conceptualization, only infrequently resorting to association, and then, only as a step toward conceptualization. The schizophrenic usually skates on the edge of immediate, rather than sustained, association, rarely utilizing conceptualization. For the most part he maintains a pattern of segmentalization.

Without generalized set in the immediate S/R context, the response is very likely to be irrelevant or "rough" because the process of generalization is integrally interrelated with apperception. Without a controlling set, the use of past experience is limited to less adaptive principles (primary rather than secondary thought processes) because selective and systematic retrieval is impaired. It is through the selective function of generalized set that the adaptive principles work. The impact of the lack of generalized set of future response derives from a failure of schematization of the response of the present with the past schemata in the interests of consolidation and integration. Consequently, learning and perceptual refinement are inhibited. Archaic needs may then gain control of the apperceptive mass—exerting excessive pressure for defensive responses that are objectively inadequate, whatever their subjective success, and thus, in the long run, maladaptive. One might surmise that, in the face of the segmentalization of generalized set function, the organism turns to segmental sets. The natural question will then be: what causes segmentalization? This question is addressed in the later section of this volume.

The behavior as a whole under segmental set is strikingly bipolar, a shifting from, or a remaining at, one extreme of response or the other, decidedly more extreme than in normals. The most effective responses usually result from a medium energy level of generalized set. But in schizophrenia, the moderate response that would be produced by the normal functioning of generalized set is rarely seen.

Discrimination and choice are earmarks of normality. When the discrimination process results in ambivalence and ambitendency, pathology exists. The workings of such ambitendency can be seen in the patient cited by Hill who, because of considerable ambivalence about drinking and non-drinking, sometimes required 30 minutes to an hour to drink a glass of orange juice (1935, p. 37). Another instance from my own experience is the patient who came to the door of the laboratory after agreeing to participate in an experiment and then alternated between forward and backward steps, seemingly unable to enter. From this state of pathological indecision, a person may easily pass into the state of being stuck at one extreme or the other of the range of conduct, because the state of ambitendency is too intolerable. (One might suppose that this inability to decide is even more upsetting to the patient than it is to the investigator!) Renee, for instance would have periods when the "slightest movement required extraordinary effort," (p. 56), causing her to "remain sitting uninterruptedly, my gaze lost in a drop of coffee fallen on the table" (p. 56). This might be replaced by "inner and outer agitation": "It was impossible to stay in bed. Singing a requiem without pause, I marched three steps forward and three steps back, an automatism which wearied me exceedingly . . . and if I stopped from exhaustion even for a moment, I felt guilty again." (pp. 61–62). Hill, again, in his insightful book on schizophrenia (1955), refers to the "futile inertia which can be punctuated by periods of intense activity" (p. 47).

A patient I worked with told of having stuck various items up his rectum such as radio tubes from his brother's and father's sets in order to acquire the knowledge of radio that his bro thers and father had. He also put some of his father's (who was a physician) sulfanilamide pills up his anus in the same way (perhaps at the same time, as a symbol of revolt against his father). This extreme behavior was manifested when he was overcome by alternating guilt and jealousy and did not dare do anything that his father or his brothers admired or accomplished, so he took this extreme and bizarre way out. He did the same thing with a British pipe, because he thought that this would be one way of acquiring the "British" ease of social conduct. He also thought that dancing with a girl meant that he was "almost married" to her, so he avoided this most of the time by staying away from girls altogether. His seeming inability to do the slightest thing without resorting to, or verbally implying extreme behavior, is characteristic of bipolar response.

Thinking of the behavior in neurological terms, one sees a failure of the integration of the organism at the central control mechanism. The central control is missing or ineffective; the superior monad is, as it were, out of commission. Under the circumstances, it is not surprising that the measured responses, when all the relevant features are taken into account, are defective. For it is the central control mechanism that is the final arbiter in these events.[3]

---

[3]More specifically, the limbic forebrain has a part in the regulation of various psychological and psychophysiological processes (Smythies, 1967). Tumors in the hippocampus give rise to behavior indistinguishable from schizophrenia (Malamud, 1967). Flor-Henry (1969a, 1969b) gives clinical reports of a schizophrenic-like psychosis in epileptics with dominant temporal lobes, as does the earlier paper by Slater and Beard (1963). I shall not go further into this area, but would recommend the reading of Thompson (1976) for those interested in further references.

PARSIMONIOUSNESS

Floyd Allport (1955) has presented, as a summary of the extensive experimental findings pertinent to normal set, 16 basic facts about normal set. The characteristics of segmental set may be elucidated by contrasting them directly with Allport's 16 "facts" (paraphrased or quoted directly).

1. The phenomenon of set involves, basically and characteristically, the following aspects: There is *some preparatory or facilitating condition* that precedes, accompanies, or sometimes even outlasts the completely aroused overt behavior, or the act of perception. In segmental set the preparatory or facilitating condition may not be present. Instead of making that process occur *with greater promptness, speed of execution, energy, or magnitude,* in segmental set, the facilating condition is likely to be delayed or not present at all.

2. In some instances the condition seems merely to *prepare* or *make ready* the full behavior process. In other cases it *sustains, prolongs, or enhances* it during its entire course. In the case of segmental set, only a *partial* process is attained.

3. The response always represents exactly the same behavior as that for which the organism is prepared by the set. In segmental set the organism may change the focus of the behavior.

4. From this and the preceding propositions it follows that set will always appear as a *selective process.* In segmental set the selection may be in the wrong direction.

5. Sets stand in an *antagonistic* relation to one another and have a *negative* or *inhibitory* as well as a positive aspect. In segmental set, there is likely to be no rationale, from the observer's viewpoint, for the antagonistic processes.

6. In preparatory and sustaining sets there is a *peripheral*

sensory as well as a *peripheral motor* aspect. In segmental set these attentional processes are likely to be disturbed.

7. When two stimuli occur simultaneously, the one to which the subject is prepared to attend is experienced first. In segmental set the principle of "prior entry" is likely to be disturbed.

8. Since set is a property of the organism rather than of the stimulus, it is possible to establish for the same series of stimuli at different times sets for quite different and mutually inhibiting types of behavior. In segmental set there is likely to be confusion between the same series of stimuli at different times.

9. Two general classes of preparatory set have been experimentally distinguished. These are sometimes known by the phenomenological terms *expectancy* and *intention*. At times, in segmental set, there may be entanglement of the two.

10. Preparatory sets may be long in preparing, or their building may occupy only a short interval. At times, in segmental set, there may be a substitution of long for short, and vice versa.

11 Getting ready for an activity may be either a voluntary or an involuntary matter, depending on the circumstances. The circumstances may in segmental set result in a confounding of voluntary and involuntary.

12. *Sets may involve or be involved in learning.* In segmental set, there may be inordinate lengths of time taken up on this learning process, especially in the early phases.

13. Although sets are specific as to their relation to the activities for which they prepare or sustain, and are unique, they can also be generalized if the activities concerned belong to a certain class. It is this process of generalization that is disturbed in segmental set.

14. Although a set can be built up either consciously or un-

consciously, and one can introspect in regard to the bodily processes involved, *it is usually very meager in its phenomenological content.*

15. *Sets can be built up and can become effective in a variety of ways.* In segmental set, the ways may be vaster or they may be much narrower than in the normal.

16. Like the full reactions of which they are a preparatory or sustaining phase, sets that have been already established, but are at the moment "inactive" or unrelated to the existing trend or events, can be "evoked" or "aroused" by appropriate stimulus conditions. The smoothness of the evoking is disturbed in the schizophrenic's use of segmental set.

CHAPTER 5

The Need-Tension Paradigm

A detailed explication of set theory must include a discussion—albeit brief—of the basic motivation underlying set, the need or tension that determines the type of set aroused. The need-tension paradigm posits a pattern of need, a need-satisfying object, and need-gratification as an order of events. When tension arises, which may be described as "disequilibrium," there follows some attempt on the part of the individual to reduce this tension. If the needed object—that is, the object toward which the need is most fundamentally directed—is present and available, gratification takes place and the tension subsides. That subsidence is relatively complete as compared to other situations of subsidence, which I shall now discuss.

When objects of need are unavailable—whether they are present and unavailable, or absent—there are a variety of possible "gratification" processes. If the person is capable of delaying the gratification, there will be an ideation of means and ends around subsequent gratification. In psychoanalytic terms, this type of response may be the basis for the development of secondary thought processes. What follows from such a response is some discharge of affect on these intermediate images of the gratification or the substitute images for the gratification, and some reduction of tension. There may also be various kinds of substitute gratification. One of these is the sublimative type, when the affect is discharged on a substitute object that is acceptable to society and one's notions of society's needs. It may be complete or it may be only partial, and the tension reduction accordingly would be of different degrees. A second type of substitution occurs when there is an immediate attempt to achieve tension reduction by way of memory *images* of gratification that do not have to be delayed, like dreams, hallucinations, or obsessions. The third type might be called *reactive,* including such responses as regression, repression, reaction-formation—various types of substitute behavior resulting in tension-reduction. In repression, no actual symptoms may be established; instead, the affect discharge is merely reduced. These various forms of response are not actually separate. Combinations of actual gratification with some of the other sorts of substitute gratification can occur, and the problem of their interrelationships should be considered.

Need, gratification, and tension-reduction also involve other aspects of the psychological process. For our present purposes I do not know of better terms to refer to them than cognitive, conative, and affective. It is crucial to recognize these in each step of this motivational process: the level of need as primarily cognitive, the attempt to reduce tension as predominately conative-cognitive, and the gratification, delay of gratification, or substitute gratification as first cognitive and then affective-conative. Tension-reduction is primarily affective, and may take place in these ways: the tension (motivation) may result in a generalized set, and gratification occurs. The tension may result directly in a segmental set, and false gratification follows, or the persons may react with segmental sets, which are ultimately based on automatized aspects of tension within the individual. Substitution (either conscious or unconscious) is involved in any case.

Dealing with the primary tensions created by external and internal needs on their road to either gratification or frustration, the essential pattern shown by the schizophrenic is quite different from that of the normal person. As the above account of Rapaport's motivation paradigm, "Conceptual Model of Psychoanalysis" (Gill, M. M., 1967, pp. 405–431), and my slight modification (Shakow, 1956) indicate, when a need object is available to the normal person, the aroused tension is reduced by gratification. When the need object is not available, his ordinary course is to delay gratification with accompanying *ideation* of the means and ends, the aroused affect being discharged on intermediate or derivative means-objects. Tension is then reduced with varying degrees of completeness or incompleteness. What, however, is the pattern in the case of the schizophrenic, when he is being typically schizophrenic? When tension is aroused by a current need, the object, even when realistically available, becomes "unavailable" to him in the sense required. He handles his tensions through a perverse "gratification" that is fundamentally substitutive rather than direct. He may hallucinate, substituting an image for the object, or he may behave in a way that may be characterized as regressive, restitutive, or reaction-formative.

CHAPTER 6

The Stimulus/Response Process

To fully examine the concepts of generalized and segmental sets, which have been briefly defined, it is necessary to consider in detail the S/R process. What follows is a detailed analysis of the stimulus/response process (or S-O-R),[1] how its phases are manifested in set, and the pathologic variations presented by the schizophrenic subject. It is my hope that this analysis will provide the base for a broader consideration of schizophrenic and normal adaptation as reflected in the concepts of generalized and segmental set.

The concept of the stimulus-response process is not a simple or passive process. White (1959) is quite correct in the exception he takes to such attitudes toward the immense variety of contextual determinants and the complexity of what consitutes the stimulus situation. Some authors discuss the stimulus only in terms of the *external*, narrow stimulus situation. The more complex view considers the *internal* state of the organism (in part available as stored memories) to be as important as the external contextual factors in understanding response. Furthermore, although the total stimulus/response process may frequently be passive, it often stems from spontaneous, active stimulus-seeking. Finally, too many analyses limit themselves to the perceptual process, particularly the

---

[1]Or input/output process, or information processing and outer control (Freides, 1974). I shall use these terms interchangeably.

cognitive aspects, when it is necessary to include the response process as part of the total complex.

The behavioral approaches to stimuli by the schizophrenic might be roughly organized into four categories: 1) withdrawal—he does not respond at all to the stimulus (or indicates that somebody else had better do it); 2) simplification—he simplifies the stimulus, reacting insufficiently to only part of it; 3) overcomplication—he makes the task much more difficult; and 4) inappropriate response—reacting poorly and peculiarly to the stimulus. His behavior represents a constant battle with the environment, whether in the home, the ward, or the temporary experimental situation. It is a battle, especially in the acute patient, between what the environment provides and perceives it has provided and what the schizophrenic "perceives" and responds to. But it must be understood that it is not strictly the sensory end of perception that is disturbed. The hue and saturation of the visual, or the tone and timbre of the auditory and the analogous levels of the other senses, are not likely to be at fault, but rather the perceptual process itself.

The schizophrenic does not continually manifest the symptoms described here, except in extreme cases or for limited periods of time; his behavior may often fall within the normal range, but he frequently manifests aberrancies of thought and conduct.

THE CONTEXT FOR THE STIMULUS/RESPONSE PROCESS

The general setting for the stimulus/response process involves the "personalness" of the stimulus, the resting state of the organism, and the stress condition of the organism. With regard to "personalness," a stimulus falls into one of three classes: neutral, impersonal, and personal. Each of these may occur under one or another of three conditions of stress: none, external, and internal. From any one of these resulting nine classes the stimulus comes to the subject in one of four "rest" conditions: sensory deprivation, basal resting, nonbasal resting, and nonresting. Whatever the stimulation—natural or experimental—it ordinarily begins with the subject in one of these background rest states for varying lengths of time. For the last three of these four, a gradual adaptational change ordinarily occurs with time. Sensory deprivation, however, is such a peculiar "rest" state that, by definiton, if invaded at all, it suffers almost immediate destruction. A more detailed examination of these categories of rest and the classes of stimulus levels are found in Appendix B. Given these aspects of the *setting* for the stimulus/response process, it is evident why even complex analyses of this process are relatively "simplistic."[2] The above says nothing, of course, about the variations within categories, and it neglects as well the fact that any realistic analysis of stimulation must really take into account the interactions of successive stimulus/response sequences. However, these classes describe only the *baseline* situations. They may, particularly in experimenter-controlled situations, be subject to further complication by many kinds of modifiers, such as the subject's explicit knowledge of the experimenter's goals or implicit knowledge derived from preliminary warning signals that are part of set.

SEVEN STAGES OF THE STIMULUS/RESPONSE PROCESS

The specific stimulus/response complex itself may be broken down into seven stages:

1. *The state of preparedness for stimulation* includes both a general and a specific form of preparation. The "general state" refers to the degree of readiness to participate in any coming stimulation. In an experimental context it might be considered the degree of "cooperativeness" of the subject— both voluntary and involuntary. It may range from active par-

[2]Cf. here Figure #11 of Allport (1967, p. 14) as another illustration of the complexity of events.

ticipation (through various degrees of indifference) to active opposition.[3] The more limited and specific nature of this readiness anticipates the immediately arriving stimulation. It may arise from awareness of the coming stimulation, resulting

[3]We have attempted to deal in part with this problem by developing the attitude scale that we used in practically all of our experimental and test studies (Shakow and Huston, 1936). The Chapmans and Salzinger have each raised some questions about this technique, but I believe that on the whole these procedures will stand up. Chapman and Chapman have said:

Shakow did not view the poor performance that results from poor cooperation as *real* schizophrenic deficit. One difficulty with this view is that one cannot really distinguish poor cooperation from psychopathology (1973, p. 231).

Our attempts to separate the effects of pathology from lack of cooperation (which we recognized) were only partially (but at least *partially*) successful. The response bias that Salzinger (1973, p. 27) talks about can be only in part eliminated. All we can say is that some attempt to answer such questions was made in a detailed study of these ratings reported in Shakow and Huston (1936) and in our deterioration monograph (1946, pp. 51–54). The following was observed:

(1) In any one experiment, the ratings were all made either by the same person or at least by persons receiving similar training in the use of the scale. There was thus some likelihood of stability in standards.

(2) Cooperation ratings correlated about .45 with adjustment ratings made independently by the psychiatrists on the ward. This served to some extent as a check on the validity of the ratings.

(3) Scores on the tests administered distributed themselves quite normally about each cooperation rating, which was considered a statistical argument supporting the ratings.

(4) The same score was given to different ratings, that is a rating was not attached to a score.

(5) The rating was not attached to a person—the same patient in different experiments at different times was given different ratings.

(6) The ratings were made by persons having considerable experience in their use.

This approach and its rigorous application leads one to place considerable faith in these findings. In any case, it is the best measure available to deal with the problem raised by variations in cooperation. The suggestions of Salzinger (1973, p. 28) although relevant, are at best only applicable for part of the problem.

from some warning signal, a degree of knowledge of the goals of the stimulation, or from the preparatory information presented by the given environment or "working memory." The factors determining the patient's particular state are manifold: they arise from a combination of the motivating factors aroused by the immediate situation, but also, more importantly, from a combination of interfering factors, internal and external, determining the subject's initial and continuing general receptivity for the potential stimulus. In the broadest sense, preparedness reflects the subject's receptivity compared to what his environment considers relevant and irrelevant.

2. *Perception*, which consists of six phases: 1) sensing, the initial awareness of the stimulus field the subject gains through the senses; 2) scanning, a quick overview; 3) articulation, where salient features of the stimulus are highlighted: 4) figure-ground distinction; 5) apperception, where the current stimulus is integrated into the larger background of past experiences with the stimulus situation and given meaning; and 6) stabilization of the particular perception.

3. *Encoding*. After these six phases the perception is ready for the central encoding process, the internuncial process, the third stage of the stimulus/response complex that connects the sensory and affective parts with the motor—the O of Woodworth's S-O-R (1929).

4. *Response to the perception*. After encoding, the subject responds to the stimulus, "choosing" one or another response. Responses may vary both in their qualitative and in their quantitative aspects of intensity or speed. Qualitatively, the schizophrenic response may be characterized as irrelevant or inefficient. As will be seen, however, these characterizations need more specific definition.

5. *Consolidation of perception/response into apperceptive mass*. After the response, the perception/response complex is consolidated by the organism into its apperceptive mass, where it is integrated with similar responses. In the need-tension paradigm, this results in some degree of tension reduction and gratification.

6. *Inhibition.* On its way to a state of general preparedness for the next stimulation, the organism usually enters into some final state of inhibition, reactive or retroactive. During reactive inhibition there is a tendency toward lessened response due to effortful activity. In retroactive inhibition the normal effects of learning are impaired by subsequent activity, particularly when they are similar. The inhibition phase may be viewed as part of the consolidation process.

7. *Return to state of preparedness (for succeeding stimulation).* The organism becomes ready again to accept the next stimulus.

Before describing these seven stages at length, I would first like to discuss *the issue of fractionation.* Is it justifiable to break up the stimulus/response complex into the stages I have listed? In advocating such a procedure am I taking what is a totality, a true gestalt, and quite arbitrarily pulling it apart into nonveridical elements? Do I regress by this action from the relative holism characterizing the psychology of the relatively recent past to an outmoded Wundtian elementalism, harking back to the kinds of discussion and controversies following Donders' subtractive procedure, Wundt's fractionation method with respect to the reaction time process, and Watt's fractionation method as applied to association processes? (See Boring's *History*, 1950, for references.)

The controversy that has raged between those who have held the perceptual process to be a unit, such as James, the gestalters, and Gibson (especially as presented in his argument that the senses should be considered perceptual systems, 1966)[4], and those who have accepted the legitimacy of the fractionation process, as recently argued by those who have been involved in the analysis of information processing (see *Acta Psychologica*, Vol. 30, 1969), has been intense. One could reasonably assume, from my suggestion of the present "stages" analysis, that I identify with the fractionaters. This

[4]Cf. John Dewey, particularly, as he states the importance of his (and Bentley's) substitution of "transaction" for "interaction"–(Letters to John Daniels, 1959, pp. 567–570.)

is, however, true only to a limited extent. Whereas, with regard to the process of perception in normal persons, my natural tendency is to agree more with those who hold that we ordinarily deal with perception holistically or "transactionally," my experience with schizophrenics supports the contrary view. It seems that, in one way or another, schizophrenics actually dismember what seems to have become, or have been from early on in the developmental process, essentially a unified and automatic process (cf. Coghill, 1933). They either give unbalanced emphasis to separate parts, or introduce distortions into various aspects of the perceptual process.

There are, I believe, two kinds of fractionation, an intellectualizing variety and a "gut" variety. The first is that indulged in by some psychologists (like Wundt), who fractionate in the scientific tradition on purely intellectual grounds, to simplify a field altogether too complex. Under these conditions, the perceptual process is weakened and artificialized. The other variety is demonstrated by psychologists who derive their evidence from observations of schizophrenics or other disturbed persons. They observe that some persons appear to find it necessary, as part of their efforts at adaptation, to pull things apart, to fractionate the life processes. Until recently, most of what could be offered in defense of this stand would of necessity have been derived from the observation of pathology, from the fact that patients appear so clearly to fractionate the stimulus/response. But developments in the neurophysiology of the input/output system, with its own complexities of internal controls, feedbacks, and reverberative processes at different stages of the system, provide further evidence of fractionating. The evidence for fractionation in clinical observation is also strongly bolstered by the movement growing out of the recent work in information processing and the numerous volumes on the attention process. From this point of view it might even be argued that a procedure like fractionation is fundamental for the analysis and understanding of behavior.[5]

---

[5]Here Donders indeed comes back to his own and achieves some degree of revenge on Külpe! See *Acta Psychologica*, Vol. 30, 1969.

In the section on overabudant stimuli (see p. 59) I shall consider a controversy between Holzman and Silverman (Shakow, unpublished, 1970) on the sensation/perception problem.

Another possibility is that these varying approaches are outgrowths of the different personalities or modes of thought of the theorists themselves. They may result from the kind of "defect" that the old Titchenerians used to label "subjective." Or, to put a better face on it, it might be accepted that some psychologists are by fundamental disposition *analyzers*, whereas others are *synthesizers*. Whatever the case, I do not see how anybody working with schizophrenics, regardless of his own personality propensities, can avoid adopting some fractionating approach if he or she is to describe accurately the phenomena presented to him or her by these patients. Therefore, it seems wisest at the outset to pay attention to what pathology magnifies and recognize the elements that enter into the total perceptual gestalting, while at the same time bearing in mind that it is a total process that synthesizes all of its elements.

This stimulus/response model, I emphasize again, is to be viewed in the context of the much broader need-tension-gratification model of which it is a part. Stimuli make different demands on the response, in relation to the nature of the needs involved. Stimuli may be essentially neutral, in the sense that they call on little beyond the minimal involvement of the subject. On the other hand, they may have additional "stimulating" qualities demanding his increased involvement, from the impersonal affective through the personal affective, the impersonal stress and impersonal affective stress to, finally, that state that is presumably most involving—personal-affective stress. The basic input/output process of the schizophrenic must be viewed not only in simple S/R terms, but with respect to its broader implications as to category of need aroused in the organism by the input, as well as the process of gratification of the need by the output.

One last preliminary comment, in the form of a warning. Despite Mark Twain's general animadversions in "The Awful

German Language" (1880), I have found it helpful to my own thinking in this area to use a set of Germanic portmanteau words attached to the prefix *Reiz* for dealing with stimulus situations. I wish, therefore, to notify the reader that I shall impose this "awful" practice on him in the present exposition.

Stage 1: Preparation for stimulation

The state preceding the actual perception of a stimulus, called "preperception" by Lewes, encompasses that "excitement from within" on which James, as I have mentioned, based his discussion of the topic (1890, Vol. I, p. 439). There is justification for postulating such a state because we rarely experience a complete equilibrium *(Reizstand)* in the waking state (and there is evidence that this may be true of the sleep state as well), a state of total rest and let-up between successive stimuli. The nearest a person comes to achieving such a state is when (not being subjected to actual stimulation) he is to some degree preparing himself, even if imperceptibly, for a potential stimulus. Thus he is always in at least a partial state of alertness. Equilibrium is a relative state, a person of necessity always being somewhat off-balance, biologically speaking.

The imbalance may stem from a state of (1) "expectancy" for a stimulus that has been aroused in the organism by some forewarning from the environment, or from (2) an "intention" to respond that has arisen from an inner state or goal that it means to carry out. Then again, it may be the result of (3) a less immediately motivated, but minimal, biological baseline level of alertness that facilitates some kind—any kind—of response should the occasion arise. (It will be noted that these are all set concepts.)

Lewes' and James' concepts of preperception are perhaps more specific than what I myself have in mind for this stage. Their concepts apparently refer to the expectancy for a structured stimulus. If this is the case, I wonder whether they have given enough attention to the generalized, unstructured preparatory state of alertness I here suggest. Before adopting their term "preperception," one must carefully examine what they imply.[6] When I use the term it is with the connotation I have indicated here.

For convenience of discussion, the preperception state may be divided into three categories: first, a *positive readiness* for stimulation, a generally adient attitude; second, essentially the opposite, an active *negative* attitude toward stimulation, a generally abient attitude; and third, representing an in-between state, an attitude of indifference. An important aspect of these processes is inhibition, or *Reizschutz*.

Positive readiness for stimulation

The person in this positive state is characterized by a readiness for stimulation that might be viewed as a "hunger" for stimulation *(Reizhunger)*. The subject is predisposed to accept stimulation *(Reizaufnahme)*, and, in fact, as is so often true of most organisms—especially the young—there may even be active excursions in search of stimuli *(Reizsuche)*.[7] The spontaneity and venturesomeness we value so much in normal persons is a striking example of this state. We must, however, carefully distinguish between "seeking" that is adaptive—the constant hunt for relevant stimulation—and "seeking" that is primarily defensive and escapist—the hunt for a change in stimulation because of the organism's difficulty in handling the present stimulation. "Any port in a storm" is perhaps a way of stating the immediate response of the normal person in such a situation. In the case of a normal person there *is* a port, though it may not be the most desirable or suitable; in the case of the schizophrenic however, it so often is a "port" of the

---

[6]Cf. James' discussion (1890, Vol. I, pp. 439, 442) and his discussion of organic adjustment, as well as pp. 434ff.

[7]Another form of *Reizsuche* involving a more subtle process, that of freefloating attention, is the one that Reik (1952, pp. 164 ff.) has called "listening with the third ear." For him, this calls for a marked sensitivity to, and searching out of, minor and transient cues that, despite their minimal stimulus intensity, carry great weight in the full appreciation of the ongoing input/output process.

Durante type.[8] An adaptive mechanism of escape thus becomes maladaptive for the schizophrenic.

We must also bear in mind that in the healthy organism the reception of stimulation is closely coupled with that most essential complementary form of biological behavior, the rejection of excessive and irrelevant stimuli in order to make selective choice possible. This concept *(Reizschutz)* is central to Freud's system, as well as to many others.[9] A similar principle is advanced in what James (1890) called "ignoring." Nature provides us with a protective device against the unsought and irrelevant stimuli that constantly bombard us from without and within. The significance of this inhibiting apparatus lies not only in the fact that it permits the organism to be selective and to *choose* (choice being the prime event) the most pertinent stimuli, but in that it serves at the same time to prevent the organism from being flooded by too much stimulation.[10]

When the normal person is in a relative state of equilibrium, a condition exists that is most favorable to the working of *Reizsuche*, the active searching for stimuli (as well as some degree of general inhibition against flooding). When he is in a similar state of disequilibrium arising from the need to consider already present stimuli, *Reizschutz* becomes transcendent. Such a state of protectiveness is directed against the appear-

[8]Jimmy Durante is taken out in a small boat in open water by a friend, when, with no land in sight, a storm suddenly springs up. He looks everywhere, finally spies the horizon, and inquires anxiously about it. When told that it is the horizon, he insists that his friend pull toward it since it is preferable to no port at all.

[9]Cf. discussion of this point by Freud (1920/1955). Diamond, Balven, and Diamond (1963, p. 166 ff.) also have important and relevant comments about inhibition.

[10]Compare in this respect the remarkable insight of a once-schizophrenic patient (MacDonald, 1960) who suffered from an "exaggerated state of awareness." Also relevant are the findings of Petrie on stimulus-government in schizophrenia (1967, pp. 66–67, 80 ff.) and in the defensive reaction of schizophrenics against auditory "bombardment." This serves to make the schizophrenic in most cases a reducer, although paranoids appear on the whole to be augmenters (See p. 157).

ance of new stimuli that might disturb whatever equilibrium exists. The attempt to hold on to the relatively undisturbed state of partial "tranquility" would appear to arise from the basic need for security.[11] In the states of disequilibrium of the schizophrenic, again unlike the normal, *Reizsuche* may take over. Under such conditions, at least among some patients, a search arises for hopefully less disturbing stimuli than those already present, presumably because adaptation to those present is found to be difficult. This results in a pathological hunt for "any port in a storm."[12]

Whereas, in the normal subject, all these processes function at balanced levels of high potency, they are markedly unbalanced in the schizophrenic. This is particularly true of the functioning of *Reizschutz*—the ability to be selective by keeping out irrelevant stimulation. The normal person impresses one, in Lewinian terms, as being provided with substantial but flexible barriers between the *Umgebung*, the outside world, and the psychological structure. The barriers of the schizophrenic, on the contrary, may be like a sieve. They may have smaller or larger gaps in them, openings that make it difficult to keep out irrelevant stimuli, as in the hebephrenic. Indeed, these gaps may at times change in size unpredictably. Or there

[11]Of possible relevance in this connection is the higher-than-normal arousal level manifested by schizophrenics during the "resting" (more precisely, preparatory) stage of stimulation (Zahn, Rosenthal, and Lawlor, 1968). At this point, when the arousal level should be at its most moderate, it is high. This inappropriately high level presumably has its effect on other stages of the stimulus/response process reflected in the lesser response to focal stimuli when they come. It has special relationship to the law of initial value (Wilder, 1967).

[12]Such an hypothesis is in part confirmed by Feffer's experiment (1961), in which his more "pooly preserved" patients sought out the less disturbing stimuli. The "better" patients went to the other extreme and appeared to seek out the *more* disturbing stimuli. In neither case, however, was the response of the type given by normal subjects, that is neutral when the stimuli were neutral, and affective when they were affective. (This experiment is described in more detail on pp. 64 ff.) Thus, in neither case were the "ports" realistic ports; there was either over-or under-reaction.

may be quite the opposite condition, the existence of narrow and rigid barriers keeping essential elements of incoming stimuli out while allowing favored ones in, as in the paranoid; inhibition appears to be working overtime.

Negative Readiness for Stimulation

In the negative state, the individual is antagonistic to stimulation. Such contrariness may be of different degrees and may stem from a range of states in the person. It may result at one extreme from a marked degree of stimulus satisfaction *(Reizzufriedenheit)*, extending from contentment with already having achieved just the right amount of stimulation to a state of definite satiation bordering on the "too much" *(Reizattigung)*, or actual overload *(Reizuberladung,)* or *(Reizentladung)*.[13] It may result in a state of active hostility to stimulation *(Reizfeindlichkeit)*, or even in an extreme state of active stimulus rejection *(Reizverwerfung)*. All but the last are reflected in one or another form of the common schizophrenic symptom of withdrawal. Or it may be reflected in an active searching for new stimuli *(Reizsuche)*, at any cost, to get away from the present stimulation. The response is essentially negative in this case.[14]

Although in normal subjects one of these reactions may occasionally appear, especially in states of temporary indisposition or fatigue, they are ordinarily absent. In schizophrenics, however, they occur frequently. Any of these states, from satiation to rejection, may describe the characteristic performance of individual schizophrenics, as well as the range found in a group of schizophrenics.

---

[13]Cf. "overloading" in Holzman and Silverman, p. 5 ff. (Shakow, unpublished, 1970).

[14]Physiological responsiveness may be another form of withdrawal. Angyal, Freeman, and Hoskins, for example, find schizophrenics to have reduced levels of autonomic responsiveness (1940).

Indifference to stimulation

In some respects, the third type of response, indifference, is a corollary of the negative attitude, although it involves much less overt activity. The attitude is one of resignation, of long-suffering "endurance" of the stimulation being piled upon the subject *(Reizleiden)*, with accompanying susceptibility to stimulation *(Reizverwunderbarkeit)*. It is as if the subject has an underlying wish to rebel, but does not have enough gumption to do so. Instead, he submissively accepts the stimulation loaded on to him and "suffers" inwardly.

This condition is also found to be much more characteristic of schizophrenic than of normal persons. Rarely, and then only under special conditions, is it to be found in the latter, except during periods of depression and extreme fatigue, or in the case of certain extremely passive personality types who still fall within the normal range. (It may also be characteristic of depressed persons.)

Thus, in the pathology manifested by the schizophrenic, with respect to receptivity, there is (1) a kind of *hyper*receptivity, a susceptibility to too much stimulation or lack of inhibition with superficial responsivity, as seen in the hebephrenic; (2) a *hypo*receptivity, which excludes too much of the stimulation with too much inhibition, but with marked responsivity to past reactions, as seen in the paranoid; and (3) an *indifference* that tolerates stimulation but is not responsive to it, as seen in the indeterminate type.

Reizschutz

Of the various principles involved in this preparatory state of reaction to the stimulus, perhaps the most important is that of *Reizschutz*. I have long considered Freud and James to be the leading exponents of this principle, although Cannon and Whitehead might also be counted among the early authors to stress its importance. The latter two, however, are perhaps more directly associated with the related concept of habituation or automatization, which I shall consider further below.

Though Freud has expressed the principle most clearly, there is much in James dealing with protection against stimulation (cf. James on "Habit," Vol. I, 1890, p. 114 ff.). Because Freud describes the working of the principle so well, I shall quote at some length from his statement about *Reizschutz*, in *Beyond the Pleasure Principle* (1920, pp. 28–29):

Protection against stimuli is an almost more important function for the living organism than *reception of* stimuli. The protective shield is supplied with its own store of energy and must above all endeavor to preserve the special modes of transformation of energy operating in it against the effects threatened by the enormous energies at work in the external world—effects which tend towards a leveling out of them and hence towards destruction. The main purpose of the reception of stimuli is to discover the direction and nature of the external stimuli; and for that it is enough to take small specimens of the external world, to sample it in small quantities. In highly developed organisms the receptive cortical layer of the former vesicle has long been withdrawn into the depths of the interior of the body, though portions of it have been left behind on the surface immediately beneath the general shield against stimuli. These are the sense organs, which consist essentially of apparatus for the reception of certain specific effects of stimulation, but which also include special arrangements for further protection against excessive amounts of stimulation and for excluding unsuitable kinds of stimuli. It is characteristic of them that they deal only with very small quantities of external stimulation and only take in *samples* of the external world. They may perhaps be compared with feelers which are all the time making tentative advances towards the external world and then drawing back from it. . . .

This sensitive cortex, however, which is later to become the system between the outside and the inside and the differences between the conditions governing the reception of excitations in the two cases have a decisive effect on the functioning of the system and of the whole mental apparatus. Towards the outside it is shielded against stimuli, and the amounts of excitation impinging on it have only a reduced effect. Towards the inside there can be no such shield; the excitations in the deeper layers extend into the system directly and in undiminished amount, in so far as certain of their characteristics give rise to feelings in the pleasure-unpleasure series. The excitations coming from within are, however, in their intensity and in other, qualitative, respects—in their amplitude, perhaps—more commensurate with the system's method of working than the stimuli which stream in from the external world. This state of things pro-

duces two definite results. First, the feelings of pleasure and unpleasure (which are an index to what is happening in the interior of
the apparatus) predominate over all external stimuli. And, secondly,
a particular way is adopted of dealing with any internal excitations
which produce too great an increase of unpleasure: there is a tendency to treat them as though they were acting, not from the inside
but from the outside, so that it may be possible to bring the shield
against stimuli into operation as a means of defence against them.
This is the origin of *projection*, which is destined to play such a large
part in the causation of pathological processes.

All that I would add to this statement is that there must exist a relationship between the shield for protection against *internal* stimuli and that for *external* stimuli. Although in many
persons the shield against the internal may be weaker,[15] it
serves to select and protect him against flooding from within.
The distinction is between outer and inner sources of interference with proper stimulus perception, although "distraction"
and "preoccupation" are sometimes difficult to distinguish
behaviorally. The shields against both outer and inner stimulation seem defective in the schizophrenic.

Whereas Freud is concerned with the dynamic-affective
primarily, James is concerned more particularly with the cognitive. He ends his chapter on "Reasoning" with the statement: "The upshot of what I say simply is that selection implies rejection as well as choice; and that the function of ignoring, or *in*attention, is as vital a factor in mental progress as
the function of attention itself" (1890, Vol. II p. 371). James'
discussion is preceded by a most interesting (and amusing)
comparison of the plebeian's need for completeness in con-
versation, his tendency to express every step of his process of
"reasoning," whether or not it be essential, as opposed to the
aristocrat's tendency "to disdain, to ignore, to overlook" all
but the high points—the essential and primary aspects. James'
description of the former carries with it much of the flavor of
certain hebephrenic behavior, including its overinclusiveness
but *excluding* (and this is very important) its fundamental

---

[15]Indeed, the differential strength of the outer and inner shields may have
important implications for personality and diagnostic classification.

superficiality. Whereas the paranoid overignores and overexcludes, worrying to death the part that he does accept (which rarely includes the essential elements) with circumstantiality, redundancy, and overexplicitness, the hebephrenic appears to find it difficult to ignore anything—*everything* is fleetingly grazed, but with utmost superficiality.

A question might be raised as to whether the "apathy" so often attributed to the schizophrenic is not a type of Jamesian "ignoring." Although there may be some surface similarity, I believe they are essentially different in character. In one case there is a defensiveness against *all* stimulation—both relevant and irrelevant, almost the obverse of James' description of the plebian; in the other, Jamesian "ignoring," there is the highest level of selection of only the most relevant. James goes on to say: "All this suppression of the secondary leaves the field clear, for higher flights—should they choose to come" (1890, Vol. II, p. 371). His statement is an excellent forecast of the detailed expansion of the theme by his student Cannon in the concept of homeostasis, especially as developed in *Wisdom of the Body* (1932).[16]

Stage 2: Perception of stimulus

Given an organism prepared for stimulation, the process of perception (and cognition) of the stimulus follows. When a stimulus is clearly presented, it is ordinarily assumed that the normal subject's perception will be veridical and his response appropriate to the perception, as well as in line with his own intention. In *aussage* (testimony) experiments, it is recognized that the subject may have perceived falsely (because of the deliberately introduced confusing and affective context), but, nevertheless, his response is expected to remain congruent with the false perception and stay in line with his own intention. The schizophrenic, however, not only tends to perceive falsely, but he also responds inappropriately to these er-

---

[16]For a further discussion by James of "inattention," see his chapter on "Attention" (1890, Vol. I, p. 455 ff.).

roneous perceptions. He may give responses incongruent with his actual perception, and perhaps not even in line with his own intention. Interpretations of the schizophrenic's behavior in specific instances are particularly difficult, because his responses may fall into any of these categories of the perception/response complex: the perception may be veridical and the response appropriate, the perception veridical and the response inappropriate, the perception false and the response appropriate to the false perception, or the perception false and the response inappropriate to the false perception.

James once said that "it is the bane of psychology to suppose that where results are similar, processes must be the same" (1890, Vol. I, p. 528). To this I might add that it is equally specious for psychology (as well as other fields) to suppose that where situations appear similar to the experimenter, they also appear similar to the subject ("the experimenter's fallacy"). Since this is not necessarily so, the experimenter must scrupulously check both the accuracy of the subject's response or report, rather than depend on his own suppositions. In the process of forming his perception, the subject may substitute "self-instructions" for the instructions of the investigator in an experiment (or the questions of the interlocutor in a clinical interview), involving modifications that may be voluntary or nonvoluntary, conscious or unconscious. These are capable of shifting the patient from a response at one of these levels of stimulation to another, without either experimenter (or interlocutor), indeed the subject himself, being aware of the change. Self-instructions may even be diametrically opposed to the instructions of the investigator or the questions of the clinical interviewer. In all studies—psychological, physiological, or even biochemical—instructions are given to the subject, usually explicitly and occasionally implicitly, to do, or not to do, something. The directive may be to lie still while a measurement is made or a reading taken, as in taking blood pressure, or it may be no more than a simple request to breathe in and out of a calorimeter. But if the subject "instructs" himself (not voluntarily, of course!), while doing such breathing, to think of some emotional incident, the likelihood of getting the "basal" reading sought is not great.

The peculiar nature of the schizophrenic makes him especially vulnerable to all varieties of stimulation. He is likely to change what is a simple neutral situation for the normal person into a highly stressful one for himself, or the reverse. Psychological studies contend with this problem constantly. The schizophrenic may, for instance, not be "in" the experimental field at all (he may be either preoccupied or distracted); he may misinterpret the instructions (because communication with schizophrenics is often difficult); or he may react with an idiosyncracy that yields incongruous results. One of our patients refused to comply with the request of an examiner to repeat "digits backwards" on the Stanford-Binet, because "it wasn't right to do things backwards." Had he not disclosed the "ethical" principles that guided his conduct and had he instead chosen only to answer incorrectly, we would have been impressed by the "typical" high scatter some have held to be characteristic of schizophrenics! (Harris and Shakow, 1938)

When it comes to the internal stimulus, the situation is both simpler and more complex. It is simpler because it is no longer necessary to place the stimulus in its environmental context, and more complex because it has no bounds—having none of the environmental constraints which it may have if it is external.

Although essentially an integral process, normal perception may still be roughly separated into the six successive phases earlier indicated: 1) sensing, 2) scanning, 3) articulation, 4) setting the stimulus against its background, 5) apperception, and, finally 6) completion and establishment of the perception—after which the stimulus is "available" and ready for response. Assuming this analysis of the perceptual process to be fundamentally correct, I shall consider each of these phases in more detail. In the discussion of the six steps, evidence is presented of pathology in the manner in which the schizophrenic subject perceives. Subsequently, interfering factors in perception characteristic of schizophrenia are considered. Quantitatively, pathology may manifest itself in the strength, the speed, and the frequency of the perception. Qualitatively, there may be marked deviance with respect to focus, duration, complexity, novelty, repetitiveness, and definition of the perception.

Sensing

The sensing part of the perceptual process involves the use of the sense organs in making contact with the world.[17] In distinguishing between sensation and perception I must reconsider the point that was constantly stressed to the older psychologists among us early in our first courses in psychology: namely, that after the first few sensations, never again does the organism experience pure sensations; thereafter, all sensations are actually perceptions. But this teaching was during the days of the simplest kind of neurophysiology. Nowadays, because of a more sophisticated neurophysiology (Shakow, 1978), there appears to be much justification for considering the sensory process as analyzable for itself, even though modified by repetition. Further, when sensory and perceptual behaviors are carefully examined initially, the clinical and experimental data are found to support the view that they are discriminable. Our findings at the Worcester Sate Hospital, coming from direct current threshold studies (Huston, 1934), from implications deriving from other studies (Shakow and Huston, 1936; Huston and Shakow, 1946), and from careful clinical observations, lead us to believe that there is little or no deficit in schizophrenic patients at the simplest sensory level. The sensing process *per se* does not appear to be disturbed, except in certain instances, whereas the perceptual part of the process is. The *primary* sensory qualities of vision,

[17]And what an amazingly rich and complicated process this is! As Dethier (1971) points out, even the lowliest of organisms, those with a marked paucity of receptors, can deal with the surfeit of varied stimuli to which they are exposed. A consideration having similar implications for more advanced organisms is presented by Gibson (1966, p. 264) with respect to equipotentiality of receptors. Cf. also Shands' (1970) discussion of the roles of distance receptors, vision, and audition.

audition, taste, smell, somesthesis, and kinesthesis appear to be normal. [When it comes to the proprioceptive sensations of the semicircular canals, more questions arise (Angyal and Blackman, 1940).]

Scanning

In the scanning part of the perceptual sequence, there is more reason to be impressed with the effect of pathology and, indeed, that of personality generally on this process.[18] Different persons undoubtedly make their first scans of the stimulating environment, or the particular reality with which they are momentarily faced, in individual ways. I am, of course, here accepting the definition of scanning as "running the eye quickly over something" (English and English, 1958), the *first* skimming of a content.[19] It seems to me preferable to limit the scanning stage to this initial, preliminary casual observation, the cursory glancing from one point to another of the total stimulus situation. For the present let us leave the "scanning" aspect defined in this way, although, as we shall see, the process may be rather more complicated than what I am here describing.

Articulation

The phase that follows scanning serves to establish sharper and more distinct boundaries among the different parts of the scanned pattern. Articulation is related to the concept of "sharpening" used by the Klein-Menninger group (Klein, 1970), just as their "leveling" has some relationship to the notion of scanning. Articulation appears to be a necessary base

[18]The findings of Holzman et al. (1974) on eyetracking of visual pursuit is a case in point.

[19]I might point out that some authors, such as Schlesinger (1954, p. 364), tend to use "scanning" in the broader sense, that of a "focusing." For me this is a confusing usage, because such an interpretation appears to include the articulation stage that follows. As the OED points out, "scan" has lost the emphasis it historically had of close analytic observation.

for the next phase, the distinguishing of figure from ground.

COMMENTS ON SCANNING/ARTICULATION

Before going on to the figure/ground phase, however, some of the pathological problems growing out of the scanning/articulation interrelationship should be considered. Here lie some important differentiations between our schizophrenic types, as well as their mutual demarcations from the normal. The varying behaviors expressed in scanning and articulation are probably demonstrated most clearly by the contrasts between hebephrenic and paranoid types. The hebephrenic leaves one with the impression that his first scan of the stimulus world is omnivorous; everything related to the stimulus situation is taken in, even much lying beyond the immediate stimulus situation. It soon becomes abundantly clear, however, that this activity is perfunctory; the hebephrenic merely brushes the surface. Those aspects selected by the patient for reacting to are unpredictable; they may not be focal at all. Such is also the case with his articulation; it does not receive anywhere near the focused attention such a process requires. (This shallow nonselectiveness is probably his defensive way of avoiding reality.) The paranoid, on the other hand, approaches his stimulus world in a distinctly different manner. His scanning process is limited for one of two reasons: either he actually does not scan the range of elements but leaps immediately to articulate a few among those scanned; or, more likely, he has developed a most refined and rapid scanning technique. This technique permits a very rapid preconscious overview of the whole situation, and the selection of only those limited elements that he is prepared to take on for further articulation. The remainder is neglected as nonexistent. (This very high selectivity may be *his* defensive way of avoiding reality.) Contrasting the two types, one might say that hebephrenics are hyperscanners who hypoarticulate, whereas paranoids are hyposcanners who hyperarticulate. The paranoids use a narrow set, but a great deal of focal attention; the hebephrenics superficially use a broad set, with little focal attention. There is a narrowed filtering in the first, a broadened filtering in the latter. There seems to be some basis for considering set as a filter, or as an allocator of attention (Broadbent, 1971; Neisser, 1967; Kahneman, 1973).

The paranoid's approach may be analogous to the hypnotized subject described by James: "He 'apperceives' it, as a preliminary to not seeing it at all!" (1890, Vol. II, pp. 607–608). In the case of the latter, of course, the selection is based on instructions from the hypnotist. Roheim has suggested in relation to mirror behavior (1919) that the paranoid suffers from a reaction-formation against a strong wish to look (having perhaps already surreptitiously looked), limiting himself to elements that might meet his defensive compulsive needs. He is thus a strong and fast scanner who rejects much, but after such rejection goes on to articulate most fully the limited elements he has selected in the scanning process.

To summarize the preceding discussion pictorially, the distinction between schizophrenic and normal response might be depicted as follows:

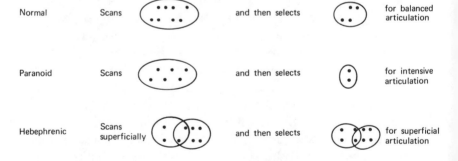

Some attention must be paid to the dynamic, defensive qualities of the situation at this point in the stimulus/response process (although it is not the entire story). It is at this level that what is permitted to enter awareness is decided on and the basis for the reaction established. The subject's encounter with reality is determined by what is readily admitted to consciousness. Viewed dynamically, part of this articulative process is the patient's propensity—already shown in the perceptual process—for being content with a very limited awareness of the outer world. In psychoanalytic terminolgy, he tends to emphasize primary rather than secondary process stimuli.

Figure/ground establishment

Having attained some degree of articulated patterning of the total perceptual presentation, the task still remains of clearly distinguishing figure from ground. Basically, the task is one of concentrating on the figure and ignoring the ground, a nuclear step in the process of establishing the percept as the basis for the response. Otherwise, contaminating effects from the latter might interfere with adequate perception. As Feffer's experiment (1961) indicates, the schizophrenic has great difficulty in keeping the ground from intruding into his perception of the figure.

Apperception

Integral at this point is the apperceptive process, wherein the percept first takes on the beginnings of the set. A variety of apperceptive processes undoubtedly accompany the steps already mentioned, particularly proprioception, bringing associations from similar or related experiences of the past to bear on each phase. Apperception is introduced at this point in order to emphasize its intimate relationship with past similar perceptions leading to the final step of the perceptive process and its important role in achieving the final perception that is to serve as the basis for the response. This is the phase at which set begins to take its final form; it predominates as the generalization emerges in the final stage, which is the response. Previously, the developing percept (which is the roughly processed stimulus information) has been the primary event. But, after apperception takes full control, with the integration of old and new instructions into a new set, the generalization, or "set," becomes predominant in determining the final form that the stimulus information (the percept) takes. In the terminology of Bruner and Postman (1949), the hypothesis is formed and confirmed, and the response follows.

The developing set may be considered to be held in abeyance until the specific apperceptive process takes place, and then the percept is tied into the preexisting, but gradually developed, set. There may be a very vague free-existing set before the sensation, or the set may follow the sensation, in the process of forming the percept. Additional neurophysiological feedback processes (including the proprioceptive) must necessarily enter in here.

The inappropriate generalizations of the schizophrenic are examined in detail in the discussion to follow. They may be partial or irrelevant, focusing on insignificant aspects of the stimulus, rather than on its major substance, or even on quite extraneous aspects of the stimulus situation.

Percept establishment

The final phase in the stimulus portion of the stimulus-response process is the full establishment of the percept. The subject now looks and listens; no longer does he merely see and hear.[20] In the progression of these steps, a transition has gradually taken place—the subject has changed from a sensing to a perceiving organism.

[20]Elizabeth Peabody, the grandmother of the kindergarten movement, whom William James called "the most dissolute woman in Boston" [!] (Matthiessen, 1947, p. 325) because of her "perennial curiosity" in attending lectures, and on whom his brother Henry likely modelled Miss Birdseye in his "Bostonians," once said, upon walking into a tree and bruising her nose while crossing Boston Common: "I saw it, but I did not realize it" (Tharp, 1950, p. 336). Do we have here a relationship among the acme of absentmindedness, unusual spontaneity, transcendental talk, and schizophrenia? One is reminded of the admonition of Sherlock Holmes to Dr. Watson in "A Scandal in Bohemia" (Annotated Sherlock Holmes, Vol. I, 1967, p. 349): "You see, but you do not observe." which brings to mind the oft-quoted statement by Yogi Berra, "You can observe a lot by just watching."

In passing, I cannot refrain from commenting on the tendency among people (cf. Hugh Sidey and others) to confuse sensation and perception. Dean Acheson, for example, has been quoted as saying that someone "listens but does not hear." If Acheson *did* say this, then a psychologist would have to object that he had the mechanics of the situation reversed.

Here again, it must be emphasized that the distinct and systematic delineation of the six phases of the perceptual process given above are only for expository purposes; the actual process is much less clear-cut and decidedly more complicated. There is much oscillation among these steps, much trial and error, many additive and subtractive sub-steps, and much feedback, both negative and positive. In the numerous phases and rephases during each of the first steps preceding the achievement of the final perception, a gradual process of refinement presumably occurs. As a result, later phases of the perceptual process may even have impact on earlier phases. Thus, in the earliest scanning phase there may be a first cursory overview to select sketchily the potentially most relevant aspects of the stimulus field. Then a preliminary phase of articulation may immediately follow, during which these elements are constructed into a rudimentary gestalt. This may be succeeded by a second process of more refined scanning. In such ways the subject gains a degree of certainty as to which elements are relevant, while simultaneously clearing out previously accepted partially irrelevant elements. A more definitive phase of articulation may follow, which provides the basis for a sound figure/ground structure. Expectant sets or rudimentary hypotheses of the stimulus will also influence the process. Such a progression illustrates the kinds of courses of action that may occur in the succession of the various foresteps and backsteps. Clearly, the proceedings are far from simple, direct, and linear.

When an expected stimulus appears suddenly or when an unexpected stimulus appears (unexpected in the sense of being completely unprepared for at that moment, or in the form of an ambiguous stimulus), the situation is modified. At such times, added rephasings or other variations in the ordering and timing may occur. Whatever the case, however, I believe the underlying fundamental processes remain the same.

Interferences in Perception

The passage through the stages of the stimulus/response process is not always smooth. The schizophrenic's perceptual processing disintegrates somewhere along the way. Perceptual interferences may arise from external sources, usually in the form of distractions, or, perhaps more frequently, from internal sources that usually originate from preoccupations, such as hallucinations. Frequently, interfering factors emerge that may be broadly classified as quantitative and qualitative. Quantitatively, the perception may suffer from scantiness or overabundance, or from extremes of speed, intensity, and duration. Qualitatively, seven major types of interference may occur, from difficulties with respect to: personalness, focus, definition, wholeness, variety, complexity, and novelty. Although such interferences may occasionally occur in the normal subject, they are ordinarily not evident in his performance. One or more of these may, however, manifest themselves characteristically in schizophrenic subjects. As is so often the case in schizophrenia, sometimes these are distributed widely over a whole group of patients, whereas at other times they may be limited to particular categories of patients. I shall identify and examine specific types of interference as they have been observed to effect stimulus perception in schizophrenic subjects.

In the present context, *perceptually* relevant interferences will be considered. A later section will focus on these two major types of difficulty with regard to response, although several aspects of the response, especially tentative try-outs of response, are already included at this point.

Quantitative Interferences

PERCEIVED STIMULI SCANTY

Some schizophrenics leave the observer with the impression that they suffer to some degree from a stimulus-starvation, a scantiness of stimulation that appears to be quite acceptable to them (*Reizzufriedenheit*), as if they had deliberately "chosen" it. Whether this condition of "stimulus-satisfaction" is derived from an excess of trivial or scantiness of meaningful stimuli, it may be acceptable because it simplifies a world that the schiozphrenic finds altogether too complex. *Reizzufriedenheit* appears often in chronic schizophrenic patients who have passed from a more to a less active phase of the psychosis ("late indeterminate").

The presence of this condition is ordinarily judged on the basis of the subject's responsiveness. Care must be taken, however, to distinguish between lack of response due to actual paucity of stimulation and lack of response in the presence of sufficient stimulation, where the response process is interfered with in such a manner as to leave the observer with a false impression of paucity. Such clinical characterizations as "apathetic," "washed out," and "nonreceptive" reflect the type of judgments about scanty stimulation often made by observers of these patients. Various physiological studies have shown numerous hyporeactivities in schizophrenic patients (Angyal, 1940). I shall consider the latter situation at greater length when dealing with the interferences on the response side of the paradigm.

OVERLY ABUNDANT STIMULI

The opposite difficulty can be observed when stimuli appear to be overly abundant; the patient seems inundated and overwhelmed by stimulation. *Reizschutz*, seems to be seriously impaired. Regardless of whether the stimulation is relevant, the torrential input interferes with adequate adaptation. Recent literature has stressed such states of excess, perhaps because of the proportionately greater frequency with which younger, more acute, and more anxiety-ridden patients are being studied. Higher GSR resting levels and similar autonomic findings have been offered as corroborative evidence for the existence of such states (Zahn et al., 1968), and some patients, as I have already indicated—MacDonald (1960) and Renée (Sechehaye, 1956, p. 63),—describe this phenomenon in themselves. Barbara Freedman has also compiled instances of this kind (1974).

In my discussion of the papers of Holzman and Silverman (Shakow, unpublished, 1970), I have raised some questions about the ubiquity of this abundance. Each of these authors emphasizes the "flooding" experience that the schizophrenic presumably undergoes. The problem must be approached in two ways, first by defining "flooding" more rigorously, and then by examining how broadly represented this state is in schizophrenia. With respect to the latter, it is necessary to know not only how veridical and common the state is, but also how persistent it is; whether, if it disappears with time, such disappearance is due to well-marshalled mechanisms developed in defense, or if it is merely the result of attrition.

In attempting to define "flooding" clearly its origins call for examination. It may arise from internal or from external sources: from either great preoccupation, or from a plethora of external stimuli and distractions, or from both. It must be recognized, further, that the patient himself often distinguishes between events in this state as either significant or trivial. Thus he may be overwhelmed by events he believes to be of "cosmic" importance, or conversely, by those he views as casual trivialities coming either from within, or from the encompassing environment. Patients have complained to me of both.

But it is particularly the universality of flooding that calls for questioning. I accept the likelihood that it may be frequent in schizophrenia, even characteristic of early schizophrenia, especially in acute states. The world, both inner and outer, in such conditions *is* indeed too much for the patient.[21] But I would point out that, with the passage of time, changes do occur, and occur differentially. In my experience with chronic patients, I have found that flooding can persist and remain almost constant, or it can be periodic in character, or, in some, adequate defenses against it can build up so that the patient is able to maintain some kind of equilibrium. Then there are patients who change sufficiently so that it no longer appears necessary for them to maintain such a defense; they seem to achieve a lower level of functional autonomy, a condition that appears to eliminate any further need to struggle with either regressive or restitutive symptoms. There is an indifference to stimuli, and a marked failure in *Reizsuche*. These are the patients who constitute the "late indeterminate" group I have mentioned.

[21]Cf. Boisen's "A Little-Known Country" in *Out of the Depths* (1960) for a subjective account of such a condition.

From another perspective, flooding may be viewed as part of the phenomenon of incidental perception. The sources of incidental perception may be either external or internal. Environmental incidental elements may be irrelevant, such as the variety of extraneous noises to which the normal person is constantly being subjected, or they may on occasion be relevant and adaptive. The incidental elements arising from inner sources are likely to arise from past experiences interfering with adaptive perception. When overloading occurs in such patients, as in the hebephrenic, then the "cluttered mind" of the schizophrenic does not result from an overabundance of relevant stimuli, but rather from a failure of *Reizschutz*, a predominance of irrelevant stimuli, in the context of a few relevant ones. Helmholtz' law of inattention appears to have been repealed, although from the point of view of the schizophrenic it is these irrelevant associations that may give the impression to the outsider of the patient's involvement in the task. But it must be emphasized that it is only when selective *inattention* is predominant, rather than selective attention, that segmental set rules.

Here, as elsewhere, one is compelled to consider a wide range of functioning represented by the complex of conditions we call schizophrenia. Although "overwhelment" may in the intital stages of the psychosis have been true of most patients, with time many of them develop one or more varied adaptive devices that tend, in some way, to reduce or modify this state. Whatever the case with regard to the absolute amount of stimulation, it is probably correct to say that the ratio of "noise" to signal is much higher in the schizophrenic—even for the paranoid, in whom both are reduced. This is to say nothing of the situation where the stimuli are abundant, but redundant, where the amount of information is small and the "noise" level great.

There are times when a patient's psyche can be characterized only by the term "seething cauldron," a state implying much stimulation not only in quantity (the amount of different kinds of motivation), but in intensity (of the motivations). But it is in response to *irrelevant* stimuli that the schizophrenic is "seething" (from a realistic standpoint).

The next three quantitative areas of interference—speed, intensity, and duration—are difficult to distinguish from one another because they often intertwine, with stimuli appearing to come either at great speed, high intensity, and enduring seemingly forever.

SPEED: OVERSLOW OR OVERFAST

The perceived stimuli may be overslow, appearing at a reduced rate, a phenomenon related to "scantiness," or they may come too fast to assimilate. The patient is so overwhelmed by the situation that he responds to only the most neutral of the presented situations.

INTENSITY: TOO INTENSE OR TOO MILD

At a certain stage of schizophrenia, usually early in the psychosis, stimuli are perceived as too intense to bear. Stimuli have a degree of intensity that appears to be extraordinary in comparison to the normal degree in both effectiveness and strength. Inherent in every stimulus is the capability of making or breaking the subject's "state of mind." This difficult state can not be sustained for long, and it inevitably leads to an opportunity for the opposite state to take over. More characteristic of the schizophrenic, especially in an advanced state, is the perception of stimuli as too mild. Barely requiring action, such a stimulus does not have sufficient demand-quality for response and is reflected in part by the lowered responsiveness to "orienting" stimuli.[22]

DURATION: TOO SHORT OR TOO LONG

In the case of duration interfering with perception, the stimuli may seem too short, too brief to be effective for inducing conduct, or they may last too long, seem drawn out, have a viscid quality, and seem never-ending. Mark Vonnegut provides an apt example of this in his book *The Eden Express* (1975, pp. 65–77):

[22]See Footnote 2 in Chapter 2.

Small tasks became incredibly intricate and complex. It started with pruning the fruit trees. One saw cut would take forever. I was completely absorbed in the sawdust floating gently to the ground, the feel of the saw in my hand, the incredible patterns in the bark, the muscles in my arm pulling back and then pushing forward. Everything stretched infinitely in all directions. Suddenly it seemed as if everything was slowing down and I would never finish sawing the limb. Then by some miracle that branch would be done and I'd have to rest, completely blown out. The same thing kept happening over and over. Then I found myself being unable to stick with any one tree. I'd take a branch here, a couple there. It seemed I had been working for hours and hours but the sun hadn't moved at all.

Qualitative Interferences

The other major category of perceptual pathology arises in the quality of the perception. Diagnosis depends heavily on observations resulting from qualitative interferences.

PERSONALNESS

Because personalness is a somewhat unique aspect of quality, I will discuss it first. In clinical situations particularly, personalness can take on crucial importance in the economy of the schizophrenic. Because of the extent to which the schizophrenic is self-centered, it may have serious consequences, as in the case of Renée, who reports:

Unhappily, Mama [her therapist] did not comprehend the intense culpability ready to sweep over me the moment I took the initiative in creating the pleasure myself. She said something dreadful: "Bathe Renée only when she wants to; she loves it, don't you Renée?"
A tearing rage against Mama rose up in me. How could she do anything like that to me, anything so shameful! To declare openly that it was I, Renée, who wanted the pleasure of a bath! The blame attached to this was immediately reawakened and I vehemently refused to bathe. (Sechehaye, 1970, p. 73)

Months passed before the relationship with Mama was restored because of this bestowing of the initiative onto the patient.

In my own experience, a patient undergoing analysis raised

the suggestion after many months of treatment that his cure lay in drinking 10 cups of coffee at one time. It would be his declaration of independence from his mother, who had dominated his life. After he had stated this on many occasions, I tentatively suggested the possibility of having this wish fulfilled. If he ever wanted to, all he had to do was ask the nurse on the ward to let him have the coffee. In the meantime, I arranged with the nurse to let him have his wish if he ever came to her. I did not hear any more of this until about a half year later, when he divulged in our daily sessions that my mention of the coffee-drinking [and his actual drinking of some 6 (!) cups] had resulted in a significant breakdown in our relationship. My tentative acceptance of his own initiative in this pleasure-seeking and his attempt to carry out the wish had reawakened the guilt. For him, drinking coffee signified a break with his mother because she had forbidden him to drink it (on the grounds that he "was not old enough"). Because his guilt had been aroused by my "permissiveness," (i.e. my recognition of his wishes) he blamed me (the tendency to blame others).

The results of our tapping experiment (Shakow and Huston, 1936) corroborated the effectiveness of giving the schizophrenic subject a certain autonomy *of which he was not aware.* Although a patient was told to respond when the "ready" signal was given, his performance was actually measured from ¾″ *after* the time he began. Therefore, when he actually tapped for 5¾″, only the last 5″ was counted. This was without his knowledge because, even in such an impersonal situation as this, knowledge alone for a schizophrenic subject is enough to awaken guilts of achieving, and lack of knowledge serves as an aid to achieving.

The interference of personalization is demonstrated clearly in the study by Feffer (1961), which has been briefly mentioned. The subjects in this investigation were two types of schizophrenics, an adequately conceptualizing group and a pathologically concrete group, and a group of normal (adequately conceptualizing) controls. Words that constituted the figure and ground in a figure/ground arrangement were presented tachistoscopically in a variety of combinations of affective and neutral contents. (The "affectiveness" or "neutrality" of content had been predetermined for each subject individually by prior testing.)

The group of schizophrenics whose thinking was characterized by concreteness *avoided* affect wherever it occurred (whether in figure or ground), whereas the conceptualizing group *sought* affect wherever it occurred (whether in figure or ground). The normal group, on the contrary, reacted only to the figure—affectively when affect was present in it, and neutrally when the figure was neutral. The schizophrenic contamination of figure by ground, whether it be positive (drawn to the affect) or negative (drawn away from the affect), represents one example of a pathological effect resulting from personalizing the stimulus.

Clearly relevant to the present argument is a point made by Shimkunas, Gynther, and Smith (1967) calling attention to Goldstein's distinction between the organic and the schizophrenic reaction to the concrete: unlike the usual case in organic patients, for schizophrenic patients, *"personal ideas enter and influence the performance"* (Goldstein, 1944/1964, p. 36, emphasis added). There is personalized thinking that is quite similar to Buss and Lang's (1965) "idiosyncratic response" and Shimkunas' "autistic response" (1970). Such personal toning plays a considerable role in schizophrenic perception; there is a marked tendency to personalize what is objectively impersonal. This characteristic may very well lie behind the striking "neophobia" shown by such patients. New situations, in particular, appear to have personal implications that must be assimilated before the schizophrenic can react at even his own (usually lower) functional level.

Contrary to this tendency and less frequent is the case in which the patient depersonalizes what is patently personal. At the clinical level, for example, he does not accept a factual statement that something calamitous has happened to a parent or that some misfortune has overtaken his plans; these events pass him by as if they had never happened. He reacts like the subjects who avoided affect in the Feffer situation; as if the calamity had not occurred.

The same tendency to depersonalize is apparent in the animation or deanimation of the percept, an aspect of personalness that is often experienced by the schizophrenic subject. Renee, for example, in describing her school class, says:

The other children heads bent over their work, were robots or puppets, moved by an invisible mechanism. On the platform, the teacher, too, talking, gesticulating, rising to write on the blackboard, was a grotesque jack-in-the-box. (Sechehaye, 1970, p. 24).

Quite the opposite may occur—inanimate things may become animate. When Renée looked at a jug or a chair, it began to exist; she writes: "it was a living, mocking thing" (p. 40). Thus the impersonal object may become "alive," whereas the human or the living may become a "thing," devoid of life.

Other pathological qualities of perceptual interference fall into six classes in which irrelevancy may appear; focus, definition, wholeness, variety, complexity, and novelty. These qualities result in percepts intrinsically unrelated to the fundamental direction and "intent" of the stimulus.

INADEQUATE FOCUS

The quality of focus is concerned with the signal-to-noise ratio of information in the system. A superfluity of noise produces a low signal-to-noise ratio. When little pertinent information is provided in a context of irrelevent stimulation, a slim basis for adequate adaptive response is available. To express the problem in figure/ground terms, the figure is so burdened with a multitude of either internally or externally derived irrelevant material from the ground that it is contaminated and overwhelmed. The peripheral aspects of the stimulus take primacy over the focal.

In many of our studies of schizophrenics, primarily those in which careful attention is important, we repeatedly found "irrelevancies" achieving prepotency against the focal stimulus demands. This problem revealed itself in a variety of ways,

including susceptibility to distractions introduced by the experimenter and spontaneous preoccupations growing out of
inner demands. For example, in the former case, the subject
would be asked to respond only to the yellow stimulus when
he was shown two stimuli (red and yellow), and the presentation of the red stimulus was enough to disturb him. In the latter case, the subject was presented with only the stimulus to
which he was to respond (the yellow stimulus) but then a passing sound distracted him.

Frequently, the schizophrenic's responses reveal a variety
of nonfocal types of responding, among which one can distinguish the following types of aberrancies:

1. The central, directly meaningful stimulus is avoided, apparently because it is disturbing; instead, the peripheral
   is endowed with meaning.

2. A casual attitude appears in which part of the field is accepted as the stimulus.

3. Prepotency is determined on "quirky" grounds. The
   subject has a "fixed" idea and resorts to it without regard for the stimulus.

4. The peripheral is accepted on the basis of what I have
   called "tcheppiness" [23]—it happens to be first at hand,
   or is selectively attended to, captures attention, and is
   adhered to.

The schizophrenic may consistently fall into the use of one of
these, or may more frequently shift from one kind of distorted
perception to another.

Inadequate Definition

The type of "interference" in which stimuli are inadequately
defined (resulting in ambiguity and unclarity) arises during a
process analogous to Head's dual sensory system, with proto-

---

[23]"Tcheppiness" is a Yiddish term that signifies a tendency to latch onto the
irrelevant and become entangled in it. This was also noted by Bingley as the
most common personality trait of psychomotor epilepsy. (*Acta Psychiatrica
et Neurologica Scandinavica*, Suppl. 120, 1958)

pathic (coarse) and epicritic (refined) levels of sensation. According to Head (1920), the protopathic system provides stimuli that are intense, diffuse, persistent, affective, and carry relatively little information. The epicritic system, on the other hand, provides stimulation that is refined, discrete, precisely localized, affectively neutral, and carries much information.[24] Without becoming involved in the neurophysiological controversy (Semmes, unpublished, 1969; Walshe, 1942) that followed Head's theorizing about the epicritic and protopathic, I might comment that, from the psychologist's standpoint, if such a notion had not been put forth by Head, someone else would soon have proposed it. Recently, Neisser (1967) suggests such a distinction in his approach to cognition. In line with the compelling argument about a "conceptual neurology" put forth by Konorski (1967), experience with schizophrenics demands hypothesizing of this kind. There appears to me to be extensive evidence (from my experience with schizophrenics) for the existence of something like a protopathic process and what might even be considered a hyperepicritic one. The evidence for the hyperepicritic process is largely based on observation of paranoid behavior, whereas the evidence for the protopathic is obtained from examination of the behavior of the hebephrenic.[25]

[24]Cf. Semmes (1969) and Simmel (unpublished, 1963) for further discussion of Head's theory. Extrapolating Head's use of protopathic and epicritic, Rivers (1922) and Sullivan (Mullahy, 1948, pp. 286–291), respectively, have developed concepts of "protopathic" and "prototaxis." Although, like mine, their terms have a general relationship to dynamic referents, their meanings refer only in a limited way to what I have in mind. Rivers comes closer to my meaning, having derived it directly from the same source, Head. However, his use of the term is not identical with Head's. When he talks about the "protopathic," Rivers seems to refer to the all-or-none character and rudeness of emotive reactions and sensibility, whereas, for him the epicritic has to do with the reasoned and adaptive. The term "prototaxis" for Sullivan describes a stage of development in the newborn, a mode of experience in which primary states are undifferentiated and stimulated.

[25]In this context, it might be appropriate to point out the analogous relationships of psychoanalytic primary process and the dream state to the protopathic, and of secondary process and the waking state (reality) to the epicritic.

In terms of the protopathic-epicritic distinction, there seem to be four major patterns of normal and pathological perceiving:

1. The subject starts with a protopathic-like perception, and then follows through with the epicritic, which he uses as the basis for response. The normal subject usually follows this course.

2. The subject is satisfied with a coarse, protopathic-like approximate kind of perceiving, and does not become involved at all with "epicritic" discrimination. He accepts anything at all similar in nature or in any way related to the stimulus as the stimulus. This is particularly exemplified by hebephrenic patients who are essentially approximators of this kind. A comment of Storch (1924) on this phenomenon, though stated in somewhat different phraseology, is pertinent. In his discussion of "Komplexqualitaten" he says: For the schizophrenic, the world of objects is often no longer composed of separate things, each distinct from the other, as it is for us: the world of inner experiences is not organized in relatively isolated groups; in place of abstract ideas, there are "perceptual analogies of ideas," diffuse complex qualities *(Komplexqualitaten)*. The mental constants which render possible the formation of definitely circumscribed representations of person and things, the complete circles of experience, clearcut concepts, are all wanting. The consciousness of objects has suffered a loss of structure and constancy and has sunk to a lower evolutional level, to that of the quality-complexes.[26]

3. The subject proceeds through both stages, but settling for epicritic perception does not seem to be sufficient. He glosses over this stage (on occasion he may even skip it entirely) and advances beyond to a kind of hyperepicritic state (of his hyperarticulation), as evidenced particularly by paranoid patients. Since the paranoid is basi-

[26]Cf. also Werner's related concept of "physiognomic perception" (1948, p. 67 ff.), an important part of his theoretical system.

cally a caviller, or, at best, an overscrupler, he has to tease out the minutest details of the already refined. His defensive system appears to require going beyond normal perceptual refinement to a kind of dismemberment (*Zergliederung*), an emphasis on fundamentally irrelevant minor elements. Even at best, when these are verdical, they are nonadaptive. Another more pronounced type of Zergliederung is discussed below.

4. Another disturbance may be seen when the subject makes an immediate jump into some partial aspect of the epicritic without going through protopathic exploration at all. He makes a sudden leap, presumably from anxiety, onto the easiest available cue—a kind of "grasping at straws"; he clings to the nearest detailed part of what is essentially a complex presentation without having gone through the preliminary stages of gross scanning and overview. Under such circumstances a truly discriminatory reaction cannot occur. Such behavior is quite often found in hebephrenics.

Viewing the issue as a whole, even if I concur with Mies van der Rohe in his pronouncement and agree that "God is in the detail,"[27] I do so only with the reservation that the accepted detail follows some previously generalized overview, and, further, that the detail is significant, not picayune—in Rorschach terms, that it is of "D" rather than "Dd" character.

IMPROPER ORGANIZATION/WHOLENESS

In a setting providing no more than a helter-skelter arrangement of elements, one which as presented does not fit together in any unified manner, the normal subject experiences great difficulty in establishing a natural gestalt to which to respond.[28] He complains of its "unorganizability." Some

[27]According to Peter Gay (1975, p. 39), it was actually Aby Warburg, the art historian and founder of the famous library, who first made this remark.
[28]Cf. Rickers-Ovsiankina (1937a, 1937b), Bennett (1941, 1942), and Shakow and Rosenzweig (impersonalizing of the personal in the play techniques, 1937).

schizophrenic subjects, on the contrary, take these in stride. By some idiosyncratic tour de force, they assemble these isolated elements into an artificial, unreal gestalt, which they then report as an acceptable structure. In many of our studies, perceptions of this kind are clearly evidenced, particularly among hebephrenics. In an experiment using play technique, a markedly jumbled placement of dolls, furniture, and blocks were designated by a patient as representing a dining room where a meal was being served and were pointed to individually as if they were elements of a genuinely organized unit (Shakow and Rosenzweig, 1937).

Conversely, in some patients a type of Zergliederung may be found. What the normal person spontaneously accepts as an obvious, natural unit is pulled apart to form a quite different stimulus. Thus, one patient complained that the cafeteria menu publicly posted excretory items, for did it not list one that said "so-you-pee!" He referred to "soup." Another instance of the cognitive Zergliederung that one finds in schizophrenia is exemplified by Renee when she saw the separate features of a face, but could not see them as a whole face (Sechehaye, 1970, p. 37).

TOO MUCH REDUNDANCY OR TOO MUCH VARIETY

Another aspect of the scantiness/abundance problem is manifested in the question of how much *sameness* there is in the stimuli. This aspect of the problem has been brought to the fore particularly by recent information theory, the physiological theorizing of Pribram (Pribram and McGuiness, 1975), and the psychological theorizing of Cromwell (1975) and Shands (1967) about schizophrenia. Some schizophrenics give the impression that they are troubled by an abundance of stimulation that is altogether too repetitive. In terms of information theory they suffer from a redundancy of stimuli that provides too much stimulation and, at the same time, little information. A subject often finds himself dunned by the monotonous quality of these stimuli. Normal persons, on the contrary, are characterized by an amount of redundancy sufficient to make adaptation easier. The opposite distortion, too much variety, is a failure likely to occur in hebephrenia. The stimuli come too quickly; the novelty is too rapid and superficial to be absorbed.

In the context of the immediately preceding discussion, it seems clear that at one extreme there may be a combination of high redundancy with either scantiness or overabundance (few stimuli of the same kind or many stimuli of the same kind), and at the other extreme there may be low redundancy combined with scantiness or abundance (few stimuli of varied kinds, or many stimuli of varied kinds).

In this category, one must also include the rigidity or looseness of the perception. On the one hand, a patient may be unable to see an object as representing something else, that is, a skein of wool as representing a color, or a picture of a horse as representing a class of animals [as in Hanfmann's (1939) patient]. On the other hand, a patient may react with extreme looseness, designating almost any symbol for any referent, as in the case of our play experiment, where the patient called both a chair and an infant, a "dead bird."

COMPLEXITY

Pathology involving variety may be related to the qualitative interferences of complexity. For the normal person, a stimulus is treated more or less according to its actual complexity. Frequently, however, a schizophrenic subject—often a hebephrenic—greatly simplifies or complicates a situation. In our study, the subject was told to represent something happening in the life of a child. He presented the scene in its very simplest terms, lining up the same type of objects in groups (e.g., dolls, blocks, furniture). He then gave a baldly simple account: "they were all happy." Conversely, we were sometimes told a story so complex, so full of irrelevancies, circumstantialities, etc., as to render it incomprehensible. The normal treats the situation realistically, simplifying some situations, complicating others, according to what is called for.

NOVELTY

To draw an extreme analogy, schizophrenics are like wild rats (Barnett, 1958a, 1958b) in that they tend to avoid genuinely novel stimuli and are perceptually sensitive to the appearance of such stimuli in the field. They may either disregard their "newness" and perceive them essentially as old, or disregard the stimulus altogether, as if it did not exist. Each is a form of the defense labelled "denial." This tendency is such a pervasive characteristic of schizophrenia that I shall postpone its detailed discussion until my discussion of general schizophrenic characteristics, but for present purposes I call attention to the theorizing about neophobia by Shands (1967, 1970a, 1970b, 1974), who offers a cogent analysis of the situation.

Stage 3: The encoding of the perception

Encoding of the perception, whereby information becomes available to the effector system, is the internal central process about which there is the least direct knowledge. Since this is a topic with which I have less than adequate acquaintance, I am not discussing it. The reader is referred to Quarton et al. (1967) and Thompson (1976).

Stage 4: Response to the stimulus: Interfering Factors

The information that has come to the output stage through the input and central processing stages contains implicitly the nature of the response of the subject to the stimulus situation. Succession of stimulus/responses as well as the individual processes are considered, since disturbance in schizophrenia is manifested particularly in the sequence of behavior. In this presentation the description, the response, and its pathology are treated together, a different approach from that utilized in the discussion of perception, because in this context I believe that it makes more sense.

Because of the striking qualitative aberrancies so prominent in the schizophrenic's responses, it is understandable that their quantitative aspects have received less attention, except notably in the studies by Buchsbaum and associates (1975). The quantitative characteristics of speed and strength (intensity), as well as the many qualitative characteristics of response, are examined here.

Quantitative aspects

SPEED

With respect to speed, responses may be roughly categorized into six classes: (1) measured reaction, which is a response appropriate in speed and intensity to the nature of the stimulus; (2) no reaction, in which no overt manifestation of responsiveness is evidenced; (3) slow reaction, in which the subject's response is drawn out—it may start promptly but has a viscid quality; (4) rapid rate of reaction, in which the reaction comes very quickly; (5) delayed reaction, in which the response, although adequate, arrives only after a relatively long interval of nonresponse or latency;[29] (6) precipitate reaction, in which the subject responds as if all triggered to react, without apparently having permitted the full information processing to take its course—responding as if he were living in a "specious present."

Although all of these varieties of response may be found in the schizophrenic, one or another of the last five kinds of nonadaptive reactions may characterize any one patient. On occasion, one of the last five categories of reaction may also be found in the normal person, but characteristically his response is measured. It must be recognized, of course, that since the normal person's response is under considerable control, he can at times deliberately distort his response by utiliz-

---

[29]Under conditions that permit such a possibility, the response may be extremely delayed. An example of this is the aptly labelled *Treppenwitz*, or "step-wit." This refers to the person who only on his return home, literally as he is ascending the steps to his dwelling, thinks of the "crushing repartee" (Princess Ida) that should have come to mind during an earlier disputation with a companion.

ing one or another of these categories for comic or dramatic effect. Such control is rare in the schizophrenic.

The speed of the schizophrenic's responses generally fall at the extremes of delay or, occasionally, of precipitateness. Quite frequently we find the response of the schizophrenic to be delayed much beyond that of the normal subject. The slowness may be in initiating the response or in executing it. The widely employed clinical symptom labels "initial" and "executive retardation" are intended to designate just such differences. In many of our experimental studies, we found the delay to be in initiating the response; it is markedly evident in reaction time. In the latter case, delay may be involved at almost each successive step of the process. In clinical situations responses frequently have the indecisive quality described in James' chapter on habit (1890). In the schizophrenic, this indecision may show itself to a highly exaggerated degree. Thus, I have seen a patient at Worcester spend almost an hour trying to "make up his mind" about entering the open door of the laboratory to which he had earlier indicated his readiness to come for an interview. His last few steps, particularly, were acted out with the highest degree of ambitendency—a step forward, a step back, forth and back, forth and back, without apparently being able to bring himself to take decisive action. (See page 24). (An important dynamic process must underlie such behavior, as Angyal pointed out in 1936).

In the normal stimulus/response process, a temporal string of stimulus signals with tentative subresponses are apparently accumulated and held in abeyance usually until the end of the chain, when they are integrated into a totality that is handled as a unit. Only then does the final response come. In the precipitate schizophrenic response, what appears to be missing is this ability to abey action—to postpone reacting until the proper amount of information for adequate response is available. This was made evident to us in the reaction/time experiment in which different preparatory intervals were used. It was impossible to get certain patients to wait for the proper interval—they would sometimes anticipate it by using a more pronounced manual reaction, as if to make up for the anticipation. Responses follow the stimulus so closely that they clearly indicate that the patient cannot possibly have gone through the cycle of steps involved in the stimulus/response process. It is as if the schizophrenic is "primed" to give a response, and, regardless of what the stimulus is, or when it occurs, he invariably gives this response. Hebephrenics are most likely to do this. Fast execution is usually associated with precipitate initiation of the response. Although it is possible to associate it with slow initiation, accelerated response is most often precipitate.

INTENSITY

The intensity of a response (which may be seen as either perceptual or responsive) may be congruent with the strength of the stimulus, or it may be either too weak or too intense. A schizophrenic subject on the one hand reports experiences of enhanced sensory stimuli, as in the case of Morag Coate (1965, Chapter II), or the opposite experience of muted sensory awareness (Sullivan, 1962). The extremes are represented by withdrawn and hyperresponsive behavior.

Withdrawal is a widespread feature of schizophrenic behavior, observed frequently at the clinical level but almost as often in experimental and test situations. In the latter, it may appear as a deliberate or an involuntary lack of cooperation, or a low level of involvement in situations, whether psychological or physiological, with consequently impaired performance. In the clinical situation the withdrawal symptom is ubiquitous, and, indeed, such behavior is used as a major diagnostic criterion for schizophrenia.

Hyperresponsivity, the contrary behavior, is seen particularly in the clinical behavior of those patients who are in the excited catatonic state. Hyperresponsivity may manifest itself in this case in the form of quite sudden and extreme outbursts. It is also occasionally observed in the behavior of hebephrenic patients, in the form of superficial flightiness demonstrated by rapid, goalless shifting of attention all over the field. Analogous behavior may be observed in the test and experimental situations in which such patients participate. The higher baseline "arousal" levels so frequently found in schizophrenics (Zahn et al., 1968) may be another reflection of this characteristic.

Qualitative aspects

It is the quality of response that is most strikingly deviant in the schizophrenic. The diagnosis is often based on it. One can categorize these qualitative aberrations under the broad rubric of "irrelevant," but it is a matter not only of degree of irrelevancy, but of its more specific nature.[30]

An appropriate response is congruent with the stimulus input and suited to the nature of the situation; it also enables the organism to proceed with the business of living by progressing sucessively from the present stimulus/response sequence on to the next, and so on. Inappropriate responses vary widely and are inadequate with respect to: (a) *structural* (formal) aspects, fundamentally cognitive, such as wholeness, complexity, refinement, control, organization, and imitativeness of the stimulus; to (b) what might be characterized as *projective* (affective) aspects, such as individuality, affectivity, and personalness; and to (c) *conative* aspects, such as spontaneity, effort and goal-orientation, or goal-direction. Usually a combination of these varieties of maladaptive response patterns occurs, depending on the degree of pathology.

STRUCTURAL QUALITIES (FORMAL COGNITION)

Disturbances in formal or structural quality are reflected in many varieties of response, frequently at bipolar extremes, with formal aspects, emphasized at the expense of the conten-

---

[30]The question of "irrelevancy" leads me to raise questions about Wishner's characterization (obviously correct) of schizophrenic behavior as inefficient (1955, 1965). Further specification of the inefficiency is needed; the qualitative range of irrelevancy includes a multiplicity of distortions that, in one way or a other, reflect maladaptive response.

tual (apparently to avoid affect). These qualities of disturbances, with their corresponding responses, may be classified as follows: (a) wholeness—overspecified/overgeneralized; (b) complexity—oversimplified/overcomplicated; (c) refinement—overformalized/overcontentualized; (d) organization—overorganized/confused; (e) flexibility—rigidity/looseness, and (f) imitativeness—echoistic/negativistic.

Wholeness. In disturbances of wholeness, responses tend to be overspecified or overgeneralized, with excessive reaction to the formal aspects of the stimulus rather than to its substance. On the one hand, the patient may generalize the stimulus, placing it in a higher category. For example, he may react to a female figure as if it were a generalized stimulus, rather than his own sister. On the other hand, the response may attach itself to one segment or another of the total, dealing with only a narrow portion of the stimulus situation, as if the person is compelled to grasp hold of the nearest detail, no matter how minute. For instance, a patient may respond only to a peculiar design in a woman's dress and entirely disregard the fact that it is his own sister wearing it. This reaction represents a kind of the "tcheppiness" to which I have referred, an apt Yiddish term for a low-level form of compulsive attachment, a kind of "snagginess." The schizophrenic, particularly the hebephrenic, is to an extraordinary degree a "clutcher at reeds," a "grasper at straws." The subject appears to treat an insignificant part of the situation as if it were the significant whole. Renee writes, "as soon as my gaze fell on a spot of any sort . . . I could not drag it away, caught and held fast by the boundless world of the infinitely small." (Sechehaye, 1970, p. 56).

It must be made clear that the responses dealing with details discussed here do not fall into the class of relevant details, acclaimed by Mies van der Rohe or Warburg, that was mentioned earlier in my consideration of the stimulus end of the paradigm. Neither do they concern the "trivials"—the transitives—that James found so important, which are significant, though small, facts of the stimulus/response situation. (Of course, the details may well be relevant and even significant, but the focal attention given to them is totally disproportionate, and the response is thereby a distortion.)

In certain patients, both in clinical and experimental situations, we find a peculiar type of circumstantiality. This deep preoccupation is especially likely to occur in paranoid patients, as seen for instance, in accessibility experiments (Rickers-Ovsiankina, 1937a, 1937b; Bennett, 1941, 1942). There may be a related type of concretization, as seen for instance in Renee, who could recognize someone she knew only if that person were in a specific setting. A patient of Hanfmann's (1939c) refused to look for the ball lost in the ball-and-field test on the Stanford-Binet, since she did now own a ball and, therefore, could not lose it. Taken more broadly, they are unable to see a thing as *representing* something else. The defect seems to be a loss of the conceptual or the categorical (categorial) attitude, which some authors consider the major deficit in schizophrenia. Allan Gregg (1957), in a talk he gave to medical students entitled "Narrative for a Specialist," closes his essay with a quotation from Socrates in Plato's Charmides, quoting a Thracian physician: "And this was the reason why most maladies evaded the physicians of Greece—that they neglected the whole on which they ought to spend their pains, for if this were out of order it was impossible for the part to be in order" (p. 97). Schizophrenics, especially paranoids, even more than Greek physicians, are *specialists*—in fact, as *emphasizers of the part and neglecters of the whole*, there are none better. The hebephrenic's great concern with detail is highly superficial by comparison to the normal's responses to the same detail. Yet, the responses of schizophrenics may also display an exasperating degree of vagueness and generality; a schizophrenic may act as if there are no trees, only forests. There may be situations when unrelated ideas are brought together in any connection, such as, for instance, when a patient smashed a window pane because the doctor who wore glasses was coming (Bleuler, 1924, p. 377). More simply, the schizophrenic often creates generalizations or "wholes" where no basis in the particulars he is presented with exists.

Complexity. Related to difficulties with respect to wholeness is the tendency to oversimplify or overcomplicate the stimulus in ways that interfere with adequate response. We are concerned here primarily with the response to the situation. It is, of course, difficult to distinguish between them—a chicken/egg question. The tendency to oversimplify, to react to only part of the veridical situation or at most only to its superficial general characteristics, may be the factor involved in causing the robot-like physiological behavior of schizophrenics—reflected in their higher correlation coefficients between oral/rectal temperatures and systolic/diastolic levels than in normals. In the psychological realm it is reflected in behavior like that of a hebephrenic patient whom I have described who, in a play situation, blithely lined up the blocks and dolls in rows and described this as "something important happening in the life of a child," (Shakow and Rosenzweig, 1937). The paranoid trims the stimulus down to what is important for him, what he "feels safe" with; the hebephrenic takes the superficial characteristics from the surface and deals with nothing in depth. Both types of "purifying" are simplistic rather than concise or essential.

The antithesis may also occur; the response is inappropriate due to the overcomplication of the stimulus. This was observed in Searles' hebephrenic patient, who saw 200–300 doctors in the room when there was only one, because every time the doctor changed posture it was another person from her past that she saw (1965, p. 307).[31]

Refinement. The coarseness or refinement of a response is another aspect of irrelevancy that corresponds to the protopathic/epicritic differentiation examined earlier in relation to the stimulus. Actually, the degree of refinement of response can describe a wide variety of the aberrancies of behavior in the schizophrenic. An "approximate" response is often offered in place of the appropriate specific response. Of

---

[31]A similar situation is demonstrated by the autistic 17-month-old Raun (Kaufman, 1976), who did not seem to be able to deal with human stimuli because they were always changing, preferring objects whose movements he could control himself.

course, all of us are familiar with this kind of response in the normal range of functioning. Expecially during states of preeoccupation, one may, for instance, turn off a light—especially if the light switch is close by—rather than the faucet one intended to shut off. When a response is called for, it is as if there is both a *general* response set—that is, to discontinue an ongoing concrete activity—and a *specific* set to make the appropriate specific response—that is to turn a faucet clockwise. In states of preoccupation (or distraction), the general set appears to be prepotent and one of the many forms of this general kind of response is carried out, instead of the specific one the situation requires. One may think of it as an hierarchical organization of stored responses, the refined selection of which has not been carried through. (This behavior would seem to have important implications for neurological theorizing.)

Thus, sometimes a patient manifests a strong tendency to simplify and confine his reactions to the formal, noncontentual, impersonal aspects of a stimulus and to disregard the complicating content, particularly when it is human in nature. As was noted earlier, Renée remarked that she lost the feeling of practical things: "children were robots moved by an invisible mechanism, the teacher was a grotesque jack in the box" (Sechehaye, 1970, p. 24). At other times, the response to content may be emphasized at the expense of formal qualities; some special aspect of the human, personal, or other part of the content is selected out for reaction without regard for the salient, formal structure in which it is embedded. Renée, for a time, would personalize the right side of the room, empty though it was, and throw things toward the persecutor (ibid., pp. 62–63).

Organization. Irrelevancy with respect to the organization of the response takes the form of confusion or overorganization. This area includes the important aspects of language and communication involvng the abstract and concrete. Regarding the latter, we see not only responses that are literal and concrete (loss of the abstract attitude), but false efforts at generalization that are not truly conceptual and might be called "pseudoepicritic." As I have indicated on another occasion:

There are some investigators who have argued that since the schizophrenic patient is the "most symbolic" of creatures (witness the patient who writes "juicy beefsteak" on a scrap of paper and swallows it with much satisfaction), that therefore he is also a conceptualizer of high degree. One need only point out the obvious fallacy of equating symbolic activity of a syncretic type (Piaget), which makes little or no distinction as to the relevancy of characterizations, with conceptualization, whose very essence is the generalization from the relevant; or of equating the vagueness so frequently found in schizophrenic thinking with abstraction. It cannot be denied that difficulty with conceptual thinking is found in schizophrenic persons, at least within the limits of the kind of activities with which we have been concerned. The possibility pointed out by Lashley (1938), in relation to brain lesions must, however, be kept in mind: that there may be many different kinds of abstractive processes (1946, p. 67).

Certain patients, especially paranoids, frequently find it necessary to organize the response to a particular environment in a meticulous way; loose ends are avoided with the greatest care. In our own experiments, we have seen this demonstrated clearly in the play constructions of paranoid patients (Shakow and Rosenzweig, 1937). For example, in using blocks for constructing the walls of a room, the patient repeatedly interrupted his execution of the task in order to return to making finically certain that the corners of the blocks he had used in the construction were so placed as to make perfect 90-degree angles. He lined them up visually and repeatedly moved them imperceptibly, while barely touching them. His obessive concern with perfection was quite striking. He was also very concerned about the role of each doll in the construction; each was to have one role and one role only.

On the other hand, particularly in the hebephrenic patients, we often find the opposite trend—marked carelessness in organizing their "worlds." It is as if anything may be associated with anything else, and usually in a most far-fetched fashion. This is observed, for instance, in the casual placements of their play constructions, in the idiosyncrasy of their associations in an association test, and, of course, in much of their clinical behavior. What appears to be an attempt to control this confusion on occasion reveals itself in the marked oversimplifications of play situations described earlier (see p. 72). It may be an effort to maintain "order," but it is so highly oversimplified, unrealistic, primitive, and irrelevant as to make it essentially meaningless.

The multiplicity of strange behaviors (or symptoms) exhibited by the schizophrenic are not independent of each other, nor are they limited to specific areas. They appear rather to be different manifestations of an underlying pervasive disorganization that may be subsumed under the concept of segmental set. Organizational pathology is quite frequently found in schizophrenia and is represented in a wide range of conduct. It is reflected particularly in the most prominent schizophrenic symptoms, those related to language and thought. It is strikingly exemplified in the emphasis on the concrete and literal in thinking, and in what has been characterized as "overinclusiveness," the inclusion of irrelevant items in conceptualizing a response. The problem of language cannot be dealt with in isolation, but should rather be viewed in its broader molar context. However, because language is so central and ubiquitous a human function, and because the peculiarities of schizophrenic language are often so arresting, it deserves a separate section; the predominant trend in the literature to deal with it separately is not surprising. Language is not considered in detail in this monograph—I leave it for another occasion—but the general principles of segmental set are applicable.

Flexibility. Another aspect of irrelevancy is reflected by the patterning of the control exerted by the subject on the response, the constraint he imposes on the response with respect to looseness or rigidity, to laxness or strictness. Normal response is rigorous and flexible. Once again, the extremes are represented in schizophrenia, from the rigidity so characteristic of the paranoid to the looseness and unboundedness of the hebephrenic. Some patients, particularly the paranoid, behave in a manner that is distinctly rigid and unyielding. This inelasticity is revealed in a wide variety of clinical and experimental situations, ranging from extremely literal interpretations of instructions (figurative phrases are taken literally) and inability to accept a hypothetical situation, to markedly obsessive-compulsive behavior in the execution of tasks, as was demonstrated, for example, when a patient of ours took five hours to dress.

Other patients, particularly the hebephrenic, characteristically give responses that are predominantly loose in character. The elements of their perception of responses are not organized or unified. Meaning is often interpreted ambiguously; a mood or an object may simultaneously carry multiple contradictory meanings. For example, a patient in the play experiment might use a doll to represent a piano. A patient of Searles (1965, pp. 306–307) "was convinced that her body was a conglomeration of parts from various other people and other people's bodies."

Imitativeness. A final type of aberrancy in the structural quality of response relates to imitativeness. In schizophrenia, one may observe "echoistic" responses that are highly compliant, imitating the stimulus. Occasionally, however, one finds the opposite, a negativistic reaction expressed in a form of extreme resistance, a contrariness that I have called "kopayerism."[32] The situation is at times a battle between compliance and contrariness that becomes truly disquieting, as revealed by Renee's account of her hospitalization, particularly the constant battle between her own feelings and those of the System (Sechehaye, 1970, p. 46).

---

[32]Indeed, at the Worcester State Hospital, during our intensive study of schizophrenics over two decades, we were so struck with this "perversity" that the "cognescenti" among us would call the schizophrenics "Moyshe Kopayers" (a person called Moyshe Kopayer who consistently did the opposite), after a cartoon character in the Yiddish Press (Rosten, 1968, p. 254). I have borrowed this term for the narrower interpretation of negativistic action. The broader term carries no implications of willfulness; rather, it is descriptive of general behavior.

PROJECTIVE QUALITIES (SOCIAL-PERSONAL, AFFECTIVE)

"Projective" aberrancies in the quality of response appear to have a somewhat different source from that of the structural abnormalities, a more personal kind of disarticulation of the person from his background that is more strictly in the social-personal sphere. I will divide these into three types, with respect to individuality, affectivity, and personalness. Although they often overlap, it is useful to consider these aspects separately.

Individuality. Unusual individuality is frequently displayed in both the behavior and speech of the schizophrenic. At its simplest, in test situations such as the association test (Kent and Rosanoff, 1910), the responses of the subject may be strikingly idiosyncratic. In spontaneous comment or in ordinary social intercourse, both the nature of the individual words and their syntactic organization may be quite different from the normal. In a study using the Kent-Rosanoff Association Test, in which the composite score reflects fundamentally the individuality and unusualness of responses as opposed to their commonness (whether "most common" by standard norms, or "common" in the sense that they are to be found in the KR tables), 200 normal subjects had a mean composite score of 9.1, whereas 100 schizophrenic subjects had a mean composite of 19.2, a highly significant difference (Shakow and Jellinek, 1965). In another study, in which 60 schizophrenic and 60 normal subjects were repeatedly reexamined, the schizophrenics maintained this same level of response over five sessions that extended over a period of 16–17 months, whereas the normals, who were reexamined after only two weeks, dropped significantly toward greater commonality from a first level of 10.2 to the second level of 8.0 (Huebner, Master's Thesis, Johns Hopkins University, 1938). In more complex behavioral situations outside of the psychometric, the idiosyncrasy of the schizophrenic is marked.

Normal subjects frequently give a great number of responses that are highly common or popular among the general population in association or similar tests. In schizophrenia, it is rather rare. When it does appear in the latter, it may very well be a reaction formation to the opposite tendency, the underlying pressure for idiosyncratization, rather than the need to belong.

When faced with contentual material in a test or experimental situation, some patients repeat what is presented to them verbatim or almost verbatim, rather than respond appropriately. Echopathy is not an uncommon clinical symptom among schizophrenics; this seems to be an avoidance technique.

Some patients do the contrary; they respond either with the opposite of the contentual material or do the converse of what is called for by the situation. I have characterized this behavior as "kopayeristic." Bleuler (1950, p. 191) gives many instances of this kind of behavior. Analogous behavior is apparently present in certain individuals or groups among the Cheyenne Indians, called "Contraries" (Grinnell, 1960). These members, usually two or three braves held in high regard, are expected by the tribe (presumably for magical reasons) to behave "perversely," that is, in ways directly opposite to conventional response. If they wished to signify assent, they would say "no"; instead of entering a lodge the right way, they would back into and out of the lodge; if asked to ride, they would walk. The essential difference between negativistic patients and Contraries lies, of course, in its social significance. Whereas for the Cheyenne, this "contrary" behavior has the support of the community because it serves some social purpose, in our culture schizophrenic behavior is isolated and individual, and out of context with at least the immediate environment. The behavior is more like that in Ganser's syndrome in that the "contrariness" is almost conscious. In schizophrenia it is not. Behavior of this kind is also seen in some children's games. Edward Everett Hale (1964, p. 69), for instance, describes a game of early New England whereby the Lord's Prayer was repeated backward either literally or figuratively in content.

Affectivity. Disturbances of response with respect to affect—the apathies, hyperpathies, and parapathies—manifested by schizophrenics in their day-by-day behavior, as well as in more formal examination situations, are striking in their range and is one of the most prominent of schizophrenic symptoms. Items from the most trivial to the most profound can carry an affective charge or completely lack it. Renee's "indescribable anguish," which "squeezed my heart," and "anguish no resolve could allay," which seized her when she refused to obey the "System" to burn her hand (Sechehaye, 1970, p. 41), or the sense that she "was devouring the head of a cat which meanwhile gnawed at my vitals," (p. 42) are instances of this involvement with affectivity. At the other extreme, there are the instances of loss of loved ones or considerable loss of money that produce "flat affect" and are dismissed as casual events. Bleuler (1950) describes the disturbances of affective response in considerable and rich detail.

Personalness. Intertwined with the problems of affectivity are those of the affective egocentricity of the schizophrenic. It appears as if almost all interactional situations are personalized, as if the subject cannot see his situation as outside himself or see himself as being evaluated and judged. He thus makes highly impersonal situations personal, and his performance tends to suffer. An extreme example of this can be seen in what Nabokov has referred to as "Referential Mania" in his short story entitled "Signs and Symbols" (*The Portable Nabokov*, 1971):

In these very rare cases the patient imagines that everything happening around him is a veiled reference to his personality and existence. He excludes real people from the conspiracy—because he considers himself to be so much more intelligent than other men. Phenomenal nature shadows him wherever he goes. Clouds in the staring sky transmit to one another, by means of slow signs, incredibly detailed information regarding him. His inmost thoughts are discussed at nightfall, by darkly gesticulating trees. Pebbles or stains or sun flecks form patterns representing in some awful way messages which he must intercept. Everything is a cipher and of everything he is the theme . . .

Renée provides another example, in which she judged the cardinal directions entirely in reference to herself (Sechehaye, 1970, p. 60) and was then not able to orient herself. Almost all situations seem novel to schizophrenics of all types. Because of their novelty, these may have personal reference, and are very disturbing in content.

At the other extreme, there may be a marked degree of depersonalization, a situation in which there does not seem to be a person, an ego, present at all, reminiscent of what James attributed to the child, who seems "to belong less to himself than to every object which happens to catch his notice" (1890, Vol. I, p. 407). This description characterizes the hebephrenic precisely. The normal person, on the other hand, with his self-esteem, intactness, pride, and barriers (in a Lewinian sense), maintains proper boundaries between the personal and impersonal, the egocentric and the allocentric.

With respect to personalization, the behavior of schizophrenic patients falls at both extremes of the response pattern. This is demonstrated particularly clearly in role-playing situations. Some patients, usually hebephrenics, when faced with situations that might resemble role-playing, are markedly facile in their ability to slip from one role to another—much more than the ordinary person. This seems to reflect a kind of impersonalization, or an extreme kind of nonpersonal reference, a looseness that implies a marked absence of a basic underlying personality structure. But most other schizophrenic patients, particularly paranoids, when faced with such role-playing situations, have the greatest difficulty in adopting the designated role at all. At best, they adopt one that is colored considerably by their own personality characteristics, an inability to dissociate themselves from themselves. This appears to be part of a general difficulty with the *als ob*—the ability to assume the hypothetical (as if) position—the quality that plays so important a role in normal functioning, particularly for problem-solving.

CONATIVE ASPECTS

The third qualitative variation in response involves striving and volition, the conative.

Spontaneity is an aspect of conative response that concerns readiness. It may range anywhere from hyperspontaneity—an absence of self-control, or impulsiveness—to a natural and normal self-initiation of response to a relevant cue from the environment, or to a complete absence of any self-initiation of activity. The hebephrenic flits around from one superficial activity to another, creating an artificial impression of spontaneity. The paranoid, on the contrary, is very chary about his spontaneity, disclosing it only reluctantly.

Effort—closely related to sponteneity, but more directly oriented toward the stimulus situation—refers to how much work the subject is willing to put forth to achieve a goal. Having a significant role in what we have termed cooperation, it may range from strong desire to respond fully, seen in normals and particularly in paranoids, to no effort to respond at all, as seen in patients who seem totally preoccupied with themselves.

In addition, there is the *goal-directedness* of the response. Is the response headed directly and with persistence toward the goal intended by the stimulus situation? Or is it pathologically distorted by being undirected or sporadic, discontinuous, or kaleidoscopic?

Rickers-Ovsiankina, in a study of accessibility of schizophrenics to environmental tasks (1937a), shows that normals, while having no outstanding response type, have a medium level of active time, time spent with the actual environmental objects provided, and a medium level of consistency (perseverance with an activity). Normals also prefer directed over undirected activities (working puzzles, for example, rather than merely ringing a bicycle bell) and spend a high percentage of their time at the deeper level (attempting to solve a puzzle as opposed to merely observing it). Paranoids have a persistent type of response, are very high in active time, very high in consistency, and very high in percent time spent on higher levels. They have low but positive means and a somewhat greater excess of directed over undirected activities. Hebephrenics show a kaleidoscopic pattern of responses, with a high active time, medium consistency, a high percentage of time spent at a deeper level, but with undirected activities exceeding the directed to a significant degree. There is thus a directedness in the normal and in the paranoid, but with regard to the latter, this is very limited in scope.

Closely related to this theme are the concepts of *ambiguity*, and tolerance for tentativity, in relation to *als ob*. Tolerance for ambiguity indicates that the subject has a strong base of security that enables him to scrutinize two interpretations on a hypothetical basis, and select a solution. It may be demonstrated by an ability to tolerate situations that are diametrically opposed to one another but clear enough in themselves, or in a tolerance for tentativity—the ability to tolerate ambiguous situations in which *neither* solution is tenable. A normal, mature person can do either under most circumstances. The schizophrenic may be able to recognize that situations are uncertain, but may not be able to assign the needed temporary value for purposes of argument to the uncertain, or to accept uncertainty as fact. Or, he may have a rigid personality that does not allow for any kind of *als ob*.

The behaviors of schizophrenics are paradoxical. On the one hand, they do not consistently adhere to a consecutive course of action. A great variety of conduct may be manifested that is often no more than a series of successive rather than consecutive actions. For example, a schizophrenic may be quite circumstantial and detailed at some times, and vague and indefinite at other times. Variability is an important characteristic of the biological organism, but the schizophrenic is inordinately variable. In our reports of empirical findings at Worcester on schizophrenics—findings from many different areas of function—we repeatedly point out that their behavior is more variable than that of the normal subject. Less frequently, their behavior may, on the other hand, be *too* consistent in a peculiar way, that is, they may be monotonously perseverative. The significant point appears to be that the schizophrenic's behavior is often inappropriate—variable when conistency or stability is adaptive, and perseverative when variety or variability is adaptive.[33]

What we see in schizophrenia are diverse efforts at coping with an extreme underlying insecurity. Occasionally these efforts may be normal and adequate, but most frequently they are inappropriate or inadequate. Much of the inappropriate behavior of schizophrenics can be described as "bipolar," because schizophrenics tend to respond at either extreme of the distribution of a function rather than in a relatively measured, balanced way toward the center. Broadly speaking, bipolar responses, as indicated earlier, represent Hughlings Jackson's principle of "compensation in excess" (1958, Vol. II, p. 35ff.). Most often the polar extremes occur in different schizophrenic patients, but both may be found in the same patient. Responses are out of balance in their cognitive, affective, and conative aspects as well as in their speed, intensity, or content.

Stage 5: Consolidation of stimuli/response

In describing the stage of consolidation, (which is actually the final stage of the stimulus/response process), it is necessary to consider the process with respect to the single stimulus as well as the succession of stimuli. This is done tentatively, because it is admittedly strictly artificial to treat consolidation in the context of only a single stimulus. The interferences (before masking by the succeeding stimulus) arise from 1) noise from the external surroundings of the stimulus, and 2) the internal noises, during (a) the preparatory stage, (b) each stage of perception process (6 steps), (c) the encoding stage, and/or (d) the response stage. The situation is discussed below at greater length in the consideration of succession of stimuli.

Stage 6: Inhibition (reactive or retroactive)

For completeness' sake, it must be mentioned that some form of inhibition may occur in the stimulus/response process—

---

[33]See footnote 32.

either reactive inhibition, the hypothesized tendency to lessen response consequent upon effortful activity, or retroactive inhibition, the impairment of the normal effects of a learning activity when it is closely followed by another, especially a similar activity. These forms of inhibition may often be disturbed in the schizophrenic.

Stage 7: Return to preparatory state for new stimulus

After the stimulus/response process has been executed, the natural tendency of the adaptive organism is to return to a new state of preparation, a state involving some degree of readiness for the appearance of a new stimulus (the state described previously in Stage I of the stimulus/response discussion). In the pathological form, there may be a readiness to respond that is contaminated by the various deficiencies in the perception process.

Succession of Stimuli and Responses

The range of responses given by the subject in the succession of stimulus/response units is a more complicated and a more realistic level of behavior than in the individual stimulus/response unit. When I say succession, I am making a distinction between *successive* and *consecutive*. The former conveys no more than the following up of one response by another, without integration; the latter indicates an interaction of responses, the influence of the past on the present or the present on the future. Often, in schizophrenia, the present situation has little or no effect on the subsequent situation, except at a rather superficial level. Consequently, I shall examine primarily the succession of stimuli.

Examining carefully the question of variety in successive responses, one can see that it entails not only the qualitative diversity of responses produced by the subject, but also their quantitative diversity in intensity and speed. A subject at one extreme may monotonously give the same response regardless of the varied nature of the stimulus situation in which he finds himself, relevant or irrelevant; his responses remain essentially univocal and redundant. Such response, without an apperceived stimulus, is called sterotypy. Conversely, a subject may be polyvocal; no matter how similar the situation he finds himself in, his responses always differ. Sometimes his reactions appear to be so random as to be completely irrelevant. The terms univocal and polyvocal have reference to perseveration and nonautomatization.

Perseveration and Nonautomatization

When the stimulus situation has changed, and the subject manifests a definite carry-over of part or all of a response he has already given—usually to the immediately preceding stimulus—he perseverates. A perseverating schizophrenic subject often reacts with apparent ease, for he is merely repeating his previous response. This lag or inertia is a negative quality, not at all like the relevant quality of persistence, which reflects a "steadfastness of purpose," as Spearman (1927) has put it. It is because the setting calls for a *change* in response, rather than irrelevant persistence of an old response, that the characteristic is pathological. Spearman considers this "general inertia" factor (c) "second in importance" only to the general factor (g). As he recognized early, "It would seem to have an extraordinary importance for education, medicine and industry" (p. 412). Indeed it has!

In the schizophrenic's perseveration, as well as in other pathological conditions, it is as if there is a commitment to the past, an unreadiness to give up a no-longer-relevant or even existing stimulus. Sometimes it is difficult to determine whether the unreadiness to deal with the new situations develops primarily from a direct commitment or attachment to the past *per se*, or indirectly from the reverse, a "neophobia," a fear of the new as new. The latter seems more likely. Insecurity, with its underlying anxiety, may result in retreat from anything new to a safer old. Then again, it may be merely the result of sensory and sensorimotor commitments, shorter or longer, as seen in the "waterfall" effect and in "mal de derangement'' (Cf. Livingston's discussion, 1967, p. 512). The source of pathology must be determined in the individual case.

Perseveration is either short-termed, that is, related to a fairly recent previous stimulus, or long-termed. In the latter case, the schizophrenic is ''past-bound'', reaching back to experiences from the past for the present response. In such instances the relatively remote past remains close to the present surface for too long, and contaminates current reactions. Fenichel (1945) gives an example of such a case: ''A fragmentary analysis in one such case demonstrated that all of the patient's fights with authorities were intended to prove that his father had done him an injustice'' (p. 434). In experimental settings, perseveration is almost always short-termed. Thus, in reaction time studies where longer preparatory intervals precede short preparatory intervals, we see this short-term perseverative effect quite clearly (Zahn, Rosenthal, and Shakow, 1963). In the clinical situation, instances of longer-term perseveration may be observed, although there may also be many evidences of the short-term phenomenon. At times the patient himself diagnoses his condition. An example is a patient of Roheim at Worcester, who told him, ''In my mind, I always linger on—I am still doing the things I have finished'' (1955, p. 198). Angyal (1935) reports a patient of his who would, when getting up from the chair he was sitting on, look behind him fearfully. It turned out that he was afraid that he had left his ''behind'' behind; he was apparently experiencing some form of depersonalization, a disturbance of his body image. In a way, this patient was literally enacting the process of perseveration, as a qualitatively inappropriate response that I am here attempting to describe figuratively. If we consider his fear from another perspective, he was fearful of giving up his anchor and strength, so he was clinging to a concrete symbol of himself, his rear. In our play experiment (Shakow and Rosenzweig, 1937), which was carried out in a room that had several one-way viewing mirrors on one wall, we occasionally saw patients, most frequently hebephrenics, look back repeatedly at their reflections in the mirrors while continuing

other tasks. Whether this was due to a depersonalization experience or some tinge of suspiciousness we cannot, of
course, say, but the phenomenon did not appear in the normal
subjects.

Donald Hall, one of our American poets, has perhaps put
his finger on this defect of long-time perseveration, especially
for irrelevant associations from the past. Some years ago, he
wrote a book of nostalgic essays about his boyhood days in
New Hampshire that he called *String too Short to be Saved*
(1961). The title of the book stems from the report of a man
who, while clearing out the attic of an old New England
house, found a box full of tiny lengths of string. On the lid of
the box was an inscription in an old hand: "String too short to
be saved." Nothing I have come across over the years has
epitomized for me as much as has this label, what I consider
to be a core behavioral characteristic of the schizophrenic—
his constant dependency on a store of behaviors that were
never adaptive but that he persists in using. Of course, he also
has available that other box, the one containing useful lengths
of string rolled up into balls of different colors and kinds—the
box most of us find so necessary to living. But he uses this
box of good string relatively infrequently in his day-by-day
psychotic states. The normal person, on the other hand, calls
upon this box constantly, rarely reverting to the other.
Gantt's "schizokinesis" (1953), the use of autonomic reactions from the past that are no longer relevant, is another example of this perseveration. But, in this case, the autonomic
responses that Gantt emphasizes, such as heart rate, were at
least adaptive in the past.

There is an interesting difference between the phenomena
of *Treppenwitz* (see footnote, p. 74) and perseveration. In the
former case there appears to be a new response, but a *delayed*
one, to an old stimulus that has perseverated; in the latter,
there appears to be an old response given immediately to a
new stimulus. If passage of time reduces anxiety sufficiently
to permit a new and appropriate response to occur, then perhaps if schizophrenics were granted a longer period in which
to respond, their performance would be much nearer the nor-

mal. Experiments on tapping, steadiness, and learning (Shakow and Huston, 1936; Huston and Shakow, 1946; Huston and Shakow, 1949) support this hypothesis. Then again, it is possible that there may be an optimal period of a certain duration in which appropriate response would occur.

NONAUTOMATIZATION

Automatization, or habituation, is a nuclear characteristic of learning. This concept is so fundamental to psychology that I shall draw upon quotations from four authorities whose approaches to the topic are quite diversified. The first is taken from William James' *Principles* (1890, Vol. I):

The great thing, then, in all education, is to make our nervous system our ally instead of our enemy. It is to fund and capitalize our acquisitions, and live at ease upon the interest of the fund. For this we must make automatic and habitual, as early as possible, as many useful actions as we can, and guard against the growing into ways that are likely to be disadvantageous to us, as we should guard against the plague. The more of the details of our daily life we can hand over to the effortless custody of automatism, the more our higher powers of mind will be set free for their own proper work. *There is no more miserable human being than one in whom nothing is habitual but indecision*, and for whom the lighting of every cigar, the drinking of every cup, the time of rising and going to bed every day, and the beginning of every bit of work, are subjects of express volitional deliberation. Full half the time of such a man goes to the deciding, or regretting, of matters which ought to be so ingrained in him as practically not to exist for his consciousness at all. If there be such daily duties not yet ingrained in any one of my readers, let him begin this very hour to set the matter right (p. 122, emphasis added).

In the *Wisdom of the Body* (1932), Walter Cannon's concept of homeostasis provides the "freedom from the activity of the higher levels of the nervous system and the muscles which they govern" to maintain control (pp. 302–303). Alfred North Whitehead, in his *Introduction to Mathematics* (1958), points out that, rather than "cultivate the habit of thinking of what we are doing, the precise opposite is the case. Civilization advances by extending the number of important operations which we can perform without thinking about them" (pp. 41–42). Finally, Heinz Hartmann, in *Ego Psychology and the*

Problem of Adaptation (1958), presents the following thesis:

Not only motor behavior, but perception and thinking, too, show automatization. Exercise automatizes methods of problem solving just as much as it does walking, speaking, or writing. . . . automatization may have economic advantages in saving attention cathexis in particular and simple cathexis of consciousness in general (pp. 88, 91).

Although described quite differently, the fundamental principle of automatization pervades these varied expressions. Whether it deals with habit, homeostasis, thought, or ego function, the expounded principle refers to the habituation that is so essential a part of biological process, particularly (though not necessarily) as related to learning.

If we were to bring this principle down to its lowest common denominator in the normal behavioral sequence, we would expect the following: a new stimulus appears, the organism manifests alertness and perception, resulting in an adequate response involving a certain energy expenditure. With repetition of the stimulus, the expenditure of energy (or effort) gradually decreases to a level at which the response is automatized (and the subject is "habituated"). Such response frees his attention for other matters—the "higher processes of the mind," as it were.

For the schizophrenic, automatization does not seem to reach anywhere near the degree it does for the normal person. The schizophrenic does not take James' admonitions at all seriously. He is the nonautomatizer, *par excellence.* Thus, besides his tendency to perseverate, the schizophrenic is further handicapped by this maladaptive response. It is as if the following dialogue takes place between a schizophrenic and an interlocutor. The interlocutor says, "Look, here is a new situation, so prepare for a new perception and a new response." The schizophrenic, who finds new stimuli anxiety-arousing, replies: "No, I cannot give a new response. I am afraid to risk it. I will respond as if the stimulus is old, with an old and safe response" (even if it were not successful before, i.e., "string too short to be saved"). Perseveration results. The scene changes. Now the interlocutor says, "This stimulus is just like the previous stimulus, so you should give the same, old response, but with less effort.'' The schizophrenic, who also finds change anxiety-arousing, replies: ''No, I dare not change my response. It is safer to give the same old response, with the same effort, which was successful just a while ago'' (as expressed by the ''match that lit alright a minute ago''). Nonhabituation results. Short-term perseveration and nonautomatization in the schizophrenic, as compared with response in the normal, may be depicted in Table I.

TABLE I   Adaptation and Automatization in the Normal and the Schizophrenic

	STATE	CURRENT STIMULUS	RESPONSE CALLED FOR	RESPONSE GIVEN
NORMAL	Adaptation	different (new)	change, no less energy	change, no less energy
	Habituation or Automatization	same (old)	same, less energy	same, less energy
SCHIZOPHRENIC	Perseveration	different (new)	change, no less energy	same, no less energy
	Non-automatization	same (old)	same, less energy	same, no less energy

The schizophrenic not only treats new as old, by perseverating, but he treats old as new, by nonautomatizing; that is, he treats every stimulus with one of a static system of responses. It is as if the schizophrenic, when faced with a choice, is forced because of his anxiety or cognitive dysfunction (which is ultimately based on anxiety) to take what appears to be the immediate way out of his dilemma. This turns out to be a maladaptive, or at least adaptive, solution to the situation. The theoretical significance of this tendency for the concept of segmental set will, I trust, become clear in the general discussions that have preceded and will follow.

CHAPTER 7

Experimental and Clinical Evidence of Segmental Set

A sampling of the experimental results of my colleagues and myself indicates that segmental responses may show up in a variety of ways in schizophrenic subjects. I shall refer to these only briefly, because I have discussed these at some length in previous publications.[1]

The empirical data included here may be classified into 4 areas according to the nature of the stimuli and their corresponding responses: (1) the physiological, where the stimulus and the response are both measured in physiological terms, that is, where thyroid is given and the blood pressure taken; (2) at the interface of physiology and psychology—(a) the physiopsychological, where the stimulus is physiological and the response psychological as in, for example, the effect of insulin on the intellectual level, and (b) the psychophysiological, where the stimulus is psychological and the response physiological, as in the effect of a "ready" signal on electrodermal response—; (3) the experimental psychological, where both the stimulus and the response, under relatively controlled conditions, fall into the psychological realm, as in

[1]This discussion is taken essentially from "Some Psychophysiological Aspects of Schizophrenia" (1967). I am limiting myself to the publications of the Worcester State Hospital and the NIMH (with a few minor exceptions) for two reasons: (1) I have greatest personal familiarity with these, and (2) other literature is so vast that it could not be given reasonable consideration. The data I have chosen to include does, I believe, convey the import of segmental set.

reaction time and learning studies (including normalizing trends); and (4) the clinical psychological (which is ordinarily termed the "psychiatric"), where the stimulus and the response are observed in more molar, less limited situations, such as behavior on the ward and during interviews.

PHYSIOLOGICAL STUDIES

Among the numerous physiological studies carried out at Worcester, many resulted in negative findings, but a significant number gave positive findings that differentiated the schizophrenic sample significantly from the normal.[2] The differences between schizophrenics and normals were of two major kinds. In one type of situation, both the basal and stimulated levels of response in schizophrenics were *lowered*; in the other, the basal and nonbasal *relationships* between two responses were *raised*. Among the differences in levels of response taken under basal conditions were oxygen consumption rates (Hoskins and Jellinek, 1932)[3]; blood pressure (Freeman, 1933; Freeman, Hoskins, and Sleeper, 1932), and circulation time (Freeman, 1934, 1938).[4] Those levels of response obtained under conditions of special stimulation included a wide range of functions that were lower:

[2] In some instances, subsequent studies carried out elsewhere did not corroborate the findings at Worcester, but the Worcester findings must be left as they are, as serious studies.

[3] I recognize that Kety (1959) indicates that basal metabolism is not lowered. My surmise here is that the later studies were carried out under different conditions, as Richter (1957) recognizes.

[4] The discrepancy between the Finesinger, Cohen, and Thompson (1938) results and those of Freeman are more difficult to reconcile, especially because the results of the Finesinger normal subjects are so close to those of previous investigators. However, a cursory examination of the Finesinger group's schizophrenic patients, divided into acute (5 years and under) and chronic (over 5 years) groups, gives means *higher* for the more acute group. This is not consistent with what would ordinarily be expected. We shall have to leave the two sets of findings as they are—inconsistent. The only thing that can be said about the Freeman results for the present is that the same technique was used for both schizophrenic and normal subjects.

1. General metabolic reaction to orally ingested stimulants such as thyroid (Cohen and Fierman, 1938), dinitrophenol (Freeman, 1934; Looney and Hoskins, 1934), and intravenous epinephrine (Freeman and Carmichael, 1935); blood pressure, heart rate, and respiratory volume reactions to the breathing of hot, moist oxygen (Freeman and Rodnick, 1940); skin temperature reactions to raised environmental temperatures (Freeman, 1939); and oral/ rectal temperature reactions to raised environmental temperatures (Gottlieb and Linder, 1935);

2. Central nervous system functioning, as reflected in nystagmic response following both caloric and rotatory stimulation (Angyal and Sherman, 1942) responses after rotation.

The other major area of difference relates not to absolute levels of response, but rather to *relationships* between two aspects of response. In all of these relationships, what is striking is the higher and more consistent parallelism in the schizophrenic between the two measures being considered than in the normal subjects. This greater consistency, as reflected in higher correlation coefficients, is found in a variety of conditions: between diastolic and systolic readings in blood pressure taken under basal conditions (Freeman et al., 1932); under a considerable variety of stimulating agents such as adrenalin (Hoskins and Jellinek, 1933), physostigmine (Jellinek, 1939), and thyroid (Hoskins and Jellinek, 1932, 1933); and in different status conditions such as acute versus chronic patients (Jellinek, 1939) or recovered versus nonrecovered patients after insulin (Cameron and Jellinek, 1939). It is also found in the relationships between oral and rectal temperature (Carmichael and Linder, 1934; Linder and Carmichael, 1935) and in the oxygen and CO_2 content of arterial and venous blood (Looney and Freeman, 1938).

In all of these conditions, when we expect variation to occur, the schizophrenics are more often consistent, and when a higher response is called for, the schizophrenics give a lower measure. In all relationships, we find a partial response, a simplification of a complex response, giving evidence of a segmentalization of set.

In viewing the physiological findings, which are, of course, only a small part of the body of experimental data concerning schizophrenia, I am struck by the amount of evidence that supports a theory of segmental set. There is evidence that when the basal and stimulated levels of response are lowered, the normal level of response is not achieved due to some interfering factor—a situation that would be expected in a state of segmental set (e.g., a state of hyperactivity or a state of apathy). When the basal and nonbasal levels are raised, other irrelevant factors (such as neophobia) interfere. I will first deal with the physiopsychological studies.

INTERFACE OF PHYSIOLOGY AND PSYCHOLOGY

Physiopsychological studies

Two experiments done during the time that pharmacological "shock" treatments were popular are relevant. The first of these is a study by Rodnick (1942) on the effect of metrazol shock on habit systems. Two groups of schizophrenics were taught to respond differentially to two tones. After the second habit was established, one group was given metrazol injections. On a retest the metrazol group reverted significantly more often than the control group to the older habit system.

Another study was more closely associated than the last with the complex habit systems of the schizophrenic (Schnack, Shakow and Lively, 1945a and 1945b). A battery of tests was administered to schizophrenic patients before and after treatment with insulin or metrazol and to a matched control group of patients who had had neither form of therapy. The results indicated that insulin and metrazol could only account for about one-third of the improvement in test scores; two-thirds were due to the ordinary hospital regime and familiarity with the test situation.

From another group of studies is an early experiment on direct current threshold (Huston, 1934). Although we finally came to the conclusion that there was no fundamental difference in the threshold level between schizophrenic and normal groups, we were impressed with one aspect of the findings that helped to emphasize a characteristic that we found pervasive in schizophrenia. This is the principle that I have called "neophobia," a tendency to do poorly on first exposure to a particular stimulus situation, but then on repetition to become "normalized."

Psychophysiological studies

There is a category of autonomic response to stimuli in the context of experiments in which the subject, in an atmosphere as relaxing as possible, is required to make no overt response. Over the years we have carried out a series of studies involving galvanic skin response, heart rate, and other such responses, as effected through repeated stimulations by verbal ready signals, noise, tone, light and pain.

In the first such study (Cohen and Patterson, 1937), conducted at Worcester, the aim was to determine the rate of adaptation of schizophrenics and normal subjects to pressure pain. Both groups of subjects started with a mean heart rate of 80. At the end of an hour of repeated stimulation the normals gradually came down to a level of 74, whereas the schizophrenic group fluctuated between 80 and 85, giving a reading of 80 again in the last trial. Their actual mean level on the ward was 74. This was interpreted as a lack of habituation in the schizophrenics (maladaptive nonautomization), whereas the normal subjects showed definite habituation.

We ran two early studies—in 1937 (Patterson, unpublished) and in 1938 (Rodnick)—on the effect of "noise" and "ready" stimulation on galvanic skin response. At that time we were using skin resistance levels in ohms as our measure of response. Although the absolute resistance levels were somewhat different in the two experiments, in both cases the patients' levels were higher than the levels of the normal subjects. We also obtained differentials in the percent decrease to the stimuli between the schizophrenic and normal subjects. In the first experiment the schizophrenics showed the same drop as the normals to the noise, but were significantly less responsive to the "ready." Actually, their response to the ready was equal to that of the noise. In the second experiment, the normal subjects gave an equal response to noise and "ready"; the schizophrenic response to noise was of equal amount, but their response to "ready" was significantly greater and more varied in adaptation. All of the ten normals adapted to the noise during the course of the experiment, whereas this was true of only one of the ten patients.

A study with 52 chronic schizophrenic and 20 normal subjects investigated the GSR orienting reactions to visual and auditory stimuli (Zahn, Rosenthal, and Lawlor, 1968). The patients showed a significantly higher arousal level using measures of base conductance and frequency of nonspecific GSR. The schizophrenics did not show the progressive adaptation to stimuli demonstrated by the normals. Nonautomization was evident when, in comparing the specific to the nonspecific GSR frequency per unit time, the normals yielded a larger ratio. One likely interpretation of this finding is that the influences of internal or self-produced stimulation in reaction to the influence of directed external stimulation is proportionately greater in schizophrenics. This ratio seems more likely to be related to "preoccupation" than to "distractibility," although the latter cannot be ruled out altogether.

A series of experiments reported by Zahn (1964) on work carried out by him and several of my other colleagues at NIMH is particularly relevant. These are concerned with the autonomic responsivity of schizophrenic and normal subjects to stimuli in relation to a certain order of arrangement of the experimental situations. The first of this series of three studies, in which GSR and heart rate orienting reactions were elicited by a series of mild visual and auditory stimuli, is the one I have just now reported.

In two further experiments, in addition to the orienting condition, we have a condition in which a tone was responded to by a voluntary response—in one case a "casual" depression of a telegraph key, and in another a quick release of a key (the reaction time situation). Skin resistance, heart rate, and finger pulse volume were monitored. The results showed that, whereas the physiological responsivity to the tone of both chronic and acute schizophrenics was equal to or greater than that of the normals in the orienting condition, it was considerably lower than that of the normals in the reaction time condition. Moreover, there was hyperarousal but hyposelection, evidence that the general arousal levels increased with increasing demand in the normal subjects but not in the patients.[5]

Thus, physiological studies such as these support major characteristics of segmental set such as fear of novelty, previously experienced but inadequate responses, and responses inappropriate to the present situation. Nowhere in these group results did we find the schizophrenics responding with a generalized set, one that is open to the wider, relevant aspects of the situation and treats the stimulus in a conceptual way. The schizophrenic typically finds ways of responding to part or irrelevant aspects of the situation.

EXPERIMENTAL PSYCHOLOGICAL STUDIES

How can one best characterize the psychological disturbance in schizophrenia as revealed by experimental and test studies? Since I have already summarized some of these data in detail on other occasions (e.g., Shakow, 1946, 1962, 1963), I shall be very brief here.

The disturbance begins to appear at a level of response in

---

[5]It is of interest in this connection that one of the relatively few physiological studies in which we attained a greater response in schizophrenic than in normal subjects was in carbohydrate metabolism (Freeman, Rodnick, Shakow, and Lebeaux, 1944). Two-thirds of the schizophrenics (who generally were of more acute status) gave diabetic type curves on the Exton-Rose, whereas this was true of only one-third of the normal subjects. However, when we placed the normal subjects in a "stress" situation, two-thirds of them had the continuing up-curve. In nondiabetic subjects, whether schizophrenic or normal, this distribution appears related to underlying tension.

which "voluntary" behavior is involved. It comes through primarily in behavior demanded by the environment, that is, behavior that is experimenter-controlled and programmed, as in reaction time (Huston, Shakow and Riggs, 1937; Rodnick and Shakow, 1940; Rosenthal, Lawlor, Zahn and Shakow, 1960). In virtually all new experimental situations the schizophrenic patient shows a difficulty with the novel, which I have already commented on. This difficulty prevents him from achieving anywhere near his capability or "capacity" level (Huston and Shakow, 1948). Under certain conditions, however, his capability level becomes more manifest and his functioning becomes closer to the normal.

The schizophrenic is generally influenced by the environment, but only in a partial and/or superficial way; he does not become involved with it to any degree similar to the normal (Rickers-Ovsiankina, 1937a, 1937b, 1938; Shakow, 1963). Even though the composite of intellectual functioning represented in mental age scores does not seem to reveal any very marked disturbance, the psychosis does apparently interfere with the balance of distribution of intellectual functions by causing a greater disturbance of the conceptual functions than the informative ones (Roe and Shakow, 1942). This inability to conceptualize (Hanfmann, 1939a, 1939b; Wegrocki, 1940) is particularly marked. For a long time our Worcester studies have dealt with one aspect or another of what might be termed the cognitive controls of attention (A. F. Angyal, 1942; Rickers-Ovsiankina, 1937a, 1937b; Shakow, Rosenzweig and Hollander, 1966), or cognitive styles. In general, our findings in this area emphasize that schizophrenic response tends to fall at the extremes of the range of function, over- or under-scanning and over- or under-articulation.[6] These responsive qualities may in general hold for between-patient comparisons, but, in some instances, they serve for within-patient functioning as well.

[6]The difference in cognitive styles between schizophrenics and normal controls appears to be a difference partially of cooperation level, causing the poorer levels of performance of schizophrenics.

In the perceptual sphere, in a tachistoscopic experiment (Angyal, 1942) in which the subjects were to report the letter of the alphabet they saw correctly, (1) the number of total errors was approximately twice that of normal subjects, (2) the use of uncommon substitution (those not used by nonpsychotic subjects) was significantly higher for schizophrenic patients, and (3) above all, there was a tendency for the schizophrenic patients to respond two ways: "pedantically" with a rigid, methodological, "obsessive" type of response, and "loosely" with an unsystematic, shifting response having little regard for objectivity and accuracy, corresponding to the distinction between paranoid and hebephrenic styles of segmentalization that I have emphasized. On the Rorschach (Rickers-Ovsiankina, 1938), in which no distinction was made between subtypes, there is a tendency for poor W- (whole), P- (popular), and O- (original responses) to occur more frequently. In other aspects of the perceptual realm, for instance in the tautophone (with which the responses are to meaningless sounds), the normal person accepts the instruction that the tautophone task is an apperceptive one (Shakow, Rosenzweig and Hollander, 1966). Thus, the schizophrenic is suggestible in a general way, responding to the stimuli according to his inner needs, whereas the normal does not distort the material to meet his needs. A normal person, who is almost always in contact with the stimulus material, makes himself the subject of many of his sentences, and chooses English words as compared to foreign or bizarre ones. Quite the opposite is typical of the schizophrenic, who may rely on bizarre responses or respond in a foreign language (a somewhat bizarre response).

In learning studies, schizophrenics show the particular learning disability of starting off handicapped in the early stages of tests and experiments, such as in the prodmeter test (Huston and Shakow, 1949), pursuitmeter (Huston and Shakow, 1948), Ferguson 5, a formboard test (unpublished), and in the Worchester 2C formboard (unpublished), and then not being able to catch up entirely during the course of an ordinary experiment. However, the capacity to perfect a new habit seems partially intact in schizophrenia *given enough time.*

Proper motivation and more time make it possible to correct at least in part the interfering factors of the earlier stages of learning.

A special and intriguing problem is raised by the reminiscence factor involved in learning. Several studies (Shakow, 1932; Venables and Tizard, 1956) provide evidence of greater reminiscence in schizophrenics than in normal subjects. As I have stated on another occasion:

The improvement in score on the first trial of the test series (in our series of tests using the prodmeter), which came after a three months' rest interval, over the best score of the preceding practice period (an improvement of as much as 120 percent in the case of the catatonic type, in whom the phenomenon is most marked) is striking. Although it is possible to account for the phenomenon in part by involving some of the factors brought together by Woodworth (*Experimental Psychology*, 1938, p. 68), it is not so easy to dismiss the role played by the process of consolidation as he does. Varying chances of recall and varying efforts to recall may play some role in the improvement, but the likelihood of review during the rest period being a factor is certainly much less in the motor function than in the verbal function with which Woodworth's review is solely concerned.

In the present motor learning task, two other principles of explanation seem more plausible, one involving the process of consolidation and the other, involving the amount of interpolated activity. Both of these factors would seem to be particularly effective in the schizophrenic subject. During the original learning period the threshold of availability of the memory, to use Lashley's term, is low in the schizophrenic patient. Actually he has learned much better than he can recall at the end of this practice period, presumably because of a multitude of interfering factors—motor, attentional, emotional—which have a blanketing effect on achievement. During the three months intervening, before recall was again demanded, these interfering factors may be supposed to have dropped out to a very considerable extent with a resultant higher threshold of availability of the memory. Book (1925), whose work seems to have been overlooked in the reminiscence literature, had already in 1908 presented a theory of this general nature to account for "an actual increase in skill during the rest interval of a year and a half" which occurred in his typewriting experiments.

An additional suggestion as to a possible effective factor is provided in the phenomena of retroactive inhibition, particularly as reported in the experiments of Jenkins and Dallenbach (*Amer. J. Psychol.*,

1924, *35*, 605–612) and Van Ormer (*Arch. Psychol.*, 1932, *21*, No. 137) on oblivescence during sleep and waking. The evidence they submit and additional arguments offered by McGeoch ("Forgetting and the law of disuse," *Psychol. Rev.*, 1932, *39*, 352–370) constitute a strong case for interpolated activity rather than mere passage of time as important for oblivescence. The findings in schizophrenia afford further evidence for this hypothesis. Schizophrenia has frequently been referred to as a dream state. Even if this characterization is not taken literally, it is certainly true that when compared with normal activity schizophrenic activity is in general much reduced. Such relative inactivity would presumably result in less oblivescence than in normal subjects. The combination of lessened interpolated activity and increased consolidation could easily account for the greater part of the reminiscence which has been found. (Shakow, 1946, pp. 60–61).[7]

A more recent article by Hovland and Weiss (1953) provides additional evidence on learning reminiscence. This study compared the learning that takes place in the presence of persons who are trusted with that when around those who are not trusted. The subjects showed poorer performance when the person who was not trusted was the experimenter. However, after the passage of time, with the fading of the context in which they learned, they showed better additional learning than those who learned from the trusted. Performance over time was differentially effected by the context. [A recent article by Aarons (1976) indicates, however, that the issues are not clear, as he reviews conflicting Soviet and American studies and the roles of sex, age, wake learning capacity, suggestibility, and other characteristics.]

In the psychological experimental studies there is particularly strong evidence of neophobia, partial responses instead of total, relative inaccessibility to the environment, and difficulties with conceptual thinking. These characteristics suggest a condition in which segmental set has replaced generalized set functioning.

---

[7]An error was corrected: "low" for "high" and "higher" for "lower" in the interpretation of Lashley, an unpardonable error only discovered in the writing of the present monograph. See section on neophobia (p. 121ff.) for further discussion.

Disturbance in the functions of language, which is supremely important for communication and thinking, produce what are probably the outstanding symptoms of schizophrenia (Hanfmann and Kasanin, 1937; Hanfmann, 1939a, 1939b). Sullivan, in his distinction between two kinds of languages (Kasanin, 1964, p. 9), gives us a key to the disturbance. He points out that language as *thought* is properly different from language as *communication*. The schizophrenic uses the first language when the second is called for—again, evidence of disorganization that may be considered in terms of segmental set.[8] The more completely cut off he is from integration with other people, the more actively novel and wholly individual and idiosyncratic he becomes, for the symbols that he uses as if they were language for communication, are actually symbols for thought. He thus does not offer any data for consensual validation, which is the prerequisite for the language of communication. [Its relationship to disturbance of the syntactical stage of language as postulated by S. R. Rochester et al. (Wynne, Cromwell and Matthysse, 1978, p. 321-328) is intriguing.] There is a deficit in conceptual thinking, as shown in the Stanford-Binet, and other items (Wegrocki, 1940 and Hanfmann, 1939), with a concomitant inability to shift or change concepts.[9]

In the personality realm, we find evidences of weak goal behavior in various experiments—for example, interruption (Rickers-Ovsiankina, 1938), substitution (Bennett, 1942), play (Shakow and Rosenzweig, 1937), and aspiration (unpublished)—in which aspiration goals are set at much higher or much lower levels than is actual achievement. There is also evidence of a "weak ego" in the tautophone responses (Shakow, Rosenzweig and Hollander, 1966) of schizophrenics, in

---

[8]G. Steiner seems to offer a similar theory in "A Note on Language and Psychoanalysis," *International Review of Psycho-Analysis*, 1976, *3*, 253.

[9]There have been some claims in the literature that the differences between normals and schizophrenics are due to educational differences. However, Hanfmann (1939) equalized her groups, using college graduates in both of them, and found the differences to remain.

which third-person responses are much greater in number than the first-person responses given by normals. There is evidence of looser affect on the Rorschach (Rickers-Ovsiankina, 1938) and greater tendency toward individuality and idiosyncracy in response on the Kent-Rosanoff (Shakow and Jellinek, 1965). Taking the psychological, psychophysiological, and experimental psychological data in at one fell swoop, I can only conclude that the concept of segmental set fits the phenomena well, as I shall shortly examine in greater detail.

A short time after the Worcester studies had been completed, an important series of experiments were conducted at the Iowa Psychopathic Hospital under Paul Huston, who had been closely associated with the earlier Worcester studies. He enlarged the concepts that we were using in some ways and sometimes used different techniques. I give here a brief description of Huston's work, essentially in his own words. (The original references are given for those who wish to follow them up.) His and his colleagues' main results were as follows:

1. Huston and Singer (1945) showed that mental set in schizophrenia can be improved by the use of intravenous amytal, but it will not rise to normal levels. Set was measured here by the Worcester reaction time method.

2. Huston and Senf (1952) showed that a set index similar to the one developed by Rodnick and Shakow almost perfectly separates schizophrenic subjects from neurotic controls and depressive controls, and that the set deficiency in schizophrenia is more pronounced in chronic than in early schizophrenia.

3. Huston, Cohen, and Senf (1955) studied shifting of set and maintenance of goal orientation by means of simple arithmetic tests. Chronic schizophrenics perform at a lower level than other groups, but no deficit in shifting or maintenance was shown in schizophrenics when compared to depressive or neurotic controls. This was assumed to be due to the nature of the task, which did not involve affect.

4. Senf, Huston, and Cohen (1955), using the Wechsler Short Form, Army Alpha Subtest 3, and Incomplete Sentences showed that schizophrenic difficulties in thinking become more apparent when greater requirements for sustained attention are present, in less structured response situations, and with tasks containing personal reference. Drugs improved the schizophrenic responses.

5. Cohen, Senf, and Huston (1956) studied perceptual accuracy by means of three tests: Gestalt Completion, Hands, and selected Rorschach items. Perceptual disturbance in schizophrenia apparently depends on the structure of the task. In early schizophrenia the disturbance is seen only in the unstructured Rorschach, but in chronic schizophrenia it is seen in both Rorschach and in Gestalt Completion. Drugs improved all groups.

6. Cohen, Senf, and Huston (1954) studied conceptual thinking by means of an object sorting test that could be made more personal by the introduction of personal items. Results indicated that impairment in schizophrenia is made worse by affective stimuli when under drugs, but neither condition alone significantly lowered the score. In depression, either drugs or affective stimuli alone make conceptual thinking poorer; in neurotic patients, drugs improve thinking in neutral situations but disrupt thinking in affective situations.

7. Senf, Huston and Cohen (1956) used comic cartoons to investigate social comprehension. The subjects were asked to describe the environment, the speakers, the action, the social roles, the motivation of the persons, and, finally, to tell why the cartoon was funny. The chronic schizophrenic showed impairment in their descriptions of all categories except environment. The early schizophrenic patients who were better than the chronic showed impairment of action, motivation, and humor.

Overall, these results corroborate the Worcester studies, and support the concept of segmental set in schizophrenia.

The amytal studies corroborate the findings of Dryud and Holzman (1973) at a later date.

Normalization

The phenomenon of "normalizing trends" should be considered here, since these findings apparently point directly away from the concept of segmentalization. I have discussed these at some length (Shakow, 1958), so I shall be brief. The subject has affinities with the whole question of vulnerability, as it is related to the possibility of the patient having another attack, once he has successfully met a previous one. Normalizing trends are revealed in studies in which the differences originally found between schizophrenic and normal subjects have either tended to disappear or have become substantially reduced under certain conditions. The normalizing factors that struck us most forcefully are the following: (a) repetition, (b) passage of time, (c) cooperation, (d) time for preparation, (e) social influence, (f) stress, and (g) shock. If one wanted to maximize the performance of schizophrenic subjects, one might do the following: 1) allow a period for acquaintance and removal of strangeness; 2) permit personal motivation to enter, either self-induced, or from the outside by providing "stress"; 3) allow the subject to control the situation without his knowing it (if he knows he is likely to do relatively poorly); 4) use extreme "shock" (or drugs) to bring the person out of his more recently acquired, maladaptive habits.

If I were to summarize what these normalizing factors indicate, I would say that these are the temporary results of differing degrees of "heroics," and "oiling of the wheels," rather than true "engine work." It does not generalize to the central area, being limited to the specific activities involved. What happens in situations in which the organism is more engrossed, where emotionality is much more a factor? Given a moderate dose of therapy (psycho- or drug or self-), does an attack of schizophrenia make the person more vulnerable because he has tasted the "freedom of psychosis," or can it serve as the basis for less vulnerability in the future? Cases such as Renée (Sechehaye, 1970) and Boisen (1960) give evidence of the latter.[10]

CLINICAL PSYCHOLOGICAL STUDIES

The clinical psychological (psychiatric) data is not considered more than superficially here, although the literature is rich and diverse, primarily because my studies have focused on the psychological studies reviewed above. Let me merely note that many psychiatric observers have been struck by facets of the behavioral characteristics I have been describing as existing in the psychological, physiological, and psychophysiological realms. They have called them examples of various conditions, such as intrapsychic incoordination, disintegration, intrapsychic ataxia, splitting, etc. I do not believe that the pervasiveness and the apparently common basis for characteristics such as the following have been sufficiently emphasized: (1) the disturbance and fragmentation of association, (2) the excessive concretization of thinking, (3) the lack of appropriateness and of modulation of affective response, and (4) the inability to maintain a state of readiness of response to incoming stimuli. All of these are explained by an underlying set difficulty. Elkes (in J. Folch-Pi, Ed., 1958) makes one attempt

[10]It would be interesting to compare this "normalizing" and normalizing that Holzman (presented at the Second Rochester International Conference on Schizophrenia, 1976) discovered when superimposing a simple cognitive task on his eye-tracking task. He found that the added task augmented the eyetracking, and the schizophrenic looked on it as a crutch. I believe this phenomenon to be a more fundamental effect, although ordinarily connected with the particular function being investigated, rather than having a generalizing value to functions of a broader nature. The likelihood exists, however, that it is similar to the "tapping situation" in that attention is diverted from the tracking test, permitting the subject to work without the consciousness of the tracking test itself. Without an awareness of responsibility for his performance, the subject is able to do much better. Another factor is the neurophysiological aspect, which is of utmost importance, but which we can not go into here.

to summarize the characteristics as stated, although I group them somewhat differently.

Comparing the two major subtypes of schizophrenia (Shakow, 1963), I have observed that the paranoid is intellectually preserved, rigid, persistent, limiting the environment in order to encompass it, responsive to personal meaning, and accurate but cautious. The hebephrenic, on the other hand, is intellectually disturbed, loose, shifting, one who broadens the environment inordinately by being at its mercy or by establishing superficial contact with it, and who is irresponsive to personal meaning, inaccurate, and venturesome. These characteristics are displayed in the examination of the psychological, physiopsychological, experimental psychological, and clinical psychological (psychiatric) findings, and all serve as evidence of what I call segmental set, as opposed to the generalized set found in normal subjects.[11]

[11]It is of interest in this context to compare the findings of an article "Are paranoid schizophrenics biologically different from other schizophrenics?" by Potkin and his associates (1978). They find paranoids to have reduced platelet MAO activity. They also cite experiments using normals who have reduced platelet MAO activity to be persons attuned to seek out stimulation from their environment. Thus the paranoids seem to be more attuned to influences from the environment than the others, and concomitantly appear to be augmenters on the auditory and visual average evoked response (Cf. to Petrie, 1967, p. 58 and Buchsbaum, 1975).

CHAPTER 8

Research

The basic task in dealing with schizophrenia is, of course, that of research—research in the experimental, physiological, psychological, and social, as well as the clinical psychological (psychiatric) areas. On another occasion I have discussed the problems of doing research in schizophrenia in the context of a chain of queries: *Why* should *who* do *what (how, when, where)* to *whom?* (Shakow, 1969).

Here I shall attempt to summarize. Under *why* in this article, I consider the motivations for doing research in this area: the understanding of schizophrenia in order to cure the individual patient; the prevention of schizophrenia; and the better understanding of pathological process, particularly for its possible contribution to the understanding of normal process. Under *who* is considered the range of disciplines relevant for research in schizophrenia, the types of interdisciplinary research and the concomitant problems each faces, and some of the special qualities needed by the individual investigator. The discussion of the *what* is quite brief, because I consider this a problem fundamentally determined by the background and perspicacity of the individual investigator. The *how* question requires proportionately the lengthiest discussion, since it encompasses so many of the difficulties of schizophrenia research. In outline these conditions include: the *method of approach* (the naturalistic, semi-naturalistic, free laboratory, and controlled laboratory); the general *time scale* (cross-sectional or longitudinal); the *modes* of approach within these specific methods (the choice of emphasis on the descriptive or theoretical, the multisimple or single recondite, the direct or inferential, the emphasis on technique or subject, method, or problem, the qualitative or quantitative, the molecular or molar, the isolated or systematic, the phenotypic or genotypic, the nomothetic or ideographic, and the contrived or spontaneous); the *background status* of the subject—his psychosis, and the less striking modifiers, from drugs to psychosocial influences; *the conditions of stimulation* seen against a background of the general conditions of stimulation (from impersonal stimulation to personal affective stimulation under stress), with varying preparatory "rest" states (from sensory deprivation through nonresting condition); the *contexts of presentation of stimuli*—their quality (focal or peripheral, brief or expanded, simple or complex, discrete or continuous, novel or old, repetitive or varied, ambiguous or defined) their intensity, and their frequency; and the *instructions of the experimenter*. Besides the stimulus situation, I consider the problems inherent in the subject's response part of the paradigm, both the portion involving his reaction to the experimenter's instructions and that deriving from his cooperation.

In relation to the *when* of the chain query I point to the problems created by internal rhythms, and to the need for keeping in mind, as well, such extrinsic factors as temporary fatigue and indisposition. The discussion of a third aspect of the temporal issue—the stage of the development of the psychosis to be studied—is left as more appropriate for consideration under *whom*.

The question of *whom*—the last link in our chain—brings us again to a topic that needs relatively more elaborate discussion. It necessitates a consideration of the problems of classification as they relate to schizophrenia—the distinction between the *whom* and *not-whom*, and the various kinds of "whoms" involved, such as the chronic-acute and the premorbid good-premorbid bad. In addition, it calls for a discussion of the problem of the relevant control groups. With regard to the first aspect, I have considered several reasonable criticisms that have been made of classification schemes, but have concluded, nevertheless, that classification in scientific activity was inevitable. However, I advocate active efforts to deal with these criticisms and suggest some steps that might be taken. Three phases of the diagnostic problem are examined: 1) accurate, initial description of patient behavior and feelings, 2) syndromization, and 3) the assignment of patients to categories. I make some suggestions for dealing with each of these phases as objectively as possible, including the use of rating scales, clear-cut criteria for syndromes, and anonymity in the process of assignment. I then consider the problems raised by possible sources of contamination in the sampling, and suggest that we are not interested in obtaining representative ("good") samples of the distribution of schizophrenia, but, rather, *pure* samples.

With regard to the second aspect of the problem—the nature of the control groups—I deal with the constitution of the schizophrenic group as a whole and the details of matching with other groups, both pathological and normal. I consider particularly the problems created by the use of class membership criteria—the differences between the superficial symbols and the referents involved. I then touch upon the problems raised by the use of dichotomies and subtypes.

I cannot, of course, go into the problems of the research ahead of us, but merely give some hints about one area with which I have been associated. Reaction time has been called the North Star of research in schizophrenia (Cancro et al., 1971), an appellation that is justified because of its ability to withstand annihilation despite broad and extensive experimental attacks. Nuechterlein *(Schizophrenia Bulletin, 3,* No. 3, 1977) has rendered the field a great service by pulling the material together creatively. I shall merely give some thoughts of Zahn (1977) on Nuechterlein's essay and add a few of my own.

Some of the advantages of reaction time should be noted. That R.T. approaches something quite fundamental in the schizophrenic seems now quite evident. That the disturbance is related to attention and set seems particularly well established. This only means that the processes involved will have to be examined more closely in the future.

The fact that schizophrenics' heart rate, arousal, and electrodermal response increase significantly less than that of controls during a period of waiting for a mental arithmetic task to start (rather than during the task itself) indicates both that the period of preparation to the response is important, and that, in schizophrenics, it is inadequate. (This is a part of the stimulus/response process that has been emphasized repeatedly in this volume.) Thus, it is necessary to distinguish attention to the stimulus from the effects of a stimulus on preparation to respond. [Broadbent (1977) offers some very pertinent suggestions here.] Further, the distinction between the persistence of memory traces and their effects on other processes has to be delineated.

The results show that schizophrenics are not qualitatively different, but are characterized by exaggerations of normal processes—their response is bipolar. Therefore, a modified version of a general normal model would be more appropriate, and the place of psychopathology in normal psychology would be enhanced. In fact, a normal psychology based on the abnormal (since there it is seen so much more clearly) is a distinct possibility and actually a necessity.[1]

In addition to complexity and competition, the question of compatibility is another variable that might be used. Marked incompatibility is another extreme stage of response, and therefore the schizophrenics' impairment may also come at this stage. The ability to shift seems involved.

Some of the remaining problems with regard to reaction time performance in schizophrenics are (1) The apparent lack of effect of anti-psychotic drugs (a clearer understanding of the *state or trait* nature of reaction time is thus called for); (2) the effects of motivation; and (3) the effects of practice,

---

[1]This point has already been made repeatedly in the past. It is seen in Bernard (1927, p. 146), Taine (1870), Galton (1883, p. 68), James (1896, in Perry, 1935, p. 123), Goldstein (1939), and Weiss (1961).

especially the effects of *considerably* extended practice. [The effect of *relatively* extended practice has been studied (Huston, Shakow, and Riggs, 1937, p. 141).]

Finally, the work of the Evarts group suggests another direction for research. They have shown (Tanji and Evarts, 1976) that pyramidal tract neurons in the motor cortex of the monkey discharge differentially prior to the elicitation of a voluntary movement, depending on which of the two movements the monkey has been instructed to make, suggesting that preparatory motor sets are represented cortically in the last supraspinal steps involved in the reaction. This is a particularly important development.

It is of great concern to us that the fields of schizophrenia and reaction time have been rather neglected by general psychologists. That an area of research producing such interesting individual differences should be felt to be lacking in appeal in its nomothetic aspects needs serious correction! Nevertheless, there is considerable evidence that the fields of psychopathology and related areas have not neglected this subject. The works of Steffy, Sutton, Zubin, Zahn, Cromwell, their associates and numerous others, provide apt examples of this.

CHAPTER 9

Vulnerability of
the Schizophrenic
to Segmental Set: Neophobia

Why is the schizophrenic so vulnerable to conditions that finally result in segmental set? It may be due to handicaps that act as an impediment to his attempts to satisfy his needs, or it may be due to his avoidance of anxiety, one result of which is his tendency to react only to items that are safe and come from parts of his past that he is relatively prepared to deal with. Both of these are aspects of neophobia, or, in positive terms, schizophilia. The schizophrenic reacts either from a fear of the new, or, at best, an attraction for the old. Two sides of one coin, these reactions are difficult at times to distinguish clinically. This predilection for the archaic may be due to defects in early conditioning or genetic factors.

One of my hypotheses with regard to the performance deficit so prevalent in schizophrenia has been the overabundance of what I have called "remorating"[1] factors—responses from

---

[1]Remorae are a genus of fish with an anterior suctorial disc on the top of the head by which they attach themselves to sharks and other large fishes and vessels. Montaigne (1908, pp. 197–198) cites Pliny's natural history as authority for the statement that Antony lost his last great naval engagement to Augustus because his vessels were "stayed in the middle of the course" by the remorae. The Emperor Caligula, sailing with a great navy on the coast of Rumania, was very angry that such a little animal could resist "the sea, the wind, and the force of all his oars," and stop his ships.

the past that are used but are no longer effective for adaptation. I discuss these types of responses in the section on perseveration (pp. 93-96). Some of these remorae were useful in the past; others never were (e.g., "string too short to be saved"). They may show up in the form of what Gantt (via Peters, who introduced the idea) has called schizokinesis, "the cleavage between the emotional, visceral, and superficial motor responses" (1953, p. 157). In this case, an autonomic function such as heart acceleration, which originally was part of an adaptive total process, is stimulated on its own and is no longer adaptive. Or it may take the form of a skeletal response that was adaptive a short time ago and is no longer adaptive. It is as if each person has an old fashioned country-store brine barrel containing not only pickles of all sizes and kinds, but also scraps of dill, bits of salt, and similar elements. For the schizophrenic, few of the juicy pickles are readily available, because they have been overwhelmed by the stresses occasioned by the irrelevant factors. Rather than floating at the top, they appear to have sunk to the bottom. Instead, only the irrelevant debris floats on the surface, readily available. In the normal subject, on the other hand, succulent pickles predominate and come easily to hand; inessential scraps have sunk to the bottom of the barrel, rarely coming to the surface.

Another form of remorae is found in situations in which a response takes into account only part of its total adaptiveness. In this respect, the schizophrenic's activity might be appropriately labelled "centipedal." He is, as in the case of the centipede of the fable, so deeply concerned about the way his feet move that he loses sight of where they should be going. If there is any creature who can be accused of not "seeing the forest for the trees," it is the schizophrenic. The paranoid sticks even more closely than the normal person to the path

---

In recent years, there has been a growing interest in remorae because of the *beneficent* effect of their operation, which, besides their delaying effects, nevertheless clear sharks of parasites (Clark, 1975). In the case of the schizophrenic, the effect of the remorae that I shall emphasize is that of the former, ancient, aspect of delay or drag.

through the forest, examining each tree along the path, sometimes even each tree's leaves, with meticulous care. The hebephrenic acts as if there were no paths, straying off the path entirely; he is attracted by any and all phenomena, even the undergrowth and floor of the forest, in a superficial, flitting way, apparently forgetting in the meantime about the place where he was going. The acute patient in the same forest usually undergoes a multitude of heightened new experiences, reacting highly affectively, for instance, to new and unusual patterns of light on the leaves, or to novel and subtle patterns of form in the branches. These are presumably expressions of the perceptive-associative powers which, under ordinary life conditions, even if aroused, are held under control, whereas in acute psychotic conditions they are brought to the surface. Once perceived, these peculiar perceptions are persisted in, despite any concurrent awareness that as far as one's job in the real world is concerned, one is dawdling, not proceeding through the forest. The experiences appear too novel, too seductive or overwhelming to ignore.[2] The terrified acute patient may have the same experiences, but reacts to them more with terror than elation.

Schizophrenics, in fact, do very little productive or goal-directed moving, despite any rich and active "yearnings" that may lie beneath the surface. The schizophrenic patient appears to be yearning for the satisfaction of fundamental needs that have never been adequately satisfied in the ordinary course of events. This schizophrenic trait brings to mind Santayana's characterization of the nineteenth century, which, he

---

[2]These feelings of the importance of the experience may suffer, of course, from the same kind of impairment of judgment that apparently takes place in dreams under ether. Oliver Wendell Holmes' account of his experience under this condition is particularly relevant. He took ether experimentally, and he reported that " . . . the key to all the mysteries that philosophy has sought in vain to solve, flashed upon me in sudden revelation. As my natural condition returned, . . . staggering to my desk, I wrote, in ill-shaped, straggling characters, the all-embracing truth. . . . The words were these . . . "*A strong smell of turpentine prevails throughout.*" (Holmes, 1871, pp. 46–47.)

says, " . . . yearned with Rousseau or speculated with Kant, while it moved with Darwin, Bismarck, and Nietzsche . . . " (Shakow, 1950, p. 387). However, when applied to the schizophrenic, Santayana's pairing must be reversed, and the movement he refers to highly attenuated. In the schizophrenic, it is the yearnings that seem to have the Bismarckian, and the "movement" the Rousseauian, quality.

Thus, the schizophrenic contends with the burden of remorae that are useless or maladaptive but which he cannot shake off. An example of a more adaptive approach to a similar burden is provided by Sinbad. In the fifth voyage of his adventures in the *Arabian Nights*, Sinbad meets a horrible old man who asks for a ride on Sinbad's shoulders over a low stream. Sinbad, in his goodness, complies. Afterwards, no matter what he does, the old man can't be dislodged. Only after several days is Sinbad able to get the man drunk, smash in his head, and get rid of him.[3]

Because of tendencies that generally have been reinforced from early childhood, there appears to have developed in schizophrenics a characteristic fear of the new, the unexpected, and a secondary clinging to the old, the previously experienced, or experienced in the past. It comes out clearly in the quote from Roheim's patient mentioned earlier, who said "In my mind I always linger on—I am still doing the things I have finished," and in Laing and Esterson's patient who said, "I don't know how to deal with the unexpected. That's why I like things neat and tidy. Nothing unexpected can happen then." (Laing and Esterson, 1964, p. 29).

It is true that normal people are sometimes reluctant to undertake something for the first time as well—witness "the universal care often passing into religious fear, about doing something for the first time, or something unusual or important," that Crawley (1960) quotes Ellis as having said (p. 218). But the normal person finally proceeds anyway, whereas the schizophrenic typically flees.

The hebephrenic patient, who seeks out the unexpected,

---

[3] It is of interest to note that Sullivan employed ethyl alcohol to induce mild intoxication in schizophrenics and achieved "considerable readjustment" (1972, p. 298 ff.).

might seem to be an exception, but he seeks *change* rather than newness in his superficial search. He doesn't seek out the unexpected for the quality of its unforeseenness. He actually does not seem to have a permanent structure (a history, if you will) to bother him in evaluating stimuli—a stimulus is a stimulus is a stimulus—without regard to their newness or oldness. The acute—especially the catatonic—patient may, on the other hand, actually be an exception, because he shows a neophilia rather than a neophobia. But it must be recognized that this neophilia is directed inwardly and *irrelevantly*, having little contact with outside stimuli that constitute veridical experience, as discussed above. In the passage from the acute to the chronic state, one sees, as it were, the shift from neophilia (of the inner life) to neophobia, from affect to apathy, the extremes of two related parameters.

At times, the neophobia becomes a phobia for *any* additional stimulation—new or old. The schizophrenic develops a "leave me alone" attitude. There is no zest for stimuli provided by himself. Thus there seems for him to be four stages of readiness for stimulation: 1) preference for internal stimuli; 2) acceptance of outside stimuli if others control the stimulation; 3) acceptance of outside stimuli with pressure from outside; and 4) withdrawal, no response.

If we were to try to epitomize the schizophrenic person's system in the most simple language with respect to his "neophobia," we might say that he has two major difficulties: first, he reacts to old and new situations as if they were recently past ones (he perseverates);[4] and, second, he is relatively unaffected by the stimulus itself, that is, he overresponds when the stimulus is relatively small and he does not respond enough when the stimulus is great.

---

[4]As Forrest (1969, p. 69) points out, uncertainties in the schizophrenic person's experience of his environment are upsetting; predictability of any kind is undesirable. The schizophrenic person enters each new situation unprepared, thus the characteristic sterotypy and monotonous repetition of ideas may be attempts to lessen the experience of surprise. The immediate assignment of idiosyncratic symbols to new and feared situations lends a semblance of control; neophobia paradoxically leads to neologism or, to the contrary, perseveration.

CHAPTER 10

The Developmental Aspects
of Segmental Set

A more detailed outline of the developmental physiological and comparative aspects of segmental set should be attempted. However, even if an adequate explanation is not forthcoming, one example from a fairly low mammalian level is relevant from an experiment by Stanley on infant dogs. It throws some light on the notion of segmental set. With regard to his hypotheses about maladaption in infant dogs, Stanley says:

> Shakow's theoretical views concerning normal and schizophrenic behavior are based on a distinction between generalized and segmental sets . . . Descriptively, the integrated sequence of key lifts followed by nipple latches and sucks, followed by key lifts, etc., is representative of a generalized set at the level of infant nonhuman animal behavior. On the other hand, the three components of the maladaptive behavioral state (tongue position, loss of directed and effective feeding movements, and stereotypic and repetitive movements) are representative of segmental sets, again at the level of infant nonhuman animal behavior. There is a striking similarity between the behavioral properties we have abstracted from the maladaptive behavioral state in infant dogs and the properties Shakow has abstracted from schizophrenic behavior (Stanley, 1972, p. 418).

An extremely different but pertinent reference from another source derives from the developmental studies of the psychology of conscience. Grim, Kohlberg, and White (1968) draw this comparison:

> The authors' attentional interpretation of the psychomotor-moral stability factor coincides with the findings with similar measures in

schizophrenics as summarized and interpreted by Shakow (1962). Schizophrenics, who are defective in a number of the psychomotor and psychophysiological variables defining the authors' stability factor, cannot be characterized as generally emotionally overreactive (or even underreactive). Instead, they appear to be unable to maintain a set to discriminate between relevant and irrelevant stimuli in a task, that is, to maintain attention (p. 251).

The human developmental aspect of set, although not developed in its schizophrenic aspects, is illustrated by the case of the child Raun described by his father in *Son-Rise* (Kaufman, 1976). Autistic Raun's performance at age one and a half years was comparable to that of an 8-month old child. He preferred handling objects to human contacts. People, who constantly change (by movement, speech, etc.), were avoided, and those manipulable objects such as the inanimate that are easily controlled were segmentally selected instead. The following excerpts from the account of this autistic boy are illustrative:

It was during the second week of our marathon observation period. Watching him for hours spinning on the kitchen floor, every round object being set into motion. Dishes, tops and plates. Pans and balls. This one time, he came upon a *rectangular shoebox.* He picked it off the floor and held it in his hands for almost twenty-five minutes. He did not move . . . just occasionally stroked it, touching the cardboard with his fingers while moving his eyes along its edges. Then, quite suddenly, he put the tip of one of the corners of the box on the floor, balanced it with his left hand and set it into motion with his right. No trial and error. He had actually used his mind analytically and with great sophistication in order to get what he had wanted. Before he moved or made a single test, he had analyzed the potential of the box as a spinning object and then synthesized a method to achieve it. Still only seventeen months old. Incredible. Amazing and slick. A significant piece of behavior hinting at the vast field of intelligence that we felt existed beneath the surface of his bizarre patterns. . . .

In contrast, when people entered the room, they were usually moving. Erratic, noisy. Unpredictable and usually uncontrollable. If one of Raun's organic deficits was a problem or deficiency with thinking—a problem of memory and recall—a problem of holding things together in time and space, then surely *objects would be easier to deal with than people.* If each person entering the room was always a new and unrelated experience to Raun, then each one of us might be a hundred different people to him.[1] What a confusing and perplexing bombardment of data we must create, a diverse spectrum of sporadic images.

He was aloof and separate from people while pouring his energy into objects. Naturally, this dilemma would produce a child who did not relate to or imitate people. Therefore, learning would be severely curtailed and, in some instances, impossible. Language acquisition which also depends on imitation, would be affected. In addition, communications and manipulating others in the environment would have no meaning in Raun's peopleless world.'' (pp. 42–43 emphasis added).

[1]A state reminiscent of Searles' patient (referred to earlier, see p. 80) who saw another therapist each time his therapist moved.

CHAPTER 11

Segmental Set and Schizophrenic States of Personality

A variety of designations have developed over the years that attempt to characterize schizophrenic behavior descriptively. Among the terms that have been proposed, the most prominent are: deterioration, regression (with its partial import of dedifferentiation), heteronomy, and depersonalization which are perhaps indicative of an underlying generalized deficit of adaptation. In the descriptions of pathology attributed to schizophrenia over the years, two aspects of segmental set are emphasized—dependence on part of the self for the total unified self, and dependence on other entities instead of oneself. Both of these represent the workings of an unintegrated human being. The dependency on part of the self is seen in such characteristics as deterioration, regression, depersonalization, and deanimation—different aspects of falling back on parts, current or past, for reactions to the environment. In behavior characterized by heteronomy and institutionalization, the schizophrenic's response is directed more by other persons or institutions than by himself.

DETERIORATION

In an extended discussion of deterioration (1946), which I need not repeat here with the exception of a few remarks, I came to the conclusion that deterioration arises not so much from a defect of the parts, but rather from a lack of integration of the whole, the situation prevailing in segmental set. The attempt to analyze the nature of this poor adaptiveness gives rise to various conjectures. The schizophrenic patient seems unable to keep the "set" (readiness to respond) necessary for the effective handling of a task for longer than a few seconds—even at his own low level of performance. He tends to fall back on minor sets of a less effective nature—sets that are easier to adopt but that result in the inefficient handling of a situation. This type of response seems to occur as well in situations involving discrete, as those involving continuous, reaction.

REGRESSION

The concept of regression presents a serious dilemma, because broadly it can subsume all the other difficulties in set and adaptation that I have been considering. The term regression is often used loosely in such expressions as "regressed behavior," referring to simpler or dedifferentiated behavior, or, in Werner's terminology, "physiognomic" behavior. But if the term is understood strictly in this sense, it would mean that an entire maturational level of behavior is nonfunctional, as if all learning and maturation of function subsequent to the earlier level has been sloughed off. It is doubtful that such pure forms of earlier behavior occur (except in rare circumstances), because they become such highly overlearned habits of response. Extreme reversals to earlier maturational levels are possible, perhaps most strikingly with neurological damage like that in the case of Ansel Bourne (see James, 1890. Vol. I, p. 391). But ordinarily, it is symbolic or dedifferentiating behavior that is interpreted as regressive.

Regression can be normal and even highly creative, as is pointed out by Kris (1950) when he uses regression as a state useful in the service of the ego. In the case of the schizophrenic, however, it occurs in the service of the id, in the form of "instinctual regression." "Archaic" needs must be satisfied in a physical and intellectual expansion that comes with chronological development and in an environment that has also changed. To provide outlets for this infantile or childish need, satisfaction, perceiving, responding, or thinking may be segmentalized, resulting in regressive behavior that is irrelevant, inappropriate, or partial, and contaminated with fragments from the past. Conative and particularly affective regression are relatively frequent, but true cognitive regression is extremely rare.

HETERONOMY

Heteronomy refers to the degree to which a person's behavior is determined directly by forces outside himself without fundamental processing within himself. Autonomy requires that the person's behavior be determined by qualities deriving from within, central to his self. Homonomy is the product of a mature socialization process (Angyal, 1941), the working of a socialized superego. Heteronomous behavior derives naturally from regression in opposition to the autonomous qualities in the personality.

Heteronomy is another deficiency in integrative control often manifested by the schizophrenic. Sometimes a schizophrenic will accept direction from the physical environment, sometimes from the human environment, and sometimes from internal forces that are clearly differentiated from the self (e.g., "voices"). The primary deficiencies in these different types of heteronomous behavior concern integration into the self and the feeling of responsibility for one's condition, which are two hallmarks of the normal autonomous person.

Heteronomous behavior reveals itself in four kinds of response: first, in the tendency to place responsibility on others, to "let George do it"; second, in the tendency to blame others, to hold others responsible for events; third, in the tendency to blame oneself entirely; and, fourth, in a reaction that might be called "time-binding."

The tendency to place the responsibility on others, and to avoid assuming it for oneself, may be seen even in simple experimental situations[1] such as reaction time. Thus, in an experiment on reaction time (Cromwell et al., 1961), when the subjects were asked which they preferred, an autonomous condition (in which they set the experimental condition themselves) or a controlled condition (in which the experimenter set the conditions), the schizophrenics chose the controlled conditions, which was consonant with their performance on the task, whereas most of the normals preferred the autonomous conditions. The difference was significant. However, if the situation is set up in such a way that the subject unknowingly assumed the responsibility and initiative for the task, the schizophrenics did better than when they knew that they were in a situation "demanded" by the outside. (The profound disturbance of the personality represented by "depersonalization" may be related to this trend.)

With respect to heteronomy, just as with other characteristics of schizophrenics, such as seen with respect to conceptualization, there is a paradox. How can one say about a schizophrenic whose behavior appears so extremely determined by inner needs, that he is directed by forces outside himself? It must be recognized that this "internal directedness" is superficial (although underlying needs are not) and does not involve integrated introjection. Rather, it is based on preoccupations with outside influences never truly assimilated and made part of one's own ego system. Exaggerated responsibility, as well as complete heteronomy, are bipolar reactions, the workings of massive defensive systems.

These alternative coping mechanisms (bipolar options) that serve to prevent the schizophrenic from being overwhelmed by genuine needs and by taking realistic responsibility, are by their very nature segmentalizing. In terms of Gordon Allport's system (1921), the response is not assimilated into his "proprium."

Institutionalization[1] represents another form of placing re-

---

[1]Over the years, increasing concern has been expressed or implied about the deleterious effects of institutionalization. The opinion of many has been

sponsibility on others. An institution can come to be a substitute for an integrated personality, because the system provides so much structure.

Delusions, which are so striking a feature of paranoid clinical behavior, often reflect the second tendency of blaming others (projection). Less extreme rationalizations for poor performance are also frequently offered by this type of pa-

---

that the effects on patients of residence in mental hospitals has been negative—that much of the illness of patients, and many of their symptoms, can be accounted for by such residence. In view of the poor quality and poor regimens of most of the institutions in which psychotic persons have been housed over the years, such a finding appears to have considerable justification and face validity. Since schizophrenics represent so large a proportion of the resident and residual patient group of such institutions, the problem is particularly relevant for this group. In the coming period, we are likely to have the requisite control studies of matched groups of hospitalized patients and groups maintained elsewhere in the community under relatively comparable regimens. These studies are now beginning to emerge (Reik, 1972, 1977). For the present, the notion of widespread deleterious effects and improvements in the community settings must rest on rather sketchy evidence, on the whole. It stems too often from clinical "impressions," and on occasion, I am afraid, even from prejudice against institutions, without adequate recognition of their immense range of qualities. (I say nothing of the economic motives behind such discharge of patients.) The matter is treated most commendably in the recent monograph by Bachrach (1976). Other recent works that shed further light on the subject are: Hersch (1969, 1972), Kirk and Therrien (1975), Becker and Schulberg (1976), Steinhart (1973), Fowlkes (1975), Rieder (1974) and Greenblatt and Glazier (1975).

Here I must make a personal aside. Having worked in a state hospital, (the only years I spent in a state hospital) from 1924 to 1925 and then again after a period for graduate work from 1928 to 1946 at the Worcester State Hospital, I must say that my experiences are quite different from others. It is true that a good deal of this period was during the depression years, when the state hospital was sought as a refuge, not only by the patients, but also by the staff. Acknowledging factors of this kind, nonetheless, the qualities of Worcester State Hospital at this time, the qualities of the superintendent and his successors, and the other characteristics of the institution that I have clarified in my monograph (1972), made my experiences there somewhat unique. But my concern was mainly with the development of the Worcester State Hospital as a research institution. With respect to institutionalization itself, the book by Bryan (1936) brings out the details of the care and the pains taken with the patients as a whole in a truly modern institution oriented around the patient.

tient in all kinds of test and experimental situations.

The tendency to take the blame for "cosmic" events on oneself is an instance of the third type of heteronomy. A seeming paradox must be dealt with at this point. I refer to the sense of responsibility for one's actions seen in the "cosmic" sense that is assumed by some psychotic persons. Although this attitude is in itself a good prognostic sign, the degree of responsibility felt is much exaggerated. For example, this sense of accountability may be a delusion of culpability for some imagined upcoming world catastrophe (Boisen, 1960). The assumption of personal responsibility for the event is of such overwhelming importance to the patient that a highly distorted perception or evaluation of the situation results. This attitude of guilt is what, on many occasions, leads the patient to eventually find his way back to relative normality. The range of attitudes observed with respect to this feeling of responsibility is of the same order as the extremes of bipolar response discussed earlier.

The problem of "time-binding," the fourth kind of response, is broader; it involves a longer-term heteronomous organization. Whereas the normal acts in a present based on his past but oriented toward the future, the time-bound schizophrenic acts in a present limited by his distorted, overdrawn view of the past, especially of its traumatic characters, and apparently has little concern for the future. Rather than being "man, the time-binder," the schizophrenic is "man, the time-bound." His behavior is controlled in a sense by the "other" of his own outmoded past.

DEPERSONALIZATION/DEREALIZATION

The terms depersonalization and derealization are sometimes used synonymously, but the term depersonalization may be assumed to concern the self, whereas derealization concerns the external world. I am considering this type of symptom as it relates to schizophrenia, although it often occurs in other pathological groups and, indeed, in normals under under certain extraordinary conditions. A fundamental theorem, as Weckowicz and Sommer (1960, pp. 17–39) point out, that seems to run through psychoanalysis, existential psychiatry, and experimental psychology, is the integrative functions of the ego, including the separation of the self from the object, as a distinction of the individual experience from their frame of reference. As Schilder puts it, in one sense depersonalization is a nuclear problem of psychology and psychopathology, because it ushers in neurosis and psychosis (1953, pp. 304–309). Deanimation (Schossberger, 1963) appears to be another form of the depersonalization/derealization system. Perhaps because it is so fundamental an aspect of depersonalization, the presence of this symptom is fraught with aspects that make for better prognosis. All of these are forms of de-differentiation, the simplification of the perception and the response, and therefore segmentalizing.

Deterioration, regression, heteronomy, depersonalization, and deanimation are all signs of coping mechanisms that are not altogether successful. As in the case of other schizophrenic characteristics, they are not generally adaptive because they serve to avoid or prevent the generalized set. Instead of taking all relevant factors into consideration, only partial and distorted features of the situation are utilized.

INEFFICIENCY (INEFFICACY)

That the schizophrenic is inefficient in carrying out tasks necessary for adaptation, and that he manifests a greater proportion of irrelevant to relevant responses, is indicated by much of the preceding exposition. Wishner (1955, 1965), in a series of papers, gives particular emphasis to this "inefficiency." He points out that it is reflected in both the means and variances of individual tasks, and in the intercorrelations among different tasks. His studies indicate that schizophrenics have not only lower means, but higher variances, and lower correlations among tasks.

White (1965), on the other hand, deals with the "inefficacy" of the schizophrenic from a dynamic point of view. He calls attention to the patient's weakness in reality-testing, his blurring of boundaries between self and nonself, his inability to block out distracting stimulation, his descent from conceptual to concrete modes of thinking, the painful fragility of his self-esteem, his limits of energy, and his gross incompetence in such matters as role-taking and being able to grasp other people's outlooks.

These factors, the "inefficiency" of Wishner and the "inefficacy" of White, may be attributed to the operations of segmental rather than generalized set. It becomes necessary to combine both the structural and dynamic views.

CHAPTER 12

Schizophrenic
Coping Behavior

The nature of coping is characteristically appropriate in the normal, but quite pathological in the schizophrenic; herein lies the crux of my theory.[1]

Under normal conditions, coping capacity requires:

1. Drive within the organism that is goal-directed
2. Freedom to cope with real changes in his environment—a resilience in meeting environmental demands
3. Multiple supports (especially in the early stages) provided by the environment
4. Temporary use of defense mechanisms (self-protection or compensatory devices) in the initial stages of coping with a situation
5. Healthy narcissism

Conversely, in schizophrenia, instead of the natural drives that develop with a person's growth, there are *archaic* drives that never were satisfied in the past and are constantly trying

---

[1]Coping may be defined as how the person mobilizes and uses his resources, and how he manipulates his resources to meet his needs. I am greatly indebted to Lois B Murphy for the creative delineation of this problem in her volume, L. B. Murphy and A. E. Moriarty, *Vulnerability, Coping and Growth* (1976). I use her descriptions unsparingly.

to achieve satisfaction anachronistically. Instead of the moderate use of a few defense mechanisms, in the schizophrenic, fantasy, denial, repression, and especially regression are rampant. In place of a capacity to delay and a tolerance for frustration, there is a tendency to show extremes of other qualities. Periods of rest, the ability to limit excess stimulation, the ability to control and limit the impact of the environment through strategic withdrawal, delay, or caution are all employed inadequately. This tends to produce bipolar extremes in his responses, manifested by either a marked rigidity or a marked looseness, as evidence of instability. The subtler forms of self-protection, compensatory measures, and a healthy narcissism, are absent. The factors contributing to health—positive self-concept, security, positive orientation to life—are all inadequate or missing. Likely to be lacking in the life history are the early supports from the environment that help to make these factors develop and grow, that is, the mother's enjoyment of the child, her encouragement and support of the child, and her active help in coping. Problems are observed in the schizophrenic's reactions to strangeness, with the preference for the already experienced manifested in repetition-choice experiments (Rosenzweig, 1945), and in his inability to accept substitutes in substitution experiments (Bennett, 1942). The developmental balance appears disturbed. (This is corroborated on the physiological side by the negatively tinged autonomic homeostatic difficulties, and at the CNS level, described briefly above.)

The concept of segmental set reflects well these characteristics of the schizophrenic. Adaptive action requires that the realistic factors involved be registered and conceptualized, leading to a form of acceptable conduct. When the schizophrenic is performing at his best, a partial consideration may be given to these pertinent individual factors. At his worst, no relevant parts of the real situation are considered. In both instances, a segmental reaction, whether in part relevant or totally irrelevant, is induced, and the response is bound to be therefore either partially or totally irrelevant. Needless to say, this judgment is from the viewpoint of the observer, society. The community expects the schizophrenic to react by consensual validation, and he, adversely, acts idiosyncratically.[2]

[2]In an interesting and here particularly pertinent account of the Grant study of normals, Vaillant (1977) describes the mature defense mechanisms of the normal persons that the Grant fund has studied and also the psychotic, immature, and neurotic mechanisms Vaillant ascribed to the pathological. Among the mature mechanisms he lists altruism, humor, suppression, anticipation, and sublimation. Among the psychotic mechanisms are delusional projection, denial, and distortion. Among the immature he lists projection, schizoid fantasy, hypochondriasis, passive-aggressive behavior, and acting-out, and among the neurotic defenses he lists intellectualization, repression, displacement, reaction formation, and dissociation. Schizophrenics typically utilize these pathological defenses.

CHAPTER 13

Symptoms and Diagnosis

The nature of segmental set is now examined in relation to the classical symptoms of schizophrenia. Its major characteristics are generally considered to be: (1) thought disorder; (2) affect disturbance; (3) hallucinations; and, (4) ego disturbance, especially as manifested in inappropriate behavior, such as poor reality testing, delusions, and hallucinations. The whole person is involved—from the biological through the psychosocial. Overall there is a striking lack of integration.

The formal properties that I have considered previously are all revealed in the symptom complex, whether they be in the realm of thought disorder, affect, or ego disturbance. The intensity of the stimulus, the focus, definition, organizability, novelty, variety, scantiness or redundancy, and personalness are all involved in these situations. And, in the schizophrenic, all are affected by segmental set. An analysis of them in their bipolar aspect gives us the schizophrenic characteristics as a whole or in one of another combination, the subtypes of schizophrenia.

The syndrome of symptoms that are categorized under the rubric of *thought disorders* are: dereistic thinking, incoherence and disconnection, delusions, bizarre ideas, and silliness. These symptoms, which collectively characterize the various types of schizophrenia, all suggest the existence of segmental set. One of the prominent ideas of the catatonic in the florid state, is the notion of cosmic catastrophe. There is all-enveloping "fire": strong, driving, motivational affect— but no matter how complete and integrated these ideas might be in and of themselves, they are, at best, only partial perceptions of the true realities of the situation. In most instances, they involve a total disregard of the actual situation. Each one of the symptoms of the schizophrenic may be examined in detail and found, at least in part, segmental. The most prominent solution used by the paranoid is that of delusions. The outstanding feature of this behavior is that, even at best, there is only a partial perception of the situation, resulting in distortion and invalid thinking. The "fire" is there, but it is limited. In other words, it is segmentalized. The marked incoherence and discontinuity of the hebephrenic show up frequently as bizarre ideas. Whereas there is no "fire," he is nevertheless everywhere at once in a hebetated way. The evidence for partial, or indeed total, neglect of the reality of the situation is obvious. His behavior is mostly a series of sputters. The indeterminate patient not only has no "fire" (like the hebephrenic), but his behavior is limited in range as well (like the paranoid).

The affective disturbances, such as apathy, instability, inappropriateness, and ambivalence, are also a function of segmental set. The inappropriateness and the sometimes pathological anger shown by the hebephrenic evidence a lack of synchrony between the cognitive and the affective mental processes. In the catatonic, self-mutilative acts, on the one hand, and negativism, on the other, are evidence of this asynchrony. In the paranoid, exaggerated affect is directed at a fraction of the environment imbued with personal meaning. These disturbances indicate the partial perceptions characteristic of segmental set functioning.

In the realm of the reality testing there is general "disintegration" in the form of "queer" and odd behavior. In the hebephrenic there are mannerisms, grimaces, silliness, hallucinations, etc.; in the catatonic there are phases of stupor or excitement; and in the paranoid there is delusional or hallucinatory development. In all of these, no general set is functional, and segmental sets prevail.

Man has appropriately been called a "time-binder," which, in the widest sense of the term, distinguishes him from the rest of the animal kingdom. But even in a narrow sense, the characterization is also apt, for the normal human being acts typically in the present, based on the past, to satisfy present but, predominantly, future needs. He does this most effectively when he is free of what has been called unhealthy narcissism. The schizophrenic appears to act in the present in the attempt to satisfy some present urgent needs, but predominantly to satisfy past needs; he leaves the impression of not having any future needs.

To turn a moment to the field of biology, in the summary from an article of Angyal, Freeman and Hoskins (1940), they conclude that schizophrenics are characterized by a hyporeactivity to metabolic stimulants, a hyporeactivity of the autonomic nervous system, and a hyporeactivity of the central nervous system. There is thus a rather general reduction of physiological responsiveness in the schizophrenic, which can be interpreted as a sign of segmental set, for as we have postulated, there is either a hypo-or a hyper-reaction with the functioning of segmental set.

CHAPTER 14

Implications of Segmental Set Theory for Therapy

The question of therapy in schizophrenia raises several issues that are of profound importance. On the one hand, there are the claims of the *echt* and extreme psychopharmacologists, who maintain that once the physical components of schizophrenia are discovered (genetic or otherwise, and this they claim is only a matter of time, considering the amount of research devoted to it), the problems will be solved with the administration of a drug. At the other extreme, there are those psychologists and sociologists who cannot perceive what part the physical aspects may play in an organism that has gone through so many long years of schizophrenic habit-formation by pathological factors in the person and in the environment. For them, an essential personality change can only come about through a surrogate reliving of the person's psychological development in an environment that is normal and highly supportive—the presence and activity of an environment that, on the one hand, breaks down the already acquired pathological habits and, on the other, helps to build up normal ones. This psycho-socio-cultural approach, they claim, is the only effective device against schizophrenia.

Although it is true that at the extremes of the distribution one or the other of these views may hold, in most instances there is a good deal to be said for the combination of these extremes. To me, the question becomes, how then can segmental set in schizophrenia be overcome: *once psychopharmocological intervention restores the capacity for integrated functioning, generalized set may not appear automatically but must be learned and encouraged in a variety of ways.*

To overcome segmental set one must deal with two kinds of anxieties and needs: *secondary anxiety* that has accumulated through the longstanding preoccupation with segmental ways of behaving (the person has hoarded up a vast accumulation of inadequate reactions and anxieties, which have to be dealt with) and *basic anxiety*, which is related to the underlying inability to meet current archaic needs. *Archaic needs* are represented by habit formations of an old kind, which require the breakdown of the segmental acts (which, in turn, must be overcome). The *new underlying needs* are constructive new needs and habits that take the place of the old needs and habits and lead to the development of generalized sets.

I will now present a prognostic classification of schizophrenics of a practical kind according to a scheme of my own combined with a scheme worked out by Erickson and Hoskins (1931), which may be useful in the formulation of therapy. First, there is a class with active symptoms—paranoids, hebephrenics, long-lasting catatonics—who remain psychotic. Then there is a second class, the "indeterminate," who no longer have symptoms, but who have settled for a lower level of adjustment and no longer manifest the need to struggle. The third class are symptom-free and may be able to get along in the community, but only at a minimal level. The fourth group are patients who return home in their original *prepsychotic* state. For all intents and purposes, these patients are substantially "cured." The fifth class are patients who have gone through the turmoil and come out of the psychosis *truly* cured. For them, there is indeed *restitutio ad integrum.* There is restitution to a state better than the original, for they have essentially dealt with their problem in its entirety. I have in mind cases like Boisen's (1960), Sechehaye's (1970), Milner's (1969), those referred to by Menninger (1963, p. 345), and by Schiff (1970), in which the patient's ego is reconstituted in such a way as to enable him to become a much more productive member of society. Segmental set is largely abandoned, and generalized set reigns. The patients in the first four "chronic" classes may have to go through a much more profound change before joining the group of the "cured." But the process is both prolonged and seemingly unending.

Stated in another way, the extensive disintegration observed in the schizophrenic, with its inevitable accompaniment of what I call segmental sets, does not necessarily imply utter pessimism. His strange behaviors carry their own kind of literal or symbolic meaning. Schizophrenic behavior, usually split-off acts of the moment, whether in the form of frights, flights, or aggressions, often indicates a reaction to underlying anxiety and deep frustration towards what the schizophrenic perceives as a lack of sympathy and understanding on the part of the environment. These feelings grow out of his underlying unsatisfied need for *love*, the never-met need for primitive security that became established during the very earliest of infantile relations, perhaps because of genetic inadequacies, or those connected with feeding and mothering. Schizophrenics, even when chronologically adult, appear to have a peculiar and exaggerated need for complete acceptance that has to be demonstrated to them in "infantile" ways, to meet the basic infantile needs that they believe they have never experienced, as is evidenced by the cases of Sechehaye (1970), Hayward (1956), and Milner. In addition, there are the Schiff cases (Schiff, 1970) and the Honig (1972) cases. In each of these it is demonstrated that profoundly anxious and frightened persons can only achieve security at a slow rate—often maddeningly slow—through the gradual development of the feelings of safety that come when understanding and love are provided, even to the extent of surrogate breastfeeding (Schiff, 1970) by persons in their environment whom they consider sufficiently strong to provide them.

In the miasma of schizophrenic disturbance, there are islands of integrity that seem to be untouched. One may, with effort, find underlying capacities for normality, both physiological and psychological. We have seen them, for instance, in

our "normalizing" studies (Shakow, 1958), which provided
evidence that schizophrenics possess functions that can reach
a normal capacity level and that there is therefore something
to work with, even though the levels achieved are limited to
the functions studied and are not transferable. In the clinical
situation, the "off-on" phenomenon is not uncommon when
the schizophrenic patient has periods of relative clarity or
normality. These may be the result of psychotherapy, or even
of "heroic" shock or drug measures. And, finally, there are
those rarer instances when recovery, or even a "cure," appears to have taken place, a "cure" that may actually make
the schizophrenic more mature than he was before his illness.
The ego of the patient appears to have been rescued and reorganized. How has this come about? How has the organism after such marked disintegration become reintegrated?

Many have a faith in the power and magic of drugs, analogous, as it is said, to the giving of L-dopa to a patient with Par-
kinsonism. I have frequently wondered if drugs alone (Wyatt,
1976), aside from their often great advantage in breaking
through the formidable barriers of schizophrenia, are sufficient, even at their best, unless they are also accompanied by
the underlying sympathy and understanding that the building
of any human relationship calls for. Only in this way, through
the encouragement gained by a lack of overwhelming anxiety,
can generalized set occur.

Others have a faith in the power and magic of a deep psychotherapy, one that recognizes the need for going through
the complex process of rebuilding the person through the
successive steps of normal development: imitation, introjection, identification, and differentiation, in both their literal and
symbolic aspects, carried out in surroundings of love and
strength[1] It is only in this reconstructive way that the tendency toward segmental set can gradually be overcome, and the
ultimate conceptual strengths of generalized set be estab-

[1]Seymour Epstein (1977) has been good enough to send me a pre-publica-
tion draft of an article that is quite relevant to this thesis.

lished. (What is being reestablished is Allport's generalized set to "perceive accurately and respond appropriately" in its fullest meaning.) The process is long, but the rewards are great.

What we can say more specifically is that, in the earlier phases of the treatment, especially when the patient is much distraught, drugs may be used to quiet him and reduce his anxieties, particularly of the secondary kind. But this should be accompanied by psychotherapy as a means of dealing with the primary anxiety, breaking down old interpersonal ways of behaving and developing new ones. It has been stated clearly by Dyrud and Holzman: "Drugs will reduce thought disorganization, quiet an unruly and excited patient, or mobilize a withdrawn patient. It remains for psychosocial interventions to teach and to train, to reassure and to raise self-confidence, and to help with skills for living that some patients may never have learned or may have learned badly" (1973). As Meltzer has put it: "There is also relevant physiological data. In states of underarousal or massive overarousal, learning is markedly inhibited, whereas it is facilitated by an appropriate level of arousal, of which anxiety may be a component (Hebb, 1966). If drugs are used wisely, they can be one means to achieve a level of anxiety which facilitates learning" (1975, p. 134).

Interpersonal skills that are dependent on generalized sets, are learned, thought disorder is reduced, social capabilities are reactivated, gradually the lack of self confidence is erased, and the skills for living that for so long have been in abeyance are built up again. The underlying anxiety has been reduced and permits generalized set to gain prominence.

CHAPTER 15

Résumé and Conclusions

The pervasive dissolution of personality in schizophrenia has been called the most disruptive and disorganizing of all psychological disorders. And rightly so. Language, metaphor, and symbolization are the ultimate skills of *homo sapiens*. The abilities to think rationally, to conceptualize across time and space, to feel accurately, and, above all, to communicate and act upon his thoughts appropriately are the distinguishing characteristics of the normal human being.[1]

[1]Despite the various extraordinary feats of Washoe (Gardner and Gardner, 1969) and his colleagues Sarah (Premack, Science, 1971, *American Scientist*, 1976) and Lana (*Language Learning by a Chimpanzee*, New York: Academic Press, 1977), the gap between human and chimpanzee (and other ape) thought processes remains for now (and forever?) insuperable, although work in this area should be carried out to the limits of investigation. Further, there is the incomparable ability of man to transmit culture.

Man is surely distinct among primates in that he, and he alone both formalizes and legalizes his social order and his social codes. He is able to do so, of course, because of his facility for language. And with that facility, he defines and predicts for his own kind what will likely happen should each part of the code be breached. Otherwise, through language man has served his ends, both for good and for bad. Through it, he has been able to make long-term predictions in relation to events that took place eons ago. Perhaps, in the appreciation of the passage of time in that perspective, he alone has become sensitive to his individual demise, and to compensate therefore, has worked apace to collapse the living of an eternity into the brief span of a single lifetime" (Savage and Rumbaugh, 1977, p. 307).

In the schizophrenic, we are faced with a person who, rather than use concept formation, indicates in his speech severe fragmentation and irrelevancies in thinking, and whose behavior is profoundly disruptive. No matter how some have tried to expand the boundaries of sanity, I believe that in all but rare instances we wish that the illness had not occurred, and that other more appropriate ways had been found to achieve similar goals.[2] As to the claims of genius in relation to schizophrenia, may I point out that the gift of genius includes

A book written by the New York Academy of Science, *Origins and Evolution of Language and Speech*, 1976 is also relevant, as is that of J. Limbar (1977). The situation is well summarized in the article by S. L. Washburn (1978). The feats of thinking and planning that the rats of NIMH exercise, which the extremely lively imagination of R. C. O'Brien makes us aware of, is a case in point! Need more be said? (O'Brien, 1971)

Yet, I do want to add one comment. We must bear in mind what Eccles says in his *Understanding the Brain* (1977) when he refers to World 3 (World 1 being the world of brain, and World 2 being the world of consciousness): "It is the world of civilization and culture. . . . World 3 is the world that uniquely relates to man. It is the world which is completely unknown to animals. They are blind to all of World 3. I say this without any reservations" (p. 195).

But, conversely, there is the World of Lilly, with his passionate but thoroughly documented claims for dolphins (and other cetacae) (Lilly, 1961, 1975). That we have underestimated (largely through our abysmal ignorance that Lilly has done so much to rectify) the intelligence of these creatures goes without saying. But that they have equal or superior intelligence with regard to man, because of their larger brains, is rather difficult to accept. In any case, we must hold more with Eccles and with Savage and Rumbaugh, extending their generalizations to other cetacae and elephants as well, that to World 3 they are blind.

[2]I cannot refrain from mentioning a case in point in a somewhat different context. It is that of Solzhenitsyn and his thesis that one can resort to an undesirable extreme to achieve a positive result. Fairlie (*New Republic*, July 29, 1978), in a thoughtful article on the subject, analyzes Solzhenitsyn's jeremiad at Harvard's 1978 commencement, which is an echo of what the West has been hearing from Russia for a thousand years—that is, the benefits of suffering. And the best way, the Russian holds, is to undergo the "benefits" of prison life, especially the harsh prison life of Russia. Here again, as in the case of the schizophrenic, one wishes that Solzhenitsyn had achieved his purpose in a more appropriate, less extreme way.

"the infinite capacity to take pains," as someone (Edison?) once opined, and the rigorous effort that this implies. The schizophrenic (as schizophrenic) lacks this requisite capacity for genius, although he may share the marked fluency of associations that superficially characterize genius.[3]

Schizophrenic disintegration appears in what I have described as a bipolarity of behavior, and what Bleuler terms

---

[3]A case in point is that of E. E. Cummings' ability to *manipulate* levels of abstraction, the absence of which faculty Bateson and his colleagues (1950) consider *the* strongest disorder of schizophrenia. And there is the further important difference found in the intense air of nonverbal expression that inheres in Cummings' writing, whereas the schizophrenic form is disconcertingly inappropriate (Forrest, 1965, pp. 16–17). As Forrest (1969b) points out elsewhere, there are four differences between the integrated poet and the disorganized schizophrenic:

1. The poet realizes that what he does with the words for things is not thereby done to the things themselves; and the schizophrenic does not always realize this. For the schizophrenic, the word for an object may acquire the properties of the object, and may be substituted for the object when the latter is not available. This is called *word magic*, and the result is that for the schizophrenic, things may be no sooner said than done.
2. The poet is a master of language, and the schizophrenic, even more than everyone else, is a slave to language. . . .
3. The poet consciously or preconsciously manipulates levels of abstraction in arriving at metaphors, but the schizophrenic tends to have difficulty distinguishing levels of abstraction and differentiating concrete from metaphorical.
4. The poet expresses emotional attitudes clearly and movingly (albeit subtly and complexly) in the tone of the poem; whereas the schizophrenic's emotional attitudes are confused and contradictory, and the tone of schizophrenic utterances seems flat or inappropriate, rather than moving in any direction (pp. 239–241).

All in all, it is that "infinite capacity to take pains" that the poet has acquired through long and hard experience that distinguishes him or her from the schizophrenic, the schizophrenic's emotional disturbances having impeded his ability to acquire this capacity. Heston (1966), who studied the genetic aspects of schizophrenia, especially with regard to foster home placement, examined experimental subjects who showed no significant psychological impairment. This does cast a modicum of doubt on the proposition. But it may be that just the implementation of foster home placement, with its peculiar hardships, draws forth the invulnerability as well as the vulnerability of those who became psychosocially impaired. The studies of Garmezy (*Schizophrenia Bulletin*, No. 8, Spring, 1974) consider this question and may advance us some distance toward answering it.

ambivalance or ambitendency (when they occur simultaneously in a patient). Polar extremes in behavior may appear in different patients or be found within the same person at different times. Whatever the case, the developmental process of such far-out behaviors is highly complex.

Need-tensions are an essential element for this formulation. In schizophrenia they are a predominant component of thought, because very primitive emotions, which may have their beginnings in infancy, must be satisfied. Anna Freud has said, "A baby wants to have its mother with all its bodily powers." One may marvel at the extent to which a schizophrenic wants to relate himself to the world in archaic emotional and physical ways (Milner, 1969).

Not only must we recognize the place of the need-tension itself on the affective side, but in all of these situations we must be prepared to attribute importance to the prelogical, nondiscursive modes of thinking that are not usually conscious. These, as well as the discursive thought processes, which *are* conscious, play a considerable role in the process we call therapy (Langer, 1948).

In the Preface, I pose the question: how can we reconcile the complexities presented by the multifaceted schizophrenic patient, with the relative paucity of even the most elaborate observational and experimental data? In attempting to address the intricacies of the problem of schizophrenia, this book conceptualizes and analyzes the major differences between schizophrenic and normal psychological processes by delineating the stimulus/internal process/response functions (the basic operations of behavior) and the accompanying processes of perception and extended response that are the groundwork for generalized and segmental sets. It describes how schizophrenic responses are out of balance in their cognitive, affective, and conative aspects, as well as in their speed, intensity, and content. The bipolarity of response is emphasized in the descriptions of interfering factors in the perception and response of schizophrenics. Quantitatively, the response may be delayed or precipitate in speed, withdrawn or hyperresponsive in intensity. The qualities of response are emphasized at the expense of the contentual. Responses may be disturbed with respect to wholeness, complexity, form content, organization, or structure (rigid or loose). In their response to content, schizophrenic responses may be defective with respect to imitativeness, popularity, personalness, and ambiguity (too much or too little tolerance for ambiguity and tentativity). Conatively, responses may be bipolar in their spontaneity, effort, or goal-directedness.

Within the schizophrenic process, this book considers particularly the paranoid and hebephrenic types as they represent the extremes of bipolar responding. Besides being essentially different from the normal in many mutual respects, they have distinctive bipolar profiles. The normal person's behavior generally approaches the means of the distributions of given characteristics rather than either extreme.

Schizophrenic behavior is contrasted with normal behavior in terms of segmental and generalized set. To recapitulate, generalized set, the fundamental system needed to deal with the world, refers to the faculty of maintaining a state of readiness to respond to an approaching stimulus and to the state that facilitates the optimal response called for by a given situation. This may at times require a readiness to respond to a specific stimulus, or a readiness to respond to a generalization from a group of stimuli. At other times it requires a readiness to respond to the final one of a series of stimuli, to organize oneself in time, whether it be a matter of milliseconds or of extended periods. It may be voluntary or involuntary, verbalized or nonverbalized, temporary or relatively permanent. It may be affective or nonaffective. It may involve awareness, or be without awareness. This unawareness may be at the level of Freud's preconscious, or at the level of either one of his two kinds of unconscious—the *nonrepressed unconscious* or his *repressed unconscious* (often called his *dynamic unconscious*). Whatever the situation, the major (general) set is constantly being gnawed at by many possible intruding segmental sets. It would appear that the difficulty for the schizophrenic lies in not being able to keep to the major set; instead, he is drawn to adopting segmental ones.

The characteristics of *segmental set* include any one or a combination of the following features. First, because so many "remorating" (oppressive) factors play a role, with accompanying anxiety, there is a slowness of response. When the tasks are of sufficient complexity, the schizophrenic's response is idiosyncratic or at least individualistic rather than popular, because of the tendency toward eccentricity. The response is also nonrealistic and variable, and shows signs of neophobia. More often than not, it is perseverative and relatively nonhabituating. Rather than maintain an aspiration level that increases after success and remains the same after failure, there is a slight tendency to decrease after success and to decrease markedly after failure (Shakow, 1963). There are signs of weakened ego control and confused and disorganized goal-behavior.

The schizophrenic is seen as vulnerable because of a neophobia resulting from long-continuing remorating factors that have accumulated from the past, but are no longer effective for adaptation. It is in this context that the terms deterioration, regression, depersonalization, deanimation, inefficiency, and institutionalization are examined. These are all considered to be different, if overlapping classes of behavior, which rely on past reactions that may or may not have been adaptive in the past, or, in severe cases, on totally irrelevant aspects of reactions to the environment.

Segmental set meets the criterion for all the models of man: the biological, the psychological, and the social. Indeed, it might be considered congruent with systems theory. On one hand, it may be thought of as a notion for the interpretation of events at the biological level, where the segmental can be dealt with through the limits that Stanley (1975) suggests with his neonatal dogs, and, on the other hand, it may be thought of in relation to the psychological and social fields. The concept has obvious theoretical significance for the segmental sets that characterize these realms.

CHAPTER 16

FINAL REMARKS

I cannot close without considering the schizophrenic as a total person. No matter how biochemical and "scientific" our description becomes in relation to disturbance, the schizophrenic must be dealt with as a person, with all that that implies. I have already stressed the importance of this issue in my detailed discussion of the psychological subtleties of the stimulus/response situation, in which the treatment of the schizophrenic as an individual is paramount. His ability to influence results, directly and indirectly, indicate how a disregard for personal characteristics may vitiate scientific findings. Schizophrenics require far more sensitive attention than the normal person. Even in their most aggressive, reactive states, schizophrenics are in many ways like timorous rabbits. The unpredictable quality of their behavior and affect appears to stem from an almost continuous state of anxiety and fright. The reaction may be to freeze or flee, to dart suddenly here or dash suddenly there, overtly or covertly, or to come out with an expression of extreme anger. When at all possible, the researcher must be prepared to help schizophrenics circumvent such inconstancies in the nature of their responses. Often, this requires great dedication, as seen in persons such as Fromm-Reichmann (1950), Sechehaye (1970), Schiff (1970), Honig (1972), Cox and Esau, (1974), and by those in the thorough overview article by Test and Stein (1978).

The prerogative of schizophrenics as persons must be fully recognized and their qualities as human beings given special respect. "Control," in the sense of manipulation, has to be reduced to the minimum if one hopes to reduce their anxiety. Insofar as possible, they should be made partners in the study process, with the explicit and implicit superior-subordinate relationships that typify research projects minimized. The fundamental spirit inherent in therapy—often called the "therapeutic attitude"—is necessary as well in research studies.

Throughout my research career, I have been impressed by how experience, suitable personality, and fundamental empathy for the patient, reflected in the behavior of persons dealing directly with schizophrenics, play a strongly positive role in promoting participation in studies. Similarly, I have found researchers without such qualities to be unsuccessful.

Further complicating this central, highly sensitive area, is the gamut of important related problems associated with doing research with human subjects, such as informed consent, violation of personality, and invasion of privacy. The fact that these are currently the subject of much controversy in both biomedical and behavioral research highlights the need for clarification of the issues underlying them. But it points, above all, to the need for treating the schizophrenic as a human being.

"*The most exciting thing in this world, perhaps in the universe, is the conceptual faculty, in all its mutations and innovations,*" Norman Cousins has said [*Saturday Review*, August 7, 1976 (emphasis added)]. In this book I take an essential aspect of this most important conceptual faculty, that of generalized set, and develop the argument that it is fundamental for normal adaptation. This system, it is argued, is bypassed by the schizophrenic in favor of segmental set systems, in which fragmented cognitive functions and irrelevenat aspects of information are dominant. It is only by forcibly pulling the schizophrenic back under the umbrella of generalized sets, or developing a capacity for such set generalizations through "more heroic" physiological and psychological means of intervention, that a cure can occur.

Because of the profound psychological dissolution in the

schizophrenic, only through the utmost dedication of the person doing the therapy, both as therapist and as human being, will results be achieved. The philosophy of the specific therapy must be of secondary importance in comparison to the general devotion and humanity necessarily consecrated to the task.

The Development of the Worcester State Hospital Classification System for Schizophrenics

At the time I joined the Worcester State Hospital staff in 1928, the research service (which had just recently started) was being expanded. Professional personnel from various relevant specialties were being recruited, and in a short time an extensive multidisciplinary activity was in operation. This work lasted for about 20 years and was probably the most continuous and extensive research on chronic schizophrenia ever undertaken. We were immediately confronted with a problem basic to psychopathology—that of selection of research subjects. It soon became obvious that we could not always depend on the routine diagnoses made by either the house service or by the Boston Psychopathic Hospital, from which we received a considerable number of our patients.

It is important to recognize the prevailing attitude toward psychiatric diagnosis at the time our experimental work on classification was being done at Worcester. Already, this was a period in psychiatry in which there was great concern with the problem of diagnosis, as well as widespread dissatisfaction with the traditional diagnostic methods. Various studies investigating the accuracy of the diagnoses made at the Boston Psychopathic Hospital compared with subsequent diagnoses made by the staffs of various State hospitals had been carried out by Southard and Stearns (1914), Lowrey (1919), and Wilson and Deming (1927). It was also at this time that Richard Cabot (1921) published an extensive study comparing the original and autopsy diagnoses of 3000 cases of physical disease.

Our examination of the psychiatric studies at the Boston Psychopathic made it plain to us that, for research purposes, we could not depend on the diagnoses made on our patients at this hospital. During the period of our own struggle with the classification problem, the article by Wilson and Deming (1927) appeared in which the authors compare psychiatric diagnoses made at the Boston Psychopathic with those of several Massachusetts State hospitals during the period of 1925 and 1926. Thirty-four percent of the diagnoses disagreed. When compared with the study by Lowrey (1919), the area of greatest disagreement was about the diagnosis of dementia praecox or schizophrenia. As Wilson and Deming pointed out, the median agreement of approximately 60% is comparable to the figure reported by Richard Cabot (1921) in his paper exploring the diagnostic pitfalls identified in a study of 3000 physical cases coming to autopsy.

We were especially impressed in the Wilson-Deming data with the differences between the classifications at the Boston State Hospital and those made at Worcester. Of the cases diagnosed dementia praecox at the Boston Psychopathic Hospital, 57 were later diagnosed at the Boston State Hospital and only 12% were called dementia praecox, whereas of the 72 seen later at Worcester, 37% were called dementia praecox. On the other hand, of the cases diagnosed by the Boston Psychopathic Hospital as manic-depressive, the Boston State Hospital placed over 28% of 134 cases in this category, whereas of the 20 sent to Worcester State Hospital so diagnosed, only 10% were called manic-depressive.

The wide variation between these two diagnostic categories made at the two hospitals were, in part, an outgrowth of the psychiatric orientations of their respective superintendents. Dr. May of Boston State Hospital [as reflected in his paper,

"The Dementia Praecox—Schizophrenia Problem, (1931)] was strongly influenced by Kraepelin's theory of dementia praecox, and he therefore included in this category only those cases who had a poor prognosis. The attitude of Dr. Bryan at the Worcester State Hospital was, conversely, more progressive. For instance, he recognized the catatonic subtype as a division of dementia praecox having a generally good prognosis. At the Boston State Hospital, under the influence of Dr. May, this type was often labelled manic-depressive. The professional attitudes of these men were reflected in the different percentages of patients at the two institutions being classified into each of these groups.

The Wilson-Deming finding that the percent of agreement on psychiatric diagnoses was no worse than the proportion of agreement Cabot found in his study of 3000 cases of physical disease might have led us to be more tolerant of the wide discrepancy we found in the classification of mental disorders. It was soon obvious, however, that we could not tolerate a 40% discrepancy in agreement in a *research* program—even if we could convince ourselves of the legitimacy of the comparison.

After much study of the statistical data of the period, we arrived at the conclusion that a strenuous effort had to be made to improve the quality of the data that served as the basis for the *initial* diagnostic work on individual patients. This policy was adopted as an integral part of our research.[1]

First, we agreed on certain ancillary criteria for the selection of patients to be used in our research. These were directed toward eliminating obvious irrelevant complicating factors. We felt justified in doing this because we were concerned with investigating the schizophrenic process itself rather than obtaining an accurate sample of existing schizophrenics. Patients were to be excluded from the study if: (1) they were over 50 years old, chiefly because of the liability of organic changes that frequently occur with advancing age; (2) there was coexisting physical disease revealed by

---

[1] A corroborative study is found at a later date in the work of Bartemeier et al. (1946).

standard diagnostic methods; (3) we were unable to obtain an adequate history; (4) there existed a marked language difficulty; (5) mental deficiency appeared to be associated with the schizophrenic condition; (6) the symptoms were predominantly those of psychoses other than schizophrenia; (7) there was recent alcoholic or other intoxication; and (8) they were female. This last restriction was adopted only because it simplified a study involving endocrine factors that were under special investigation in the early years of our study. The endocrine complexity of women is so much greater than that of men that it seemed expedient to exclude them from an already complex study. (Later, I might add, we did carry out a study of female patients to provide a control group for special purposes.)

Our criterion for *inclusion* was based on our observation that the process of classification could be broken down into several stages, culminating in a diagnostic categorization: (1) the initial mental status examination; (2) the decision about criteria for placement in the schizophrenic category and, beyond that, in a subtype group; and (3) the final diagnostic process—both for the individual diagnostician and for the whole group of investigators. We first began to consider the diagnostic process by examining the merits and defects of earlier approaches to systematic classification.

Previous to our own efforts, attempts had been made to develop descriptive rating scales to help with the classification problem. The works of Kempf (1915), Plant (1922), and the Boston Psychopathic Hospital study of Kasanin (1938), Bowman and Raymond (1931) and their associates (1931, 1933) were the only studies we found in which the attempt to describe psychotic patients had reached the stage of formal presentation. E. J. Kempf, at Hopkins, constructed a pictorial behavior chart of mental diseases in the tradition of the work that Adolf Meyer had carried out at Phipps, following out work previously done at Kankakee, Worcester, and in the New York State Hospital systems. Plant's method, devised for use of the nursing staff at the McLean Hospital and closely approximating a degree rating scheme method, consisted of statements describing concrete forms of behavior that involved little subjective interpretation on the part of the rater. The types of behavior covered were: attitude toward taking food, reaction toward nurses, emotional reaction, hallucinations, and recent memory. A rating system emphasizing personality traits was constructed at the Boston Psychopathic Hospital. Since it had been devised for a study of the sociological aspects of mental diseases (Kasanin and Rosen, 1933), the scale emphasized this kind of material and the ratings were done primarily by social workers. The scheme was the most carefully constructed of the rating methods we investigated before our attempt. Unfortunately, the ratings were based on historical material from more or less biased observers (relatives, friends, etc.), so that the prejudice represented went beyond the difficulty encountered by even an unbiased person in the attempt to report objectively in the complex subjective area of personality evaluation.

Consideration of the then current mental status evaluation techniques routinely used by psychiatrists or even those employed in elaborately worked-up case studies could not but leave us dissatisfied. Our analysis of diagnostic methods uncovered several reasons for this dissatisfaction. First of all, the methods lacked quantifying possibilities. The absence of a system for the quantitative determination of an individual's clinically derived psychological characteristics made it difficult to correlate these factors with quantitatively expressed variables such as the different aspects of experimental psychological and physiological functioning that were a major part of our research. The use of the traditional classification for types of psychoses was also, in general, unsatisfactory—a dilemma frequently recognized by the investigator and not infrequently accompanied by an apology.

There was also an inexactitude of definition in the qualitative use of the terms used for psychiatric symptoms and traits. From the psychological viewpoint, the definitions used were often inadequate and unreliable. Individual psychiatrists were found to characterize the same behavior differently in different patients, or even at different times in the same patients, and different psychiatrists would describe divergent types of behavior with identical or similar terms.

We concluded that an adequate rating method would offer the most satisfactory quantitative technique for certain aspects of psychiatric work. Psychiatrists had, in general, shied away from any attempts at the quantification of their professional techniques and had argued long and vehemently against what they termed "oversimplification." While acknowledging the theoretical desirability of accuracy and quantification, they had tended to ignore these criteria as an impractical "counsel of perfection." There was, of course, some justification for their distrust of oversimplication and the reliance on quantitative rating. Nevertheless, it would be difficult for anyone involved with psychiatric classification not to agree with Gordon Allport's opinion that, "Notwithstanding the dangers and difficulties encountered in devising and employing rating scales, we are forced to recognize this method as the only available objective criterion of personality. The sources of error must be gradually overcome by the improvement of the technic of rating" (G. W. Allport 1921, p. 449).

Some of the specific advantages of a workable mental status rating scale that particularly impressed us were the following:

1. The roughly quantitative material of psychiatric characteristics obtained from it would be suitable for correlation with data from quantitative studies in other areas made on the same patient. For a single patient, one could use the ratings of one psychiatrist, or the composite (average) ratings of a group of psychiatrists (which has been found to be more reliable from a technical standpoint).

2. Reasonably dependable qualitative material for following up the same cases would be made available.

3. The personal factor, which interfered with the objectivity of the then-current evaluative system, would be eliminated. Although this personal factor might be important in therapy, it often proved to be a marked handicap in investigation.

4. A working mental status scale would offer more dependable material for the determination of syndromes, and
even in the determination of diagnostic types.

5. A method for evaluating psychiatrists would be offered.
One of the primary qualities of a good psychiatrist is his
ability to utilize his "peculiar" professional language accurately in the description of the patient. The reliability
of this use of professional phraseology could be checked
by his successive ratings on the same patient and be
compared with the composite ratings on the same patient
of a group of other psychiatrists of known ability.

6. A method for training resident psychiatrists would be
offered as well, because the use of a mental status rating
scale emphasizes the need for accuracy in symptom description and classification. It would make it possible for
an individual student to check his use of psychiatric
terms against the ratings of experienced observers on the
same patient. The mental status scale also keeps the psychiatrist alert to the particular items of information that
he should try to obtain during the course of a mental status examination. Eventually, the scale might even serve
as the basis for a "standard interview" that would preserve the flexibility and open-endedness in administration that any reasonable use of the interview technique
calls for.

With these goals in mind, we undertook several preliminary
studies. For the first of the studies, we made up a list of 104
traits, symptoms, and response patterns (which I shall he-
reafter call"traits") of all types of psychoses. These were
based on data taken from leading psychiatric texts, and the
contemporary periodical literature. Kraepelin, Bleuler, W. A.
White, Jelliffe and White, Kempf, Rosanoff, Henderson and
Gillespie, and Strecker and Ebaugh were among the authorities consulted. The clinical experience of the psychiatric and
psychological staff at the hospital was also called on in the
construction of the initial scale. First attempts at definitions
of these traits were adopted from textbooks, dictionaries

(psychiatric and psychological), and other similar sources, and a scale of the degree of the presence or absence of the different traits was established. In general, we tried to fit the traits into a 5-point scale, with descriptive characterizations for the different degrees wherever possible. (There was also a "0" (zero) category to indicate that a certain trait could not be rated.) In order to eliminate any possibility of the rater consistently checking one of the extremes, the "most marked" presence of a trait was sometimes set at 1, sometimes at 5. Rating forms for the traits and instructions for the use of the scale were gradually developed, together with a trait dictionary containing the definitions of both the traits and their degrees of intensity. Approximately 70 patients were rated by the scale once, some 25 of these taking part in two studies spaced 3 months apart. The comments and criticisms of the psychiatrists and others using the scale were collected for each of the traits. A preliminary statistical analysis was made of the collected ratings to determine such problems as the items that were difficult to rate and the items on which there was considerable disagreement. On the basis of our work with the first preliminary form, we found that the definitions of the traits were the most unsatisfactory part of the scale. Modifications of this aspect of the rating device were, therefore, given primary attention in the construction of the second scale.

When the material was collected and the comments and criticisms organized for the second study, the four psychiatrists, the Chief Biometrician, the Resident Director of Research, and I held an extended series of active conferences on the project. As a result of these discussions, a second rating scale was organized along the following lines:

1. After detailed discussion on each characteristic, the definitions were changed to meet the consensus of opinion of the group. Considerable weight was, however, accorded by the group to the opinion of authorities in the field.

2. Many new items were added, a few were omitted, the final number totalling 138.

3. In this scale, the descriptive characterization of the degree of presence of traits, except for the normal distribution basis represented by the categories of "very marked," "marked," "considerable," "some," and "none," was eliminated. It was felt that this part of the scale should depend on a large accumulated body of clinical experience, and that, while this was being collected, it was best to leave the matter open.

4. Each staff member working on the second study used a notebook in which he recorded comments, difficulties, or criticisms that occurred to him while using the scale. We hoped in this way to compile a detailed description of each degree of a single psychiatric trait, together with a series of actual examples of behavior included under each degree. The primary purpose of making such detailed characterizations of the traits was to reduce the element of personal bias in determining the intensity of the traits—probably the most difficult part in the construction of any personality rating method.

5. New forms, a new set of instructions, and a new dictionary were organized. A special place was left in the new form for the rater to record sources of information on which the judgment was based. We hoped that after a time it would be possible to specify the sources of information for most of the traits, and that we might even weight the ratings according to source.

The scale was subsequently used in our research program. Except for minor modifications, further plans to refine the system were never executed. One project was not implemented because of the lack of needed outside financial support.

In the course of work on this project, we recognized various sources of error common in such an enterprise and the need for certain controls to meet them.

1. Differences in the length and depth of acquaintance of the psychiatrists with their patients was one source of difficulty. We partially controlled for this through corrections based on a statistical (correlation) study of the

effect on the ratings of the varying lengths of time the psychiatrist had a particular patient under treatment.

2. The 5-point "very marked" to "none" scale to describe to what degree traits are present appeared inadequate. A more satisfactory detailed *descriptive* scale for each of the degrees based on examples given in text books, personal experience, etc., was continuously being evolved.

3. Differences in the difficulty of rating traits were another source of error. Traits were defined and redefined, but if it was impossible to achieve agreement, the given trait was finally eliminated.

4. To counteract the "halo" effect in rating, traits were defined as exactly as possible. The insidiousness of this personal effect on rating was stressed in training the observers.

5. Another source of error was the observer's use of "expected" rather than actual performance as the criterion for rating. Emphasis was repeatedly placed on the importance of making *actual* performance the basis for a rating in order to determine the bases on which judgments of behavior were made. The psychiatrists were frequently called on to give the rationale for their particular rating of a trait.

6. Variations existed in the standards used by individual psychiatrists. There was an attempt to correct for these differences by making distribution curves of each observer's ratings for each trait rated. The need for constancy of standards was stressed in the training of the observers. Rechecks were made of previous ratings at regular intervals, and emphasis was placed on the use of the average as the standard.

7. Ratings were always made independently to prevent the influence of raters on one another.

8. To control the influence of previous results on successive ratings, the raters were instructed to fill out the

forms without referring to earlier ones they had filled out on the same patient.

9. The intra-individual variability of each patient also posed a constant problem. The instructions to the raters were, therefore, to consider variability as an expected characteristic, but one calling for continuous scrutiny.

10. Frequent conferences on procedure and additional training sessions were held to detect general errors that tended to creep into the work.

The material was then treated statistically. The following points, which resulted from this statistical analysis, were among those kept in mind by the participants in the project:

1. Which items lent themselves to a rating scale technique? Items that consistently yielded zero ratings (i.e. "cannot be determined"), even after attempts at redefinition, were eliminated. The differences among psychiatrists might occasionally indicate that one or another had a superior technique for dealing with certain items. A subsequent discussion of these differences often resulted in a redefinition of the item.

2. The reliability of ratings took into consideration the variation of the individual psychiatrist, the variation among psychiatrists, and the study of differences in successive examinations by the same psychiatrists. These variations were carefully analyzed to make certain that they were not due to shifts in scoring standards.

3. Personal bias was dealt with by self-ratings of observers, which were compared with ratings by other psychiatrists and sophisticated raters not engaged in the psychiatric work.

4. The statistical determination of the syndromes used such methods as inter-correlation of the various traits. The traits resulting from this statistical treatment were again redefined and their degrees more descriptively stated. There was also some attempt to weight traits by the

pooled judgment of experts on their relative importance, or their reliability, and by a combination of both.

Thus far, only the first of the three aspects of the problem of classification has been discussed: the raw data of the characteristics that make up the syndromes and how they might be obtained with some reasonable degree of dependability. The next step in development of the diagnostic process was how to determine the syndromes of traits that were to be the basis for diagnosing a patient as schizophrenic and to place him, whenever possible, in one of the subcategories of schizophrenia. Again we relied on the standard texts and other literature, together with the experiences of our own staff, to compile a list of symptoms that were regarded as characteristic of the schizophrenic disorder and additional lists for the various standard subtypes of schizophrenia: simple, catatonic, paranoid, and hebephrenic. This diagnostic scheme was circulated among the psychiatrists and other members of the staff and finally resulted in a list that seemed generally acceptable and that all participants in the study agreed to use for diagnosis. Then, having both the raw traits for characterization and the basis for combining these into syndromes, we came to the third aspect of the diagnostic process—the actual procedure we utilized in the final classification of the patient. Our procedure was determined only after considerable trial-and-error experimentation with other methods. The classification of a patient was decided on at a diagnostic staff conference that was attended by the four psychiatrists, the Director and the Associate Director of Research, the Chief of Internal Medicine (the last three being internists), and the two senior psychologists. Information on a particular patient was presented by one of the four psychiatrists to whom that patient had been assigned in accordance with the established procedure of rotation. He discussed the psychiatric material on the patient together with the data from the patient's social history. This was followed by a presentation of the results from an extensive battery of psychological tests. The patient was then interviewed before the group (unless contraindicated by his condition), and an interpretative discussion of the case followed.

On the basis of these data, three decisions were made— about diagnosis, prognosis, and suitability for the research program. All these decisions were carried out anonymously. The value of anonymity should be clear to those who have had experience with the manner in which staff conferences are ordinarily conducted as well as the errors introduced under these conditions. In his personal evaluation, each member of the staff wrote down his opinion of the patient under consideration on the three topics mentioned and passed it on to the Chairman of the meeting. The final results of the vote were tabulated and announced by the Chairman. There had to be a practically unanimous agreement about the suitability of the patient for the research and about the diagnosis of schizophrenia. With regard to subdivision, the standard subtype was used if there was substantial agreement on the subtype classification of the patient. If not, then the categories of "mixed" and "unclassified" were used liberally. In addition, we developed a category called "late indeterminate." This subdivision was used for chronic patients who had at one time clearly belonged to one of the standard subtype classifications, but who did not currently demonstrate any of the classic symptoms of that subtype. The Worcester State Hospital classification for schizophrenia and the major subtypes is presented in Table 2.

If accepted as suitable for the study, the patient was interviewed daily by the psychiatrist throughout 3 months of active investigation, and notations, which were incorporated into weekly notes, were made of his mental state and behavior. The rating scale system previously described was used over a considerable period of the study. When necessary, changes in the original diagnosis and subtype category of any patient were made at diagnostic conferences assembled for the purpose. In addition to the psychiatrist's observations, daily notes were also kept by the nursing staff and by two specially trained ward observers, who were instructed to report selected aspects of a patient's behavior. Notations were made less frequently during the "rest" periods—the periods in between those in which active study of the patient was going on.

Table 2

Characteristics of Schizophrenia and its Subtypes

General Characteristics of Schizophrenia	Subtype Classification Simple	Hebephrenic	Catatonic	Paranoid
1. Outstanding Characteristics Abnormal development, instincts and feelings Defects of interest Blunting of emotions Ambivalence Disturbances of association and thought Autistic-thinking Incoherence, disconnection General "disintegration"—in sense of queer and odd behavior 2. Anamnestic Waning of interest Seclusiveness Dreaminess Oddness Overpiety Overconscientiousness Overdefensiveness Emotional instability Suspiciousness	Gradual loss of interest	Thought—marked incoherence Bizarre ideas—changeable Mannerisms and grimaces Silliness	Phases of stupor and/or excitement Negativism	Delusional development Hallucinatory development

3. Onset Usually in adolescence, (with change of disposition), few after 40 Slow and insidious (except some cases, particularly, catatonic)	Early adolescence Insidious	Earlier than catatonic or paranoid Usually insidious, with change of disposition, de-pression, or irritability shown early	Acute, usually with change of disposition Initiated by depres-sion, or excitement followed by stupor	Usually later than other types May begin as such or follow manic or acute catatonic state
4. Course Usually chronic (except catatonic)	Chronic	Chronic	Frequently recover or go on to other type	Usually chronic
5. Personality Sensitiveness Exaggerated self-con-sciousness	Good-natured Lackadaisical	Generally dis-integrated	Marked regression Acute	Suspicious Evasive
6. General Behavior Odd, impulsive, apparently purpose-less acts	Lazy, neglectful conduct Tractable	Manneristic Slovenly Silly	Stupor: (two groups of symptoms) Negativism: Muscular tension Mutism Active opposition Diminution of activity	Secondary in-tractability Meticulousness Homicidal (sometimes)

171

Table 2 —*continued*

Characteristics of Schizophrenia and its Subtypes

Generai Characteristics of Schizophrenia	**Subtype Classification** Simple	Hebephrenic	Catatonic	Paranoid
			Retention Hypersuggestibility: Cerea flexibilitas Automatic obedience Automatism Echopraxia Echolalia Excitement Increased psycho-motor activity Markedly impulsive and compulsive acts Assaultive, destructive, suicidal, homicidal, or auto-mutilative acts Mannerisms Stereotypy	
7. Illusions and Hallucinations Frequent in Most forms in most fields—especially auditory	Rare, fleeting, commonly unexpressed	Generally present Numerous kinds—visual and auditory especially Bizarre—dominant in early stages	Common	Common Particularly auditory and somatic

8. Stream of Mental Activity Tendency to disconnection Tendency to irrelevancies Intelligence ambivalence	Lowered level of cognitive activity	Incoherence marked Neologisms common	Incoherence marked Stereotypy Perseveration	Peculiar phraseology (e.g., stiltedness) Neologisms
9. Mental Content Autistic thinking (dereism)	Poverty of significant content	Poverty of significant content	Ideas of cosmic catastrophe	Grandiose ideas Persecutory ideas
10. Delusions Common	Rare, mild, never grandiose	Fantastic, silly, changeable Often religious, sexual, somatic	Death and rebirth Ego expansion and contraction	Always present and dominant (but may be concealed) Toward coherent and systematized Often bizarre Commonly persecution and vengeance Commonly grandiose
11. Affective/Emotional Reactions Pathologic: Apathy, instability, ambivalence	Apathy, relatively marked	Inappropriateness in quality and degree Pathological anger	Marked extremes	Relatively normal, but some inappropriateness of degree
12. Orientation Commonly undisturbed for person and place	Undisturbed	May be disturbed	May be disturbed, especially in	Commonly undisturbed

Table 2 —*continued*

Characteristics of Schizophrenia and its Subtypes

General Characteristics of Schizophrenia	Subtype Classification Simple	Hebephrenic	Catatonic excited states	Paranoid
May be disoriented for time Sometimes double orientation				
13. Attention Active attention generally poor Passive attention generally good	Undisturbed	Active: poor Passive: moderate	Active: poor Passive: good	Active attention may be relatively the best
14. Memory Usually good	Usually good	Usually good	Usually good	Good— hypermnesia or paramnesia sometimes
15. Consciousness Generally clear	Clear	Clear	Apparently clouded in stuporous states	Clear
16. Judgment and Insight Serious defects common	Not prominent	May have insight in early stages	May have insight in certain stages	Markedly absent
17. General Deterioration Some degree present	Slow or arrested	Rapid or arrested	Variable: from none to marked	Commonly not marked

174

And what did this effort in classification amount to—what results did we achieve? It is my opinion that, in spite of its incompleteness and its many failings and inadequacies, the study was one of the most carefully carried-out, large-scale projects ever attempted in the classification of chronic schizophrenia. I must point out, however, that, because our study was directed at the chronic group, our problem was made much easier than if we had been dealing with the whole range of mental disorders, or even with only the full group of schizophrenic or schizophreniform conditions. The results of the project may be considered under the heading of both overall and specific effects. In general, the atomosphere of the study fostered intimate knowledge of the individual patients and accuracy in clinical investigation, as well as calling for objective evidence in establishing the criteria for diagnosis and emphasizing the importance of unambiguous psychiatric categories. The research group developed a sensitivity both for the complexity of the problem and for the need for accurate characterization of the syndromes.[2] The project resulted in the evolution of a common area of agreement about psychiatric classification among the psychiatrists, as well as among the rest of the staff, despite the different philosophic backgrounds represented, varying from psychoanalytic through structural to organic orientations. In short, we were able to minimize significantly what is inevitably a sort of Gresham's law of psychiatric discourse—the tendency for loose talk to drive out rigorous talk.

The specific effects of the project were many. First, criteria were developed that offered considerable realiability in evaluation. We were also able, on the basis of these evaluations and classifications, to establish reasonably homogeneous groups of psychiatric subtypes, so that these subtypes cor-

[2]Anna Freud, on a visit to the National Institutes of Health (1965), described what took place at Hampstead as a result of the establishment of their Index—a marked increase in the understanding of the phenomena they were studying. This same general effect of our procedure was noticed in the Worcester group.

related with quite independent psychological studies made of these same patients. We were able to differentiate the schizophrenic group from both other psychoses and from normal subjects, and even to differentiate the various subtypes *within* the psychosis.

Another specific result that we achieved was a fairly high correlation between items on the mental status examination and the results of a wide variety of psychological experiments and tests. Needless to say, the study was terminated before completion. Such an outcome is almost inevitable with any project in this most complicated area. I am certain that even if we had obtained the necessary financial support for the elaborate study of the current mental status system I have mentioned, we would not have been able to achieve conclusive results. The task is an immensely difficult one, it has many steps, it takes a long time, and for that reason the battlefield is strewn with bodies of only partially viable projects abandoned to eventual death. I am convinced that only from a long succession of such systematically organized careful studies will any meaningful solution of this problem be achieved.

During an experiment using the play technique (Shakow and Rosenzweig, 1937), Rosenzweig and I observed how clearly the behavior of normal, paranoid, and hebephrenic subjects in the assigned task differed from each other. Having selected the subjects for our experiment according to their mental status and the other criteria used in the psychiatric classification, we were impressed with how distinctly the independent psychological data differentiated these categorized groups.

A question that probably occurs to many of you is why we did not use factor analysis in our study of classification. It seems so natural an approach, especially to psychologists. At the time we were planning the study, I discussed the problem with Morton Jellinek, who was Chief of Biometrics in our research group during 8 of its most intensive years. He advised against the use of factor analysis. His reasons for discouraging us were similar to those that Thurstone gave in his own early discussions of the use of this technique, namely, that the results obtained from a factor analysis depended entirely on the quality of the data put into the statistical hopper (Thurstone, 1937). Jellinek agreed with us that our primary task at the time was to collect a body of dependable and accurate descriptive date.

The characteristics of the particular educational process involved in the development of such a classification system seem to be essentially these: (1) the intitally great differences in the criteria for diagnostic judgment that exist among the participants; (2) the minimization of these differences as a result of the participants' discussions of their differences in professional opinion, and the resulting achievement of an optimal degree of agreement and reconciliation; (3) the dilemma: are the judgments veridical, or are they merely group-accepted stereotypes or group-adopted mental sets? In the end, I suppose, we must accept a minimal level of stereotypy. This will not, I believe, be a critical disadvantage if the participants have already employed both selfcriticism and mutual criticism in the attempt to clarify the concepts they use. Some of the obstacles in dealing with this problem lie in the initial wide divergence in the professional knowledge and personal background and orientation of the participants in the project.

APPENDIX B

The Context for the Stimulus/Response Process

As I have indicated, the general setting for the stimulus/response process involves the resting state of the organism, the personalness of the stimuli, and the stress condition of the organism. There are four basic "resting states:"

1. *Sensory deprivation.* By definition, this condition is almost entirely devoid of external stimulation, whether directed or undirected.

2. *Basal Resting.* Under these conditions, the subject undergoes a substantial period of both physiological and psychological "rest."[1] This includes at least 12 hours of food abstinence since the last meal preceding the stimulating situation.

3. *Non-basal resting.* Although food intake is not limited in this condition, a substantial, carefully controlled rest period (of at least 30 minutes duration) precedes the stimulating situation.

[1]Of course, this regime may be *physiologically correct, but psychologically stressful.* A careful review of the situation must be made on each case to prevent this situation from occurring. Rest is defined as the minimization (but not elimination) of both directed and undirected (casual) stimulation, since some external and internal undirected stimulation is unavoidable.

4. *Non-resting.* In this condition, the subject is placed in a stimulating situation without any general preparatory rest period; he enters into it directly from occupation with previous ordinary day-by-day activities.

There are nine classes of stimulation: combinations of three levels of personalness—neutral, impersonal, and personal—and three levels of stress—none, external, and internal.

The nine specific stimulus settings I suggest are as follows:

1. *Neutral (N)*—stimulation is of a neutral nature under conditions of no stress

2. *Impersonal (I)*—stimulation is of a general affective nature, *not* related to the person stimulated, under conditions of no stress

3. *Personal (P)*—stimulation is of an affective nature, related in some way to the person being stimulated, but under conditions of no stress

4. *Neutral, external stress (NE)*—the neutral stimulus occurs under a condition of external stress by an environmental distractor, such as noise or other forms of interruption

5. *Impersonal, external stress (IE)*—the impersonal affective stimulus occurs under a condition of external stress of the kind just mentioned

6. *Personal, external stress (PE)*—the stimulation is of an affective nature related to the person stimulated under conditions of external stress of the kind mentioned

7. *Neutral, internal stress (NI)*—the stimulation of neutral nature occurs under conditions of internal stress in which emotional significance is given to the stimulus and the subject of the stimulation is, implicitly or explicitly, held personally responsible

8. *Impersonal, internal stress (II)*—the stimulation is of an impersonal kind under conditions of internal stress of the kind indicated in the last category

9. *Personal, internal stress (PI)*—the stimulation is of a per-

sonal kind under conditions of stress such as that indicated in the last category.

The concept of specific stimulus "settings" was developed in two early experiments carried out in our laboratories. The first, which recognized these distinctions in part, was the "Luria" study we conducted over four decades ago (Huston, Shakow, and Erickson, 1934). In attempting to determine whether emotional "complexes" could be investigated in the laboratory setting, we used hypnotically induced "complexes." An association test was constructed that utilized words related to known stressful events for the individual as well as neutral words.

The second experiment that attempted to categorize the different stimulating conditions was carried out some dozen years after the first. It was part of a broader study of the biological and psychological effects of stress on the 17-ketosteroids (Pincus, 1947; Pincus et al., 1949). In this study we attempted to ascertain the effects on 17-ketosteroids of placing the subject into various actual situations: neutral, impersonal, and personal, both under free and stressful conditions. In this latter study, we came even closer to the categorization I am here proposing.

SPECIFIC CONTENTS

Aside from the *general* rest background against which the subject is stimulated, there is, particularly in experimental situations, the *specific* context in which the actual stimulation takes place. I have in mind such contextual modifiers as rest periods preceding the actual experiment, knowledge about the goals of the particular experiment, warnings of coming stimulation, concurrent stimulation, frequency of stimulation, and the nature of the physical surroundings in which the stimulation occurs.

Unless a study is deliberately designed to be of a continuous (nonstop) type, stimuli are usually presented in intervening periods of nonstimulation. It must be pointed out, however, that these are not periods of nonactivity. The response process itself, as delineated in this book, may be said to consist of repeated successions of stimulus/ response/rest/preparation for the next stimulus/stimulus/response/rest, etc. Interpolated periods of nonstimulation, perhaps seen at their simplest in reactive and retroactive inhibition or in refractory phase, appear to be an important, probably essential, part of ordinary information processing. (Cf. reactive inhibition discussion of Steffy and Cromwell, unpublished.) In the experimental situation, even when not provided by the experimenter as part of the procedure, intervening periods are likely to be worked into the response process by the subject himself, whether deliberately, surreptitiously, or automatically, without awareness. A basic organic need for such intervals of nonstimulation, of "rest," appears to be involved. The nature of these periods, their length, distribution in relation to the stimuli, and similar characteristics are all significant aspects of the total stimulus/response process.

Another contextual variable is knowledge of the nature and purpose of the experiment. On rare occasions such information is provided "fully" to the subject by the experimenter; most frequently this is done in part, and sometimes not at all. (Occasionally, even erroneous information may be provided, whether implicitly or explicitly, to attain certain experimental ends. Because of ethical considerations, such experimental manipulation is ordinarily revealed to the subject post-experimentally.) Even when not deliberately imparted by the experimenter, some degree of knowledge may be acquired by the subject on his own during the progress of the experiment. This knowledge may be correct or erroneous. There are even occasions when the experimenter has described the aim accurately to the subject, but the latter has nonetheless ascribed a radically different goal to the experiment. Whatever the case, the experimenter must recognize that different degrees of knowledge, lack of knowledge, or assumed knowledge have varying effects on the results. These may range from negligible to very considerable effects.[2]

[2]The works of R. Rosenthal (1966) and R. Rosenthal and R. Rosnow (Eds.) (1969) have such aspects of research in mind. The findings they report are even more applicable to schizophrenia.

Still another feature of experimental context, *warning* of an approaching stimulus, is also important in determining the response. Sometimes this preparatory warning is given by the experimenter at the beginning of the experiment as a whole, sometimes before a group of stimuli, and sometimes before each separate stimulus. Both the importance of keeping conditions constant across subjects, as well as providing warnings at points appropriate to achieve the purposes of the study, must be kept in mind.

The particular physical *surroundings* in which the stimulation takes place is another contextual variable. Many experiments have shown that such specific environmental characteristics as the nature of the experimental room, the personality and sex of the experimenter, and similar variables tend to have considerable effect on the results (e.g., H. L. Rheingold and E. S. Kip, unpublished).

Finally, another contextual variable requiring attention is *concurrent stimulation*, a variable at times experimenter determined, but usually arising unintentionally. I do not, of course, refer here to studies in disparate attention in which the experimenter deliberately provides competing focal or focal/peripheral stimuli to determine the effects of divided attention, but, rather, to the accidental, unintended stimuli originating in the environment, the extra-experimental stimulation provided by the subject himself, or on occasion, even unwittingly, by the experimenter. All of these may have similarly disturbing effects on the findings.

Set and Schema Theory in Twentieth Century American and British Psychology: A Brief Review*

Ann S. Masten

Set and *schema*, two related concepts that continue to reappear in the psychological literature, have been called on in multifarious contexts to explain integrated, purposeful, or selective behavior. *Set*, which came into common usage in American psychology, usually refers to the process of becoming prepared or the state of preparedness for selective behavior. *Schema*, which has been more popular in British psychology, usually refers to an organization of past experiences that provides the organism with some sort of orientation. As will be seen, definitions or applications of both these concepts have differed considerably, and interpretations vary widely in their emphasis.

Reviewing 40 years of experiments on set, Gibson (1941) critically indicates many ambiguities and contradictions in the uses of the concept: "Apparently the term set denotes a large

---

*Adapted from a longer review available from the author at Elliott Hall, Room N446, University of Minnesota, 75 East River Road, Minneapolis, Minnesota, 55455.

and heterogeneous body of experimental facts and connotes rather different things to different psychologists" (p. 782). Some of the unresolved questions that Gibson points out are: whether sets determine action or are forms of action; whether set is temporary or persisting; whether it is central or peripheral; what its relation is to motivation and to conditioning. Two "crucial ambiguities," as Gibson describes them, are the relation of set to past experience or habit and its voluntary or involuntary character (p. 811). Allport (1955), on the contrary, does not seem to worry about the discrepancies that Gibson finds in different experimental uses of set. Instead, drawing on Gibson's review in listing 16 "facts" about set (1955, p. 213 ff.), he extends the definition to include all the phenomena. Allport looks to a formulation of set encompassing all these possibilities, interpreting the variety of phenomena ascribed to set as an indication of the fundamental nature of the process.

The purpose of this survey is to present several theories that have utilized set or schema as a fundamental principle in their approach to the function and/or structure of some aspect of normal human behavior. Pathological set functioning is not considered. Another major omission is the topic of set in learning, particularly in human conditioning. Shakow elucidates pathological set functioning in this book and reviews the few theoretical treatments of it. Gibson (1941) describes the earlier experimental work involving set in human learning, and his paper should provide the initial references necessary to pursue this topic.

HISTORICAL BACKGROUND

The history of the psychological concept of set closely parallels the history of experimental psychology in the nineteenth and early twentieth centuries. Apperception, reaction time, attention, and selection are some of its prominent relatives that drew much experimental and theoretical attention in this period. Boring's *History* (1950) considers all of the following topics, which are pertinent to the history of set: individual reaction time, from its discovery in astronomy and the "personal equation," to Donders (subtractive method), to Wundt's laboratory (Lange, Kulpe); apperception and the apperceptive mass (Leibnitz, Herbart, Wundt); Helmholtz' "unconscious inference" in perception; "imageless thought"; and James' ideas of the "fringes of consciousness," transitive states, attention, selection, and relevance.

The "Wurzburg school of imageless thought," which established the experimental study of what was to be called generally "set," is considered by Boring in some detail. Watt calls the new introspective method "fractionation" and emphasizes the *Aufgabe* or task as instructed to the subject. The *Aufgabe* results in the subject becoming *eingestellt*, or set. [1] Ach gives the name "determining tendency" to the unconscious process between preparation and completion of the prepared response, or unconscious predisposition. The Wurzburg group brought the thought process under scrutiny, directing their studies toward aspects of consciousness (such as "attitude") that had been described before, as in James' transitive states, but not studied systematically; they also studied unconscious influences on response.

In Great Britain, the concepts of Carpenter, Lewes, and Maudsley seem to have particularly anticipated the ideas taken up for study by the Wurzburg school and later developed in the studies of schema and set. Hearnshaw's history (1964) considers both Carpenter's role in spreading the idea of the unconscious, and noting that he discussed determining tendencies "years before the Wurzburg psychologists" (p. 24), and Maudsley's concept of "residua," which resembles the later "schemata." Maudsley emphasizes the organizing capacity of the mind, which unconsciously builds up organized structures (p. 28; cf. Head's and Bartlett's schemata). The directive influence of past experience (residua) is called "preperception" by Lewes (a term James was to borrow), who also recognized the role of "motor intuitions" in movement,

---

[1] Boring indicates that *Einstellung* was translated "set" (1950, pp. 404, 716).

similar to the later concept of postural schema.

In America, James and his textbook (1890) were extraordinarily popular. His chapters on the Stream of Thought and Attention are important antecedents of concepts, particularly relating to set, that came to the forefront of psychological theory and experimentation in the twentieth century. The concepts stream of consciousness, transitive as opposed to substantive thought, tendency and intention, fringes of consciousness, selective attention, anticipatory preparation, inhibition, preperception, and inattention may be found in these, as well as other, chapters.

SCHEMA IN BRITISH PSYCHOLOGY

Head: Postural Schemata

In *Studies in Neurology* (1920, Vol. II), Henry Head (with Holmes) asserts that posture cannot be perceived directly from immediately present postural sensations, but only in relation to postural sensations that have come before; there is a standard against which change in position is measured that itself changes with each successive change in position. This standard, which is physiological and "outside consciousness," is called the "schema." [2] The schemata (plural) are active organizations of past impressions taking the role of the sensory cortex as "storehouse of past impressions" (1920, Vol. II, p. 607). New sensations are related to past impressions by means of the organizing function of the schema. There may be one schema for limb position, another for localization of sensation. New sensations from a change in posture are integrated with the postural schema of past impressions before "recognition" or conscious "appreciation" of the new posture can take place. It is the integration that produces the

[2] In "The Concept of Schema in Neurology and Psychiatry," Brain (1950) discusses Kant's schema concept as it relates to the British concept, noting that Head and Holmes borrowed the term from Kant.

conscious sensation of position or location of passive movement. "Every recognizable change in posture enters consciousness already charged with its relation to something
which has gone before, and the final product is directly perceived as a measured postural change" (Head, 1920, Vol. II,
p. 669). Voluntary movement depends on appropriate posture
or tonus. The schemata are said to provide a continuous record of body position that facilitates voluntary movement,
making coordinated movement possible.

Bartlett: Schema in Remembering

Frederic C. Bartlett developed his theory of remembering on
the concept of "schema" adopted from Head, with whom he
had a personal as well as academic relationship (Northway,
1940). At Cambridge, Bartlett in turn taught Oldfield and
Zangwill, whose treatment of "schema," as it developed
from Head through Wolters (Oldfield and Zangwill, 1942,
1943, Parts I-IV), is an important review and analysis of the
concept.

   In *Remembering* (1932), Bartlett describes many of the experiments on perceiving, recognizing, and recall that he had
begun in 1913 and carried out over some years. In his studies,
Bartlett observed several outstanding features in common
among these cognitive processes, noting for example that perception and recall are usually selective, constructive, and characterized by an attitude that is often affective. Perception,
recognition, and recall are viewed by Bartlett as aspects along
a continuum. Perception has two major features: a sensory
pattern and an orientation that has a constructive function.
Recognition (knowing that what is currently perceived has
been perceived before) requires a current sensory pattern (the
stimulus for recognition is immediate and sensory) and an
orientation that corresponds with a previous occurrence of
the pattern and the orientation. The same orientation must
have been maintained. However, recognition must also have
an aspect of content to explain the increasingly selective dis-
criminations possible in human learning. The orientation that

is preserved from an original to another stimulus situation does not involve the storage of specific content in certain places as in trace theory, but the maintenance of an organized mass of material. An organized mass of past experiences is called a "schema." In recognition, past perceptions affect the present by means of the orientation provided by this persisting organized mass or schema, although the organism is not aware of the mass functioning in this way. In remembering, this mass is reacted to and part of the organism directs itself at the mass; an "attitude" emerges toward this material rather than being formed by it.

In the concept of schema, Bartlett adapts Head's postural notion for a psychological concept of how past experiences affect present response. Such schemata applied to recall would be organized chronologically but dominated by the most recent responses (just as in postural change the most recent position must have the greatest influence on the next movement). Bartlett suggests that, in human cognition, a change has taken place that enables man to reconstruct the schemata according to need or interest. The process in which the schemata become the objects of organization, rather than the organizers of experience, is called "turning round" upon the schemata. This turning round process allows the transcendence of chronological sequence in remembering, thereby obviating much redundancy in the use of past experience and the dominance of recency, allowing relevance (interest or need) to dominate recall. "Turning round" is said to be the origin and purpose of consciousness (Bartlett, 1932, p. 206). When the organism turns round upon its schemata and becomes conscious, what emerges is the "attitude" discussed above.

The prevalence of "attitude" in Bartlett's experimental subjects led him to conclude that constructive recall is selectively determined by attitude. In his theoretical discussion, he bases his assertion that construction in remembering is in effect a "justification of the attitude" (p. 207), on the series of reproductions he obtained experimentally, in which the attitude of the subject toward the stimulus was seen to affect his later reproductions so as to conform (often stereotypically) with the attitude.

Bartlett's schema concept has been criticized particularly by Northway (1940) and by Oldfield and Zangwill (1942, Part III). Northway points out that he uses "schemata" four different ways: as forces (that determine the influence of past response on the present), as forms (organized settings for preserving material), as storehouses (of content), and as apperceptive mass (p. 317). Another major difficulty in Bartlett's theory is how "turning round" comes about, along with the concomitant "emergence" of attitude and consciousness. Bartlett only provides the barest outline of what he considers a "crucial" step in organic development. Oldfield and Zangwill point out that unless this process is explained, it amounts to no more than stating that the organism remembers (1942, Part III).

How set arises and how it functions are chronic problems in set theory. The results of the process are more readily described, and analyses of set often begin by describing a behavioral situation. Attitude is similarly difficult to study experimentally. Bartlett describes what appears to be a mediating function between past and present perception and cognition in his experiments but has trouble addressing the phenomenon theoretically, although attitude plays a key role in his theory. He himself remarks that attitude "names a complex psychological state or process which is very hard to describe in more elementary psychological terms" (p. 206).

Paul: Replicating Bartlett

In America, psychologist I. H. Paul has studied remembering in terms of schemata (1959) and compared trace and schema theories of remembering (1967). In *"Studies in Remembering"* (1959), Paul reports on several experiments he carried out replicating or modifying Bartlett's methods, in which he attempted to analyze the data more systematically than Bartlett. Quantifying the set is considered by Paul to be a less active, preparatory activity that is "too general and all-embracing, referring as it often does to postures of a purely muscular and physical kind" to encompass "schema"—whereas he considers schema to be more limited and dynamic—designating "only cognitive factors" (1959, p. 142). In the later paper, Paul (1967) calls set the "psychological equivalent of the original schema concept" (p. 241), "set" representing the more passive, postural schema of Head.

Wolters: Schema in Thinking

Wolters, in several papers (1933, 1936, 1943), develops the role of schema in the thinking process. He treats thinking as a skill and as a response to some sort of problem or demand (as does Bartlett), and he maintains that thinking has much in common with other cognitive behavior. Wolters begins by assuming that there are universal or general ways of thinking. These "universals" or concepts are not mental entities, but organizations of reaction tendencies that are manifested in behavior that indicates a readiness or preparation for response, differing from habit in its flexibility. Whereas habit is a preparation for a limited range of response to a limited range of stimuli, the "universals" are more generally adaptive. The universals are schemata, but without the material aspect of Bartlett's schemata. Wolters is interested in how we think rather than the content of thought, and therefore his universals are functions.

Wolters adopts Bartlett's concept of "turning round" with modifications. "Turning round" for him consists of the organism reacting to "itself as schematized" (1933, p. 140). He views the schema as a way or organizing experience that is more adaptable than repetition or habit. Schemata can be of different levels, schematic organizations ranging from the lowest instinctual behaving to the highest level of abstract thinking. Animals have limited levels of schematic organization of responses; only man attains the highest level, which involves the deliberate schematic organization (or reorganization) of *schemata* themselves. The highest levels of schematic activity unique to man involve "reflections upon the manner of one's behaving" (1933, p. 140). This level is achieved when "deliberate self-modification" takes place (1943, p. 181). Consciousness is considered a way of behaving schematically, just as perceiving and thinking are schematic behavior.

The striking difference between Bartlett's and Wolters' use of schema lies in the "material" aspect of Bartlett's concept that is not part of Wolters'. For Wolters there is no content of thought except the "knowing" of ways of doing, acting, and behaving, with regard to stimuli. Oldfield and Zangwill have compared the schema theories of Wolters and Bartlett (1943, Part IV).

Vernon: Schema in Perception

M. D. Vernon has discussed the role of schemata in perception (1952, 1955, 1957). The storage and use of perceptual data is said to require an "organized procedure." Vernon applies Bartlett's concept to this classification system, regarding schemata as "persistent, deep-rooted, and well-organized classifications of ways of perceiving, thinking, and behaving" (1955, p. 181). These schemata have built up since infancy (and thus are skills improved by practice, as described by Wolters). Piaget's studies of "schemes" are considered to be examples treating the development of schema (see Vernon, 1952 in particular).

Vernon regards the schema as having two functions in perception: providing the expectancy that acts to select relevant data from among the mass of sensory data available, and giving meaning to selected data. When there are no appropriate schemata to deal with a situation, Vernon suggests that then short-term cognitive sets develop based on the situation. Given the right circumstances (such as, presumably, repetition or advantageous consequences), these sets can develop into schemata. Thus, Vernon appears to distinguish between set and schema primarily on the basis of permanence. A set develops from the immediate situation and may endure to become a schema. (A set is also implicitly more stimulus-bound.)

Broadbent: Filtering

Although information processing theories are not reviewed here, some mention should be made of theorists in this area to indicate to a limited extent the relation of set and schema to this approach. In *Perception and Communication* (1958), in which Broadbent describes the nervous system as a "communication channel" with limited capacity that functions selectively upon the environment, he points out that his filtering mechanism is related to Bartlett's schema (pp. 61–67). Broadbent emphasizes the similarity of their approaches as to the importance of selective use of past stimuli or information in present response. Another relationship between filter and schema lies in the concept of a selectively set mechanism with which stimulus information either does or does not fit, a fit being necessary for perception or further processing. In his revision of the earlier theory (1971), Broadbent adds other mechanisms of selection to the simple filtering, among them "pigeon-holing," a process that increases the likelihood of certain responses (decreases that of others).

The concept of attention in information processing theories could be considered at length. Broadbent's filter theory would be central to such a discussion. Neisser (1967) and Kahneman (1973) have treated Broadbent's theory and others in their attempts to integrate these concepts. Oldfield's paper (1954), "Memory Mechanisms and the Theory of Schemata," outlining a computer model of schemata functioning, might also be considered in the context of information theory.

Schema: In Summary

The concept of schema is basically an attempt to explain how past experience is involved in present cognition. It refers to an active, ongoing organization either of content (Bartlett, 1932) or response patterns (Wolters, 1943). Organization can take place at different levels: perceptual or imaginal or ideational, abstract thought being the highest level of schematic organization. The higher cognitive levels require the organization of the schemata themselves ("turning round"). Such high levels of activity are associated with consciousness, with cor scious effort or will, but the process of schematic organization itself is usually considered unconscious.

The schematizing of experience facilitates adaptation by reducing repetitious cognition (as in remembering or thinking), by making relevant data available more quickly, by preparing the organism for response in a broader and more flexible way than habit, and by providing the basis for abstract thinking.

In relation to set, schema is usually considered a more permanent condition or structure, although it is continually developing and changing. Schemata may produce temporary preparatory sets to respond selectively, including postural preparation. An "attitude" may arise from the schemata, then serve in turn to activate additional schemata (Bartlett, 1932). In the context of an experiment, instructions can activate a schema that provides the attitude (Zangwill, 1937). Responses are incorporated into existing schemata and thereby effect future sets and responses.

Schemata may be built up from infancy. Bartlett, who suggests that there are some innate schemata that are later dominated by acquired schemata, does not examine the development or learning of schemata in detail. Piaget's approach to cognitive development is a logical direction in which to pursue the developmental aspect of schema theory.

SET AND SCHEMA IN AMERICAN PSYCHOLOGY

In American psychology, the influence of several early textbook authors has established a place for the concept of set. In *Psychology*, Woodworth (1929) discusses preparatory set, which is considered the "essential response in attending" (p. 366). In *The Essentials of Psychology*, Pillsbury (1920) considers the selective and facilitative role of set in attention. Dashiell, who considered set the "neglected fourth dimension to psychological research" (1940), gives considerable attention to set in his textbooks, *Fundamentals of Objective Psychology* (1928) and *Fundamentals of General Psychology* (1937). One of the salient features of set in these three authors is its selective role in attention. The role of set in selective attention and differential readiness continues to be central to theories of set in American psychology—for example, in the information processing approach.

Set has dominated the American approaches, particularly to motor response and perception; "schema" has been used in approaching remembering (as in Paul's work, discussed in the previous section) and other higher cognitive functions, as well as having been influential in the interpretations of set.

Motor Theory: Freeman

Two "motor" theories of response are considered here, those of Freeman and Davis, who both emphasize the physiological, motor character of set.

Freeman's theoretical considerations of set (1938b, 1939, 1940a, 1940b, 1948) are founded in large part on his experimental studies of motor aspects of the stimulus/response process, reported primarily from 1930 to 1940 (e.g., 1931a, 1931b, 1933, 1938a; Freeman and Kendall, 1940). These studies might be divided into two groups: those intending to show that there is measurable neuromuscular activity that precedes, accompanies, and follows a range of responses, from peripheral, overt motor responses (e.g., in reaction time experiments) to mental acts (e.g., arithmetic); second, those intending to demonstrate that this neglected motor aspect of response not only accompanies, but affects the quality of the response in that it may facilitate or inhibit performance of both primarily motor and primarily mental tasks. In the first group, his method usually involved the measurement of neuromuscular activity before, during, or after a response, or during the preparation or performance of a task. The second group of experiments usually involved the inducement of tension in order to observe the effects on performance. These two basic groups of experiments, the experimental foundation for Freeman's "motor" view of set, demonstrate that motor activity corresponding to "preparation" precedes response and that various induced "patterns" of this tonic tension have a differential effect on simple motor and also cognitive performances. Sets are patterns of tonic activity that facilitate overt acts like pressing the lever in a reaction time experiment and covert acts like multiplication. In the former case, sets can increase the efficiency of performance by focusing tension in the areas of the body needed to make the response.

Sets play a selective channeling role for the discharge of energy in the neuromuscular homeostatic system postulated by Freeman in *The Energetics of Human Behavior* (1948). Sets are those patterns that prepare the organism for certain kinds of responses, rather than a general unprepared "startle" response. The proprioceptive backlash from these patterns are also part of the set process. Some degree of preparation or selection antecedent to overt response is involved when the organism is said to be "set." The nature of set effects is neuromuscular, although Freeman uses "set" to refer to both neuromuscular patterns and central facilitation resulting from their backlash.

After a response, the organism does not just return to a previous equilibrium condition unchanged; it is different by virtue of the effect of proprioceptive backlash on the neural control centers ("principle of backlash action"). The development of sets and learning are explained by means of residual proprioceptive effects, better adaptation being the normal result of set differentiation. Sets develop from diffuse muscular tension (general alertness) to specific expectancies; with repeated stimulus/response situations, sets become more selective, narrowing down available channels by preparing some and inhibiting others. Timing, amount, and locus of set are factors important to this differential channeling. Freeman presents this generalization about sets:

Set-expectancies are tentative and antecedent homeostatic adjustment acts, developed in response to minimally displacing stimulus cues and preparing the channelization of discharge through some particular response outlets which, if not so prepared, would function only through a greater displacement to general equilibrium. (1948, p. 220)

Sets are thus particular though modifiable patterns of preparation and inhibition (enduring in the organism) that form
tension-sets preparatory to response and built up from response (cf. Head, Bartlett).

Motor Theory: Davis

During approximately the same period that Freeman developed his motor theory of set, R. C. Davis, at Indiana University, was carrying out related experiments in the area of motor
response and formulating his own theory of muscular influence on set. Davis appears to base his interpretation of set, as
presented in "The Psychophysiology of Set" (1946), primarily on his experimental work in the preceding decade, during
which he studied muscular tension patterns in different experimental situations, from reaction time to "mental work"
(e.g., 1937, 1938, 1939).

When Davis studies set, he defines it in terms of experimental situations. [Freeman, in his functional "working hypothesis" of set (1939), dealt similarly with the problem of definition.] In the first of his two major papers on set (1940), he uses
reaction time as an index of set and finds a good correspondence between properties of set in reaction time and the pattern of muscular tension development he observes in his experiments. He concludes that muscular tension is the beginning of the response, that "sets are patterns of incipient muscular and glandular activity" (p. 29). The great variety of sets
is considered to be the result of different overall tension patterns. In "The Psychophysiology of Set" (1946), Davis
defines set by two experimental situations: the foreperiod in
reaction time and the time error in stimulus judgment of lifted
weights. The patterns of muscular tension are compared with
well-observed properties of set in these situations, showing a
strong correspondence of the set phenomena and patterns of
tension.

Davis' view of set is physiological and peripheral; he directs his experimental studies and hypotheses toward describ-

ing these aspects of the set process. Preparatory sets are patterns of excitation manifested in the muscular system (where he and others have detected differential qualities of tension for different responses) that, in effect, lower the threshold for a particular response. Davis focuses on the "sets" he can partially measure rather than theorizing to any length on their "neural correlates." Although Davis measures the muscular accompaniments of mental work, he does not explore the development of the phenomena or the relationship between motor set and cognitive set. Although he suggests in his paper on pattern development (1943) that psychological processes may have motor patterns that are "vestigial remnants of overt movement," (a provocative statement), he does not develop this idea theoretically. Davis does not present a theory of set; rather, he contributes what he undertakes to consider: the "psychophysiology of set." Together with Freeman's work, his experimental studies of tension and set lay a foundation for a peripheral aspect of set that was often overlooked at the time. Both Davis and Freeman took similar stands against the central-only theories of set, such as that espoused by Mowrer, Rayman, and Bliss (1940), in the "central-peripheral" controversy. (The "motor" theories of Freeman and Davis are compared in the unabridged review by this author.)

Perceptual Set Theory—Introduction

Two major theoretical approaches to perception in which set is a central concept are considered in this section: Bruner and Postman's hypothesis theory and Allport's structural theory. Neisser's approach to perception is also briefly described in reference to his schema-like concept of cognitive construction of synthesis.

Allport's theory is basically a transformation of hypothesis theory into the broader terminology of his understanding of set, which includes aspects of motor theory as well as features from sensory-tonic theory. Although it will not be discussed here, Werner and Wapner's sensory-tonic field theory of perception (Wapner and Werner, 1957; Werner and Wapner, 1949, 1952) bridges the peripheral tonic theories and the central perceptual set theories.

Perceptual Set Theory : Bruner and Postman

Jerome Bruner and Leo Postman are identified with the "new look"[3] approach to perception, which was the movement, occurring about mid-century, to bring the individual perceiver and particularly his motivational state to the forefront in understanding perception. In the late forties, Bruner and Postman were spokesmen for a "directive-state" theory (1949b) approach; a little later, in the early fifties, they advocated a revised version of their earlier concepts, referred to as "hypothesis theory."

Many of the experimental studies undertaken from the perspective of "new look" or directive-state concepts were related to set, but this discussion focuses on the work of Bruner, Postman, and associates because they singled out the mediating role of set as the perceptual hypothesis in their studies and later formulated a more general cognitive theory of perception in terms of this role.[4]

A group of early experiments investigated the general directive-state hypothesis that motivational factors play a selective role in perception (e.g., Bruner and Goodman, 19-47; Bruner

[3]See Luchins (1951) and Bruner's "reply" (1951a).
[4]For a detailed consideration of the directive-state contribution to perceptual theory, consult Allport (1955). The collection of papers in the volume *Perception and Personality: A Symposium* (Bruner and Krech, 1968; a reprint of the *Journal of Personality*, 1949, *18:* 1 and 2—"Interrelationships between Perception and Personality: A Symposium"), provides a range of the experimental findings and theoretical viewpoints characterizing this movement. Luchins (1951) criticizes the New Look at some length by defending the Gestalt concepts attacked by it. Haber (1966) summarizes the evidence for two basic hypotheses regarding the effect of set on perception: (a) "set enhances the percept directly"—the perceptual tuning hypothesis (a New Look approach), and (b) set has no effect on perception itself but on memory traces or responses. Steinfeld (1967) attempts to integrate these two hypotheses through an "availability" theory of set.

and Postman, 1947, 1948; Postman, Bruner, and McGinnies, 1948; Postman and Schneider, 1951). They examine the effects of social, personal, and symbolic value, or need, on the size and speed with which objects are perceived. In these early experiments three adaptive processes in perception are formulated and studied: selection, fixation, and accentuation. The selective process is called a "perceptual hypothesis" or "systematic response tendency," which, they propose, becomes "fixated" if rewarded, growing stronger and more "accentuated" (e.g., bigger, clearer, brighter).

The Bruner-Postman group also carried out experiments directly concerning set (Postman and Senders, 1946; Postman and Postman, 1948; Postman and Bruner, 1949; and Bruner and Postman, 1949a). One aspect of set that is particularly important to hypothesis theory is what Postman and Bruner (1949) refer to as "multiplicity": "the range or extent of alternative stimuli for which the organism is perceptually prepared" or the "sharpness of tuning" (p. 369).

A later group of experiments are based on the concept of sets as hypotheses, the intervening variables involved in selective response, with stimuli serving to arouse, confirm, and deny" these sets (e.g., Postman, Bruner, and Walk, 1951).

Perceiving in hypothesis theory is conceived of as a three-step cycle. An hypothesis (or expectancy or set) is aroused by partial stimulus information or cues. If the relevant or appropriate stimulus information matches the hypothesis, then it is "confirmed," resulting in a stable perception; if not, the hypothesis changes until confirmation is achieved. The determinants of hypothesis arousal that lead to confirmation with appropriate information are discussed by Bruner and Postman in terms of hypothesis *strength.*

Bruner defines the hypothesis as *generalized* because it can "govern all cognitive activity" during its functioning (1951b, p. 125). However, the *selectivity* of the hypothesis can be "tuned" finely or broadly (tuned, for example, by the arousing stimulus cues or by instructions). Postman (1951) develops the concept of a system of hypotheses as structural and functional, active and stored, in much the same way as Bartlett conceives of schema—Postman calls these systems schemata in recognition of the close relationship with Bartlett's concept. However, Postman and Bruner do not, up to this time, develop the other cognitive aspects of hypothesis theory to any great extent. Although Postman (1951) discusses remembering and suggests that thinking would involve similar hypothesis-information processes, he provides little detail.

Set in this conceptualization has a central, organizing (active) function, linking past experience, personality, drives, to the present stimulus or problem, for integrated adaptation to the environment. It is a state of selective preparation varying in specificity and strength, inferred from perceptual experiments and applied to the problem of how "directive-states" affect perception and other forms of cognition.

Perceptual Set Theory: Allport

Among perceptual theories, hypothesis theory is regarded by Floyd Allport as the "one outstanding exception to the general neglect of set" (1955, p. 240). With regard to Allport and set, perhaps the most important point to be made is that nowhere in his monograph does Allport criticize the use of set as an explanatory principle except to encourage a better and more significant utilization of it. The importance he ascribes to the role of set is a salient feature of his treatment of perceptual theory.

Allport's theory of set is essentially a synthesis of hypothesis theory and Freeman's tonic theory from Allport's structural perspective. The concepts of set confirmation and stimulus cues (structure) are integrated with a dynamic concept of set facilitation.

Allport's "structural theory of set dynamics and interaction" has the stated goal of translating the "language of 'hypotheses' into some of the more explicit concepts which the facts of set are capable of providing" (p. 407). Allport begins by bringing the concept of energy explicit into the hypothesis. Hypothesis strength becomes set energy. The stimulus provides additional energy to the set so that the preparatory set can rise above a threshold level of energy. But the stimulus also provides a "structure" or pattern for this energy that does or does not fit with the "structure" or "format" of the set, to complete it in the process of stimulus-information or -deformation. Appropriate information is "confirmed," because it provides the energy necessary to raise the current set above threshold, and its energy is structured in such a way that it will fit with the structure of the set and can be added to it [reflecting Allport's attempt to integrate the hypothesis of Bruner and Postman with implications of the facilitative pattern of Freeman's tonic set; cf. also, Woodworth's (1937) concept of sets as resonators.] To clarify this concept, Allport uses the analogy of a carpenter placing in a house a final beam that completes both its structure and increases its supporting strength (p. 408).

In the final chapter of his monograph on perception, Allport (1955) describes his Event-Structure theory, which in part attempts to explain how sets might operate and be stored. This theory is too complex to describe here; a brief description may be found in the longer review of set and schema theories by this author.

Allport's approach to set is among the broadest of the theories under consideration. As such, it leaves itself open to questions regarding the many roles of set and its seemingly contradictory characteristics. Allport, however, does indicate one pathway toward unifying cognitive and motor set theories.

Perceptual Set Theory: Neisser's Constructive Cognition

Ulric Neisser (1967) proposes a general theory of cognition based on constructive concepts resembling Bartlett's approach to remembering, a theoretical debt he acknowledges. Neisser discusses visual and auditory perception, and, to a lesser extent, recall and thinking, in terms of this constructive process, referred to as "analysis-by-synthesis." A two-stage theory of cognitive construction is suggested: a preattentive, "fast, crude, wholistic, and parallel" stage; and a "deliberate, attentive, detailed, and sequential" stage (p. 10). Neisser suggests that perceptual set may affect perception by controlling the order of analysis from one stage to the next, those items selected first for further analysis (focal attention) having a better chance of surviving to affect perception. Focal attention involves synthesis, an active, constructive, and sequential process (sequential because only one thing at a time can be given attention.) Remembering and thinking are assumed, in the final chapter, to have analogous constructive stages, although Neisser does not go into as much detail. The stored information in long-term memory has a role like that of the stimulus in perception; it is used constructively. Information in these higher processes consists of traces of previous processes of construction. A third level of cognitive construction is proposed in this final section that consists of constructed context—the where, when, and what (meaning) frames of reference that characterize a percept. This third level is a schema or "cognitive structure." Neisser defines this as a "nonspecific but organized representation of prior experiences" (p. 287). Cognitive structures, compared with Bartlett's schemata by Neisser, are the form of remembering. He emphasizes, as does Bartlett, that recall is not the revival of traces, the arousal of earlier experiences. Neisser suggests that an appropriate set is necessary for (or greatly facilitative of) reestablishing a schema, or remembering (as is Bartlett's "attitude").

In *Cognition and Reality*, Neisser (1976) develops the role of "anticipatory schemata' in perception, that is, constantly changing cognitive structures in the tradition of Head's postural schemata and encompassing hypothesis theory. In the "perceptual cycle," schemata mediate the access of information: "At each moment the perceiver is constructing anticipations of certain kinds of information. . . . the information picked up—modifies the original schema. Thus modified, it directs further exploration and becomes ready for more information" (pp. 20–21). In this perceptual cycle, anticipated information can be sharpened or "tuned" by the information picked up. Schemata selectively affect what information is picked up, and then are in turn modified by that information.

Perceptual Theory: In Summary

Set and schema processes in these perceptual theories act selectively upon stimulus information to affect perception. For Bruner and Postman, and Allport, the set process consists of a matching of stimulus information and set structure that increases the strength or energy of a hypothesis or set toward the threshold of perception. This "matching" or "fitting" of stimulus cues to an organismic structure resembles the "effort after meaning" or matching process in Bartlettian schema theories. In Neisser (1976), schemata determine what information is picked up.

The maintenance of sets and their relation to memory are construed differently by these theorists. Hypotheses, like Bartlett's schemata, are actively "stored" for continual utilization. Memory traces of stimulus information are also stored and become the information for remembering in a process considered similar to hypothesis confirmation (which is not detailed). For Allport, sets are memory traces. Allport adopts a concept of energy loops, as the form of sets, much like Freeman's motor sets, but centralized. These can continue to exist indefinitely, although they may change and develop through interaction with other sets and stimulus information. Set is not a mediator for traces of past experience, it is the stored form of the past experience.

Neisser's (1967, 1976) approach to perception and remembering with regard to set or schema is very much like Bartlett's. The roles of set (1967) in selecting parts of the stimulus for processing, determining the objects of focal attention, and in "searching" for the appropriate cognitive structure for remembering, resemble the roles of attitude in Bartlett's theory. The cognitive structuring is, of course, Bartlettian. Perceiving is constructive, and remembering is reconstructive. The role of schemata in the perceptual cycle (1976) is also in the British tradition of schemata.

Language: Werner and Kaplan

Werner and Kaplan use a set or schema concept in their organismic-developmental approach to language (1963). Symbol formation is conceptualized as a "dynamic schematizing activity." Dynamic schematizing is a medium in which object-meaning and linguistic meaning develop. This theory of symbolic meaning has interesting parallels with Allport's (1955) view of linguistic meaning in his dynamic-structural theory. Most of the volume on *Symbol Formation* (1963) by Werner and Kaplan is given to detailed analysis of the development of language, in which the focus is on a relatively high linguistic level rather than on the underlying process of schematization; therefore, their theory is not discussed further here.

CONCLUSIONS

Is there "no common meaning" of set or schema in the theories discussed above, as Gibson (1941) maintains, for the experimental usages of set? Many of the same difficulties that Gibson describes can be observed among these theories; there are numerous "ambiguities and contradictions" remaining in the concepts of set and schema. Because part of the difficulty no doubt stems from the many different roles attributed to set and schema, an approach for at least some systematization of these roles is suggested. Before such an attempt, however, there are several general qualities usually attributed to set and schema that might be reviewed.

Both "schemata" and "sets" *prepare* the organism for adaptive activity by *organizing* (internally) past and present information. The postural schemata (Head) integrate proprioceptive information for conscious awareness of posture. Bartlett's schema is an organized mass that can be reorganized for more advantageous remembering. Wolters' schema is an organization of reaction tendencies that can also be reorganized for the purposes of thinking. Vernon discusses the storage, organization, and use of percepts in terms of schemata. Freeman and Davis consider set a preparatory pattern of tonic activity. Bruner and Postman emphasize the organization and utilization of stimulus information by the hypothesis process. And Allport's set is a "structuring of events."

Both concepts imply a *selective* ability or effect upon behavior. The preparation for activity is selective, although the types of behavior referred to may differ greatly. Freeman's set, for example, provides the selective preparation of neuromuscular channels for energy discharge, whereas the hypothesis of Bruner and Postman provides selective "tuning" for perception. The selective preparation for activity has been applied specifically to the preparation for receiving sensory information and the preparation of the motor system to respond. Processes such as remembering and thinking require selective utilization of information already stored.

By this organized and selective preparation, schema and set serve to *orient* or *direct* behavior. They are not usually considered the sole determinant of behavior, but a fundamental influence on movement, remembering, thinking, and/or perception.

Schema and set are also *determined by experience*, although there is a question of whether all schemata are learned, or whether some are innate. In Bartlett's schemata system, as for Head's postural schemata, each new experience is integrated with the existing schemata so that a schema may be constantly changing. Bartlett's system, however, undergoes the additional alterations of the "turning round" process of reorganization. For Wolters and, similarly, Vernon, thinking and perception, respectively, are like skills, built up from experience. Freeman's "residuals" (via proprioceptive feedback) lead to the reformulation of sets. In the system of Bruner and Postman the hypothesis process links past to present behavior, and, through "cognitive support," hypotheses are strengthened from experience. In Allport's theory of perception, sets are refined and stored in the form of energy systems.

There seem to be three major types of activity that are described by these theories. The *set function* is a temporary preparation of the organism for selective action, serving to orient the organism's receptor and response systems for efficient perception and response (e.g., by bringing a high level of attention to a particular modality or by mobilizing energy for appropriate tonus), or to orient "consciousness" for selective recall or directed thinking. A temporary organizing condition of the entire organism, a set is normally not "stored," but it does influence the storage of stimulus and response information, and thereby effects future set formation. Each normal set is unique, because it reflects the cumulative experience of the organism, as well as the present stimulus situation and organismic state. The range of specificity of set to the stimulus is extensive, but, with each stimulus/response occurrence, learning tends to occur that produces a capacity for very "fine tuning" of set to stimulus cues.

A set may change rapidly into another set with the introduction of new stimulus information or changing organismic conditions. Change can occur readily because of the schematizing function, a general, constructive, integrative, and flexible activity characteristic of human cognition. Schematizing is analogous to Head's postural schema function and is generalized in the sense of providing a broad organization of the human organism's faculties. The schematizing function is always active in the conscious organism (and perhaps in sleep; cf. Freud's dynamic dream construction process). It may be passive, as often the case in the outer-directed schematizing of perceiving, or active, as in the inward-directed schematizing of remembering and thinking. Like set functioning, schematizing is a phenomenon of the present (cf. James, 1890, stream of consciousness).

The third type of function is schema, the stored form of past sets or modes of schematizing that have made their way into an enduring form of "memory," made up of the accumulated ways of perceiving, responding, remembering, and thinking, "constructive" by nature because the pervasive schematizing function was active during their formation. Schemata underlie sets, which often are temporary manifestations of these stored "ways of acting." In turn, each set leaves an impression on the schemata structuring, the degree of impact depending on such qualitative features as the attention, emotion, or drive involved in the prepared-for act.

When a schema is well-established (by whatever process), the sets produced from it may function like habits because they are so similar to past sets. Such a set may perseverate in the face of conflicting stimulus cues, such as happens when a playing card has the suit color reversed, causing the subject to misperceive it as a standard card or with an inbetween color (Bruner and Postman, 1949a). This tendency becomes pathological when it causes constant misinterpretation of stimuli and poor adaptation. (Shakow suggests such pathological perservation of segmental sets is schizophrenia.)

Although these three levels are rudimentary, they serve to clarify the assortment of roles attributed to set or schema in the aforementioned theories.

The classifaction of *set function* would include: Bartlett's (1932) orientation and "attitude," Zangwill's (1937) set, Vernon's expectancy or cognitive sets (1955), Broadbent's filter (stimulus set) and response set (1958, 1971), Bruner and Postman's (1949b) hypothesis in perception, Freeman's (1948) tonic set expectancy, Davis' (1946) motor set, the set function in Neisser's (1967) first level of cognitive construction, wherein units from the preattentive persistence of the stimulus (e.g., "iconic" or "echoic" memory) are selected for second level processing by the allocation of attention, and Neisser's (1976) anticipatory schema in the perceptual cycle.

The *schematizing function* would include: Bartlett's constructive remembering (1932), the "effort after meaning," and the search and match process in perception; Wolters' (1933) "universal" thinking; Allport's structuring of "events" and the operation of his generalized set to "perceive accurately and to respond effectively" (1955, p. 417); Werner and Kaplan's (1963) dynamic schematization in symbol formation; Bruner's (1951b) and Postman's (1951) hypothesis functioning, particularly in remembering and as a generalized intervening or mediating mechanism; Bruner's (1951b) concept of categorizing; and Neisser's (1967) analysis-by-synthesis cognitive constructive process and the constructive anticipations of information in Neisser's (1967) schema process. It would also include the formation of schemata implicit in Vernon's (1955) approach to perception and perhaps the formation of category states implicit in Broadbent's (1958) approach.

The *schemata or storage level* of set/schema functioning would include: Bartlett's (1932) schemata as utilized in remembering and in "turning round"; Zangwill's (1937) and Vernon's (1955) schemata underlying set; Broadbent's (1958) category states; Allport's (1955) event-structures, Freeman's (1948) set residuals; Bruner's (1951b) and Postman's (1951) systems of hypotheses or categories, and Neisser's (1967) cognitive structures. Some such storage function is implicit as well in Wolters' (1933) "ways of thinking" and Werner and Kaplan's (1963) concept of linguistic meaning, since these involve learning and are multiple abilities that are maintained by the organism and are available to consciousness upon need.

This tripartite division of set/schema functions provides only one suggestion of an approach for further analysis of these hypothetical processes. Major theoretical difficulties remain to be ironed out in set or schema theories.

Several of the most salient questions regard the formation of sets and schemata. If set is a derivative of schema, although modified by environmental and organismic circumstances, there is the question of how a "setting" is achieved. Then one must ask how sets leave an impression on the underlying schemata. Regarding the formation of schemata, there are questions such as how percepts, thoughts, or other information become actively stored in schemata, and how affect and motivation affect their formation and "activation," that is, what determines their accessibility or strength (and how do these qualities of *schemata* affect the *sets* that may arise from them).

There is also the fundamental question of how a percept is initially organized. How do new percepts derive from schemata of the past "meeting" with new stimulation? Does set always play a role in new perceptions?

Then there is the relation of schematizing to schema and to set. Schematizing appears to be a widely recognized functional characteristic of cognition. Set and schemata appear to have characteristics encompassed by this general function as if both are manifestations of its activity: set being a temporary product derived from the schematizing of the stimulus situation, organismic state, and schemata (or from some combination of these) for the purpose of orienting for response (whether perceiving, remembering, thinking, or moving); the latter being an enduring record or schematized experience, although active and cumulative. The question of such interrelationships appears to be quite open for theoretical development.

Other troublesome areas include the relationships of attention and memory to set or schema and the question of how motor and cognitive sets are related.

These are a few of the questions that might be raised about the use of set and schema as they are related to the limited aspects of behavior touched on in this review. The "most crucial ambiguities" that Gibson finds in his review of the experimental treatment of set are "the relation of set to past experience or habit" and "the characterization of a set as voluntary or involuntary" (1941, p. 811).[5] The former remains a crucial ambiguity; there are presently numerous debates over the latter, in which more significant questions than that of voluntariness arise. Chief among them perhaps is the interrelationship of set, schema, and schematizing.

[5]The second ambiguity derives primarily from his review of conditioning experiments, an area omitted from this survey.

References

Aarons, L. "Sleep-assisted Instruction." *Psychological Bulletin*, **83**, 1–40 (1976).

Acta Psychologica, 30 (1969). Donders Centenary Symposium on Reaction Time. Eindhoven, The Netherlands. July 29–August 2, 1968. Under auspices of Institute of Perception Research IPO, Eindhoven.

Allport, F.H. "A Theory of Enestruence (Event-structure Theory): Report of Progress." *American Psychologist*, **22**, 1–24 (1967).

Allport, F. H. "A Theory of Enestruence (Event-structure Theory): Report 441–445 (1921).

Angyal, A., Freeman, H. and Hoskins, R. G. "Physiologic Aspects of Schizophrenia." *Archives of Neurology and Psychiatry*, **34**, 270–279 (1935).

Angyal, A. "The Experience of the Body Self in Schizophrenia." *Archives of Neurology and Psychiatry*, **35**, 1029–1053 (1936).

Angyal, A. *Foundations for a Science of Personality*. New York: The Commonwealth Fund, 1941.

Angyal, A. and Blackman, N. "Vestibular Reactivity in Schizophrenia." *Archives of Neurology and Psychiatry*, **44**, 611–620 (1940).

Angyal, A., Freeman, H. and Hoskins, R.G. "Physiologic Aspects of Schizophrenic Withdrawal." *Archives of Neurology and Psychiatry*, **44**, 621–626 (1940).

Angyal, A. and Sherman, M.A. "Postural Reactions to Vestibular Stimulation in Schizophrenic and Normal Subjects." *American Journal of Psychiatry*, **98**, 857–862 (1942).

Angyal, A. F. "Speed and Pattern of Perception in Schizophrenic and Normal Persons." *Character and Personality*, **11**, 108–127 (1942).

Bachrach, L. L. *Deinstitutionalization: An Analytical Review and Sociological Perspective*. Washington, D. C.: U.S. Government Printing Office, DHEW Publication No. (ADM), 76–351, 1976.

Badger, R. G. *The Doris Case of Quintuple Personality and Others*. Boston: Gorham Press, 1916/1917.

Baring-Gould, W. S. (Ed.) *Annotated Sherlock Holmes, Vol I*. New York: Clarkson & Potter, Inc., 1967.

Barlett, F. C. *Remembering: A Study in Experimental and Social Psychology*. Cambridge at the University Press, 1932.

Barnett, S. A. "Experiments on 'Neophobia' in Wild and Laboratory Rats." *British Journal of Psychology*, **49**, 195–201 (1958a).

Barnett, S. A. "Exploratory Behavior." *British Journal of Psychology*, **49**, 286–310 (1958b).

Bartemeier, L. H. et al. "Combat Exhaustion." *Journal of Nervous and Mental Disease*, **104**, 358–389 (1946).

Bateson, G., Jackson, D. D., Haley, J., and Weakland, J. "Towards a theory of schizophrenia." *Behavioral Science*, 251–264 (1956).

Becker, A. and Schulberg, H. C. "Phasing Out State Hospitals: A Psychiatric Dilemma." *New England Journal of Medicine*, **294**, 255–261 (1976).

Bennett, G. "Structural Factors Related to the Substitute Value of Activities in Normal and Schizophrenic Persons: I. A technique for the Investigation of Central Areas of the Personality." *Character and Personality*, **10**, 42–50 (1941).

Bennett, G. "Structural Factors Related to the Substitute Value of Activities in Normal and Schizophrenic Persons: II. An Experimental Investigation of Central Areas of the Personality." *Character and Personality*, **10**, 227–245 (1942).

Bernard, C. *An Introduction to the Study of Experimental Medicine*. New York: Macmillan, 1927 (1868).

Bernstein, B. *Thurber: A Biography*. New York: Dodd Mead, 1975.

Bingley, T. "The Concept of Temporal Lobe Epilepsy." *Acta Psychiatrica et Neurologica Scandinavica*, **Suppl. 120**, 1–151 (1958).

Blackman, N. "Experiences with a Literary Club in the Group Treatment of Schizophrenia." *Occupational Therapy and Rehabilitation*, **19**, 293–305 (1940).

Bleuler, E. *Textbook of Psychiatry*. New York: Macmillan, 1924.

Bleuler, E. *Dementia Praecox or the Group of Schizophrenias*. New York: International Universities Press, 1950.

Boisen, A. T. "Personality Changes and Upheavals Arising Out of the Sense of Personal Failure." *American Journal of Psychiatry*, **5**, 531–551 (1926).

Boisen, A. T. *Out of the Depths*. New York: Harper, 1960.

Book, W. F. *The Psychology of Skill*. New York: Gregg, 1925.

Boring, E. G. *A History of Experimental Psychology*, 2nd. ed. New York: Appleton-Century-Crofts, 1950.

Bowman, K. M. and Raymond, A. F. "A Statistical Study of the Personality in Schizophrenic Patients." In G. H. Kirby, T. K. Davis and H. A. Riley (Eds.) *Schizophrenia (Dementia Praecox): An Investigation of the Most Recent Advances*. Baltimore: Williams & Wilkins, 1931, 48–74.

Broadbent, D. E. *Decision and Stress*. London and New York: Academic, 1971.

Broadbent, D. E. "The Hidden Preattentive Processes." *American Psychologist*, **32**, 109–118 (1977).

Bruner, J. S. "Personality Dynamics and the Process of Perceiving." In R. R. Blake and G. V. Ramsey (Eds.), *Perception: An Approach to Personality*. New York: Ronald, 1951.

Bruner, J. S. and Goodman, C.C. "Value and Need as Organizing Factors in Perception." *Journal of Abnormal and Social Psychology*, **42**, 33–44 (1947).

Bruner, J. S. and Postman, L. "Perception, Cognition, and Behavior." *Journal of Personality*, **18**, 14–31 (1949).

Bryan, W. A. *Administrative Psychiatry*. New York: Norton, 1936.

Buchsbaum, M. S. "Average Evoked Response Augmenting/Reducing in Schizophrenia and Affective Disorders." In D. X. Freedman (Ed.), *The Biology of the Major Psychoses: A Comparative Analysis*. Long Island, New York: Raven Press, pp. 129-142, 1975.

Buss, A. H. and Lang, P. J. "Psychological Deficit in Schizophrenia: I. Affect, Reinforcement, and Concept Attainment." *Journal of Abnormal Psychology*, **70**, 2–24 (1965).

Cabot, R. C. "Diagnostic Pitfalls Identified During a Study of Three Thousand Autopsies." *Journal of the American Medical Association*, **59**, 2295–2298 (1921).

Cameron, D. E. and Jellinek, E. M. "Pulse Rate and Blood Pressure." *Endocrinology*, **25**, 100–104 (1939).

Cancro, R. *Schizophrenic Reactions: Critique of the Concept, Hospital Treatment, and Current Research: Proceedings of the Menninger Foundation Conference on the Schizophrenic Syndrome*. New York: Brunner/Mazel, 1970.

Cancro, R., Sutton, S., Kerr, J., and Sugarman, A. A. "Reaction Time and Prognosis in Acute Schizophrenics." *Journal of Nervous and Mental Disease*, **153**, 351–359 (1971).

Cannon, W. B. *The Wisdom of the Body*. New York: Norton, 1932.

Carmichael, H. T. and Linder, F. E. "The Relation Between Oral and Rectal Temperatures in Normal and Schizophrenic Subjects." *American Journal of the Medical Sciences*, **188**, 68–75 (1934).

Chapman, L. J. and Chapman, J. P. *Disordered Thought in Schizophrenia*. New York: Appleton-Century-Crofts, 1973.

Clark, E. "Into the Lairs of Sleeping Sharks." *National Geographic*, 570–584, April, 1975.

Coate, M. *Beyond All Reason*. Philadelphia: Lippincott, 1965.

Coghill, G. E. "The Neuro-Embryologic Study of Behavior: Principles, Perspective and Aim." *Science*, **78**, 131–138 (1933).

Cohen, B. D., Senf, R. and Huston, P. E. "Effect of Amobarbital (Amytal) and Affect on Conceptual Thinking in Schizophrenia, Depression, and Neurosis." *Archives of Neurology and Psychiatry*, **71**, 171–180 (1954).

Cohen, B. D., Senf, R. and Huston, P. E. "Perceptual Accuracy in Schizophrenia, Depression, and Neurosis, and Effects of Amytal." *Journal of Abnormal and Social Psychology*, **52**, 363–367 (1956).

Cohen, L. H. and Fierman, J. H. "Metabolic, Cardiovascular, and Biochemical Changes Associated with Experimentally Induced Hyperthyroidism in Schizophrenia." *Endocrinology*, **22**, 548–558 (1938).

Cohen, L. H. and Patterson, M. "Effect of Pain on the Heart Rate of Normal and Schizophrenic Individuals." *Journal of General Psychology*, **17**, 273–289 (1937).

Cole, M. and Maltzman, I. (Eds.) *A Handbook of Contemporary Soviet Psychology*. New York: Basic Books, 1969.

Cousins, N. "Editorial." *Saturday Review*, 8/7/76.

Cox, R. H. and Esau, T. G. *Regressive Therapy: Therapeutic Regression of Schizophrenic Children, Adolescents and Young Adults*. New York: Brunner/Mazel, 1974.

Crawley, E. *The Mystic Rose*. New York: Meridian Books, 1960.

Cromwell, R. L. "Assessment of Schizophrenia." *Annual Review of Psychology*, **26** (1975).

Cromwell, R. L., Rosenthal, D., Shakow, D., and Zahn, T. P. "Reaction Time, Locus of Control, Choice Behavior, and Descriptions of Parental Behavior in Schizophrenic and Normal Subjects. *Journal of Personality*, **29**, 363–379 (1961).

Crozier, W. J. "The Study of Living Organisms." In C. Murchison, Ed., *The Foundations of Experimental Psychology*. Worcester, Ma: Clark University Press, 1929.

Dashiell, J. F. "A Neglected Fourth Dimension to Psychological Research." *Psychological Review*, **47**, 289–305 (1940).

Davis, R. C. "Modification of the Galvanic Reflex by Daily Repetition of a Stimulus." *Journal of Experimental Psychology*, **27**, 504–535 (1934).

Davis, R. C. "Set and Muscular Tension." *Indiana University Publications: Science Series*, No. 10 (1940).

Davis, R. C. "The Psychophysiology of Set." In P. L. Harriman (Ed.), *Twentieth Century Psychology*. New York: The Philosophical Library, 1946, pp. 387–404.

Dethier, V. G. "A Surfeit of Stimuli: A Paucity of Receptors." *American Scientist*, **59**, 706–715 (1971).

Dewey, J. "Letters of John Dewey to Robert V. Daniels, 1946–1950." *Journal of the History of Ideas*, **20**, 569–576 (1959).

Diamond, S., Balvin, R. S. and Diamond, F. R. *Inhibition and Choice*. New York: Harper Row, 1963.

Dyrud, J. E. and Holzman, P. S. "The Psychotherapy of Schizophrenia: Does it Work?" *American Journal of Psychiatry*, **130**, 670–673 (1973).

Eccles, J. C. *The Understanding of the Brain*, 2nd. Ed. New York: McGraw-Hill, 1977, 2nd ed. Journal of Psychiatry, **126**, 400–404, (1969).

Eissler, R. S. et al. (Eds.) *The Psychoanalytic Study of the Child*, Vol. 31. New Haven: Yale University Press, 1976.

Elkes, J. "Schizophrenic Disorder in Relation to Levels of Neural Organi-

214   References

zation: The Need for Some Conceptual Points of Reference. In J. Folch-Pi, Ed., *The Chemical Pathology of the Nervous System*. London: Pergamon Press, 1958.

English, H. B. and English, A. C. *A Comprehensive Dictionary of Psychological and Psychoanalytic Terms*. New York: Longmans, Green, & Co., 1958.

Epstein, S. "Natural Healing Processes of the Mind." To appear in H. Lowenleim (Ed.), *Meanings of Madness*. Behavioral Publications, 1977.

Erickson, M. H. and Hoskins, R. C. "Grading of Patients in Mental Hospitals as a Therapeutic Measure." *American Journal of Psychiatry*, **11**, 103–109 (1931).

Fairlie, H. "Mother Russia's Prodigal Son." *The New Republic*, 18–20, July 29 (1978).

Feffer, M. H. "The Influence of Affective Factors on Conceptualization in Schizophrenia." *Journal of Abnormal and Social Psychology*, **63**, 588–596 (1961).

Fenichel, O. *The Psychoanalytic Theory of Neurosis*. New York: Norton, 1945.

Finesinger, J. E., Cohen, M. W. and Thompson, K. J. "Velocity of Blood Flow in Schizophrenia." *Archives of Neurology and Psychiatry*, **24**, 24–36, (1938).

Flor-Henry P. "Psychosis and Temporal Lobe Epilepsy: A Controlled Investigation." *Epilepsia*. Amsterdam, The Netherlands: Elsevier, 1969a.

Flor-Henry, P. "Schizophrenic-like Reactions and Affective Psychoses Associated with Temporal Lobe Epilepsy: Etiological Factors." *American Journal of Psychiatry*, **126**, 400–404 (1969).

Forrest, D. V. "Poiesis and the Language of Schizophrenia." *Psychiatry*, **28**, 1–18 (1965).

Forrest, D. V. "New Words and Neologisms." *Psychiatry*, **32** (1), 44–73 (1969a).

Forrest, D. V. "The Patient's Sense of the Poem: Affinities and Ambiguities." In J. L. Leedy (Ed.), *Poetry Therapy*. Philadelphia: Lippincott, 1969b.

Fowlkes, M. "Business as Usual—at the State Mental Hospital." *Psychiatry*, **38**, 55–64 (1975).

Frank, G. *Psychiatric Diagnosis: A Review of Research*. Oxford: Pergamon Press, 1975.

Freedman, B. J. "The Subjective Experience of Perceptual and Cognitive Disturbances in Schizophrenia. *Archives of General Psychiatry*, **30**, 333–340, (1974).

Freeman, G. L. "The Problem of Set." *American Journal of Psychology*, **52**, 16–30 (1939).

Freeman, G. L. " 'Central' vs. 'peripheral' locus of set; A critique of the Mowrer, Rayman, and Bliss 'demonstration.' " *Journal of Experimental Psychology*, **26**, 622–628 (1940a).

Freeman, G. L. "Concerning the 'Field' in 'Field' Psychology." *Psychological Review*, **47**, 416–424 (1940b).

Freeman, G. L. *The Energetics of Human Behavior*. Ithaca, New York: The Cornell University Press, 1948.

Freeman, G. L. and Kendall, W. E. "The Effect Upon Reaction Time of Muscular Tension Induced at Various Preparatory Intervals." *Journal of Experimental Psychology*, **27**, 136–148 (1940).

Freeman, H. "Effect of 'Habituation' on Blood Pressure in Schizophrenia." *Archives of Neurology and Psychiatry*, **29**, 139–147 (1933).

Freeman, H. "The Arm-to-Carotid Circulation Time in Normal and Schizophrenic Subjects." *Psychiatric Quarterly*, **8**, 290–299 (1934).

Freeman, H. "Variability of Circulation Time in Normal and Schizophrenic Subjects." *Archives of Neurolgy and Psychiatry*, **39**, 488–493 (1938).

Freeman, H. "Skin and Body Temperatures of Schizophrenic and Normal Subjects under Varying Environmental Conditions." *Archives of Neurology and Psychiatry*, **42**, 724–734 (1939).

Freeman, H. and Carmichael, H. T. "A Pharmacodynamic Investigation of the Autonomic Nervous System in Schizophrenia. I. Effect of Intravenous Injections of Epinephrine on the Blood Pressure and Pulse Rate." *Archives of Neurology and Psychiatry*, **33**, 342–352 (1935).

Freeman, H., Hoskins, R. G., and Sleeper, F. H. "The Blood Pressure in Schizophrenia." *Archives of Neurology and Psychiatry*, **27**, 333–351 (1932).

Freeman, H. and Rodnick, E. H. "Autonomic and Respiratory Responses of Schizophrenic and Normal Subjects to Changes of Intra-Pulmonary Atmosphere." *Psychosomatic Medicine*, **2**, 101–109 (1940).

Freeman, H., Rodnick, E. H., Shakow, D. and Lebeaux, T. "The Carbohydrate Tolerance of Mentally Disturbed Soldiers." *Psychosomatic Medicine*, **6**, 311–317 (1944).

Freides, D. "Human Information Processing and Sensory Modality: Cross-modal Functions, Information Complexity, Memory, and Deficit." *Psychological Bulletin*, **81**, 284–310 (1974).

Freud, S. "Beyond the Pleasure Principle" (1920). In J. Strachey (Ed.), *Standard Edition of the Complete Psychological Works of Sigmund Freud*, Vol. 18. London: Hogarth Press, 1955, pp. 1–64.

Fromm-Reichmann, F. *Principles of Intensive Psychotherapy*. Chicago: University of Chicago Press, 1950.

Galton, F. *Inquiries into Human Faculty*. New York: Macmillan, 1883.

Gantt, W. H. "Principles of Nervous Breakdown in Schizokinesis and Autokinesis." *Annals of the New York Academy of Sciences*, **56**, 143–163 (1953).

Gardner, B. T. and Gardner, R. A. "Teaching Sign Language to a Chimpanzee." *Science*, **165**, 644–672 (1969).

Garmezy, N. and Streitman, S. "Children at Risk: The Search for the Antecedents of Schizophrenia. Part 1. Conceptual Models and Research Methods." *Schizophrenia Bulletin*, Issue No. 8, 14–90, Spring (1974)

Gay, P. "Encounter with Modernism: German Jews in German Culture, 1888–1914." *Midstream*, **21**, 23–65 (1975).

Gewirtz, J. "Some Contextual Determinants of Stimulus Potency." In R. D. Parke (Ed.), *Recent Trends in Social Learning Theory*. New York: Academic, 1972, pp. 7–33.

Gibson, J. J. "A Critical Review of the Concept of Set in Contemporary Experimental Psychology." *Psychological Bulletin*, **38**, 781–817 (1941).

Gibson, J. J. *The Senses Considered as Perceptual Systems*. Boston: Houghton Mifflin, 1966.

Gill, M. M. (Ed.), *The Collected Papers of David Rapaport*. New York: Basic Books, Inc. 1967.

Goldstein, K. *The Organism*. New York: American Book Co., 1939.

Goldstein, K. "Methodological Approach to the Study of Schizophrenic Thought Disorder." In J. S. Kasanin (Ed.), *Language and Thought in Schizophrenia*, Norton, 1964, pp. 17–40.

Gottlieb, J. S. and Linder, F. E. "Body Temperatures of Persons with Schizophrenia and Normal Subjects. Effect of Changes in Environmental Temperature." *Archives of Neurology and Psychiatry*, **33**, 755–785 (1935).

Greenblatt, M. and Glazier, E. "The Phasing Out of Mental Hospitals in the United States." *American Journal of Psychiatry*, **132**, 1135–1140 (1975).

Gregg, A. *For Future Doctors*. Chicago: The University of Chicago Press, 1957.

Grim, P. F., Kohlberg, L., and White, S. H. "Some Relationships between Conscience and Attentional Processes." *Journal of Personality and Social Psychology*, **8**, 239–252, (1968).

Grinnell, G. B. "The Cheyenne Indians." In M. Mead and R. Bunzel (Eds.), *The Golden Age of American Anthropology*. New York: George Braziller, 1960, pp. 139-148.

Hale, E. E. *A New England Boyhood*. Boston: Little, Brown, 1964.

Hall, C. E. "The Position of the Paranoids in the Schizophrenic Group." Unpublished Master's Thesis, Clark University, 1933.

Hall, D. *String Too Short to be Saved*. New York: Viking 1961.

Hanfmann, E. "A qualitative Analysis of the Healy Pictorial Completion Test II." *American Journal of Orthopsychiatry*, **9**, 325–329 (1939a).

Hanfmann, E. "Thought Disturbances in Schizophrenia as Revealed by Performance in a Picture Completion Test." *Journal of Abnormal and Social Psychology*, **34**, 249–264 (1939b).

Hanfmann, E. "Analysis of the Thinking Disorder in a Case of Schizophrenia." *Archives of Neurology and Psychiatry*, **41**, 568–579 (1939c).

Hanfmann, E. and Kasanin, J. "A Method for the Study of Concept Formation." *Journal of Psychology*, **3**, 521–540, (1937).

Harris, A. J. and Shakow, D. "Scatter on the Stanford-Binet in Schizophrenic, Normal, and Delinquent Adults." *Journal of Abnormal and Social Psychology*, 33, 100-111 (1938).

Hartmann, H. *Ego Psychology and the Problem of Adaptation.* New York: International Universities Press, 1958.

Hayward, M. L. and Taylor, J. E. "A Schizophrenic Patient Describes the Action of Intensive Psychotherapy." *Psychiatric Quarterly*, 30, 211–248 (1956).

Head, H. *Studies in Neurology* (2 volumes). London: Oxford University Press, 1920.

Hebb, D. O. *A Textbook of Psychology*, 2nd Ed. Philadelphia, Pa: W. B. Saunders, 1966.

Hersch, C. "From Mental Health to Social Action: Clinical Psychology in Historical Perspective." *American Psychologist*, 24, 909–916, (1969).

Hersch, C. "Social History, Mental Health, and Community Control." *American Psychologist*, 27, 749–754 (1972).

Herzog, R. L. and Hritzuk, J. "Set: A Concept in General Psychology. Review of D. N. Uznadze's *The psychology of set.*" *Contemporary Psychology*, 13, 451–452 (1968).

Heston, L. L. "Psychiatric Disorders in Foster Home Reared Children of Schizophrenic Mothers." *British Journal of Psychiatry*, 112, 819–825 (1966).

Hill, L. B. "A Psychoanalytic Observation on Essential Hypertension." *Psychoanalytic Review*, 22, 60–64 (1935).

Hill, L. B. *Psychotherapeutic Intervention in Schizophrenia.* Chicago: University of Chicago Press, 1955.

Holmes, O. W. *Mechanism in Thought and Morals.* Boston: James R. Osgood & Co., 1871.

Holzman, P. S. "Personality." *Annual Review of Psychology*, 25, 247–276 (1974).

Holzman, P. S., Proctor, L. R., Levy, D. L., Yasillo, N. J., Meltzer, H. Y. and Hurt, S. W. "Eye-tracking Dysfunction in Schizophrenic Patients, and their Relatives." *Archives of General Psychiatry*, 31, 143–151 (1974).

Honig, A. *The Awakening Nightmare.* Rockaway, New Jersey: American Faculty Press, 1972.

Hoskins, R. G. and Jellinek, E. M. "Studies on Thyroid Medication. I. Some Conditions Determining the Haematopoietic Effects." *Endocrinology*, 16, 455–486 (1932).

Hoskins, R. G. and Jellinek, E. M. "The Schizophrenic Personality with Special Regard to Psychologic and Organic Concomitants." *Proceedings of the Association for Research in Nervous and Mental Disease*, 14, 211–233 (1933).

Hovland, C. I. and Weiss, W. "The Influence of Source Credibility on Communication Effectiveness." *Public Opinion Quarterly*, 15, 634–650 (1951).

Hovland, C. I. and Weiss, W. "Transmission of Information Concerning

Concepts through Positive and Negative Instances." *Journal of Experimental Psychology,* **45,** 175–182 (1953).

Huebner, D. M. "A Comparative Study of Verbal Associations of Normal Adults and Schizophrenic Patients in Repetitions of the Kent-Rosanoff Association Test." Unpublished Master's Thesis, Johns Hopkins University, 1938.

Huston, P. E. "Sensory Threshold to Direct Current Stimulation in Schizophrenic and in Normal Subjects." *Archives of Neurology and Psychiatry,* **31,** 590–596 (1934).

Huston, P. E. "Psychopathology of Schizophrenia and Depression. I. Effect of Amytal and Amphetamine Sulfate on Level and Maintenance of Attention." *American Journal of Psychiatry,* **109,** 131–138, (1952).

Huston, P. E., Cohen, B. D., and Senf, R. "Shifting of Set and Goal Orientation in Schizophrenia." *Journal of Mental Science,* **101,** 344–350 (1955).

Huston, P. and Senf, R. "Psychopathology of Schizophrenia and Depression (I)." *American Journal of Psychiatry,* **109** (2), 131–138, (1952).

Huston, P. E. and Singer, M. "Effect of Sodium Amytal and Amphetamine Sulfate on Mental Set in Schizophrenia." *Archives of Neurology and Psychiatry,* **53,** 365–369 (1945).

Huston, P. E. and Shakow, D. "Studies of Motor Function in Schizophrenia: III. Steadiness." *Journal of General Psychology,* **34,** 119–126 (1946).

Huston, P. E. and Shakow, D. "Learning in Schizophrenia. II. Pursuit Learning." *Journal of Personality,* **17,** 52–74 (1948).

Huston, P. E. and Shakow, D. "Learning Capacity in Schizophrenia: With Special Reference to the Concept of Deterioration." *American Journal of Psychiatry,* **105,** 881–888 (1949).

Huston, P. E., Shakow, D. and Erickson, M. H. "A Study of Hypnotically Induced Complexes by Means of the Luria Technique." *Journal of General Psychology,* **11,** 65–87 (1934).

Huston, P. E., Shakow, D. and Riggs, L. A. "Studies of Motor Function in Schizophrenia. II. Reaction Time." *Journal of General Psychology,* **16,** 39–82 (1937).

Jackson, J. H. *Selected Writings of John Hughlings Jackson* (2 volumes). New York: Basic Books, 1958.

James, W. *The Principles of Psychology* (2 volumes). New York: Holt, 1890.

Jellinek, E. M. "The Function of Biometric Methodology in Psychiatric Research." In F. R. Moulton and P. O. Komora (Eds.), *Mental Health* (American Association for the Advancement of the Sciences Publication No. 9). Lancaster, Pa.: Science Press, 1939.

Jenkins, J. C. and Dallenbach, K. M. "Oblivescence During Sleep and Waking." *American Journal of Psychology,* **35,** 605–612 (1924).

Kahneman, D. *Attention and Effort.* Englewood Cliffs, New Jersey: Prentice-Hall, 1973.

Kasanin, J. S. (Ed.) *Language and Thought in Schizophrenia.* New York: Norton, 1944 (paperback edition, 1964).

Kasanin, J. S. and Hanfmann, E. "An Experimental Study of Concept Formation in Schizophrenia. 1. Quantitative Analysis of the Results." *American Journal of Psychiatry,* **95,** 35–48 (1938).

Kasanin, J. S. and Rosen, Z. A. "Clinical Variables in Schizoid Personalities." *Archives of Neurology and Psychiatry,* **30,** 538–566 (1933).

Kaufman, B. N. *Son-rise.* New York: Harper & Row, 1976.

Kempf, E. J. "The Behavior Chart in Mental Diseases." *American Journal of Insanity,* **71,** 761–772 (1915).

Kent, G. H. and Rosanoff, A. J. "A Study of Association in Insanity." *American Journal of Insanity,* **67,** (1910).

Kety, S. "Biochemical Theories of Schizophrenia. Part I." *Science,* **129,** 1528–1532 (1959).

Kety, S. "Biochemical Theories of Schizophrenia. Part II." *Science,* **129,** 1590-1596 (1959).

Kirk, S. A. and Therrien, M. E. "Community Mental Health Myths and the Fate of Former Hospitalized Patients." *Psychiatry,* **38,** 209–217 (1975).

Klein, G. S. *Perception, Motives, and Personality.* New York: Knopf, 1970.

Konorski, J. *Integrative Activity of the Brain: An Interdisciplinary Approach.* Chicago: University of Chicago Press, 1967.

Krech, D. and Klein, G. S. (Eds.) *Theoretical Models and Personality Theory.* Durham, North Carolina: Duke University Press, 1952.

Kris, E. "On Preconscious Mental Processes." *Psychoanalytic Quarterly,* **19,** 551–552 (1950).

Laing, R. D. and Esterson, A. *Sanity, madness, and the family.* New York: Basic Books, 1964.

Landau, S. G., Buchsbaum, M. S., Carpenter, W., Strauss, J., and Sacks, M. "Schizophrenia and Stimulus Intensity Control." *Archives of General Psychiatry,* **32,** 1239–1245, 1975.

Langer, S. *Philosophy in a New Key.* New York: Penguin, 1948.

Lashley, K. S. "Factors Limiting Recovery after Central Nervous Lesions." *Journal of Nervous and Mental Disease,* **88,** 733–755, 1938.

Lewes, G. S. *Problems of Life and Mind,* Vols. I-II. Boston: Houghton, Osgood & Co., 1880.

Lilly, J. C. *Man and Dolphin.* New York: Doubleday, 1961.

Lilly, J. C. *Lilly on Dolphins.* New York: Doubleday, 1975.

Lilly, J. C. and Lilly, A. *The Dyadic Cyclone.* New York: Simon & Schuster, 1975.

Limbar, J. "Language in Child and Chimp." *American Psychologist,* **32,** 280–295 (1977).

Linder, F. E. and Carmichael, H. T. "A Biometric Study of the Relation Between Oral and Rectal Temperatures in Normal and Schizophrenic Subjects." *Human Biology,* **7,** 24–46 (1935).

Livingston, R. B. "Brain Circuitry Relating to Complex Behavior." In G.

C. Quarton, T. Melnechuk, and F. O. Schmitt (Eds.), *The Neurosciences.* New York: Rockefeller University Press, 1967, pp. 499–515.

Looney, J. M. and Freeman, H. "Oxygen and Carbon Dioxide Contents of Arterial and Venous Blood of Schizophrenic Patients." *Archives of Neurology and Psychiatry*, **39**, 276–283 (1938).

Looney, J. M. and Hoskins, R. G. "The Effect of Dinitrophenol on the Metabolism as Seen in Schizophrenic Patients." *New England Journal of Medicine*, **210**, 1206–1213 (1934).

Lowrey, L. G. "An Analysis of the Accuracy of Psychopathic Hospital Diagnoses." *Bulletin Mass. Commission Ment. Dis.*, **3**, 67–85 (1919).

Luria, A. R. *The Nature of Human Conflicts.* New York: Liveright, 1932.

MacDonald, N. "Living with Schizophrenia." *Canadian Medical Association Journal*, **82**, 218–221, 678–681 (1960).

Malamud, N. "Psychiatric Disorder with Intracranial Tumors of Limbic System." *Archives of Neurology*, **17**, 113–123 (1967).

Masten, A. S. "A Review of Set and Schema Theory in American and British Psychology." Unpublished, 1976.

Matthiessen, F. O. *The James Family.* New York: Knopf, 1947.

May, J. V. "The Dementia Praecox—Schizophrenia Problem." *American Journal of Psychiatry.* **11**, 401–446 (1931).

McDougall, W. *Outline of Abnormal Psychology.* New York: Charles Scribner's Sons, 1926.

McGeoch, J. A. "Forgetting and the Law of Disuse." *Psychological Review*, **39**, 352–370 (1932).

McWhirter and McWhirter (Eds.) *Guinness Book of World Records.* New York: Bantam, 1977.

Mead, M. and Calas, N. *Primitive Heritage.* New York: Random House, 1953.

Meltzer, H. J. "Regression is Unnecessary." In J. C. Gunderson and L. R. Mosher (Eds.), *Psychotherapy of Schizophrenia.* New York: Jason Aronson, 1975, pp. 123–137.

Menninger, K., Mayman, M. and Pruyser, P. *The Vital Balance.* New York: Viking, 1963.

Milner, M. *The Hands of the Living God.* New York: International Universities Press, 1969.

Montaigne. *Essays of Michael, Lord of Montaigne.* Second Book. London: Grant Richards, 1908.

Mullahy, P. *Oedipus Myth and Complex: A Review of Psychoanalytic Theory.* New York: Hermitage Press, 1948.

Murchison, C. (Ed.) *Foundations of Experimental Psychology.* Worcester, Mass.: Clark University Press, 1929.

Murphy, G. and Kovach, J. K. *Historical Introduction to Modern Psychology*, 3rd. ed. New York: Harcourt Brace Jovanovich, 1972.

Murphy, L. B. and Moriarty, A. E. *Vulnerability, Coping and Growth.* New Haven: Yale University Press, 1976.

Nabokov, V. *The Portable Nabokov*, Page Stegner, Ed. New York: Viking Portable Library, 1971.

Neisser, U. *Cognitive Psychology*. New York: Appleton-Century-Crofts, 1967.

Nuechterlein, K. H. "Reaction Time and Attention in Schizophrenia: A Critical Evaluation of the Data and Theories." *Schizophrenia Bulletin*, 3 (3), 358–428 (1977).

O'Brien, R. C. *Mrs. Frisby and the Rats of NIMH*. New York: Atheneum, 1971.

Oxford English Dictionary. (13 volumes). Oxford: Clarendon Press, 1933.

Paschal, F. C. "The Trend in Theories of Attention." *Psychological Review*, 48, 383–403 (1941).

Patterson, M. "Skin Resistance of Schizophrenic Patients and Normal Controls." Unpublished, 1937.

Perry, R. B. *The Thought and Character of William James*. Vol. II. *Philosophy and Psychology*. Boston: Little, Brown, 1935.

Petrie, A. *Individuality in Pain and Suffering*. Chicago: University of Chicago Press, 1967.

Pillsbury, W. B. *The Essentials of Psychology*. (rev. cd.). New York: Macmillan, 1921.

Pincus, G. "Studies of the Role of the Adrenal Cortex in the Stress of Human Subjects." *Recent Progress in Hormone Research*, 1, 123–145 (1947).

Pincus, G. et al. "Adrenal Function in Mental Disease." In *Recent Progress in Hormone Research, Proceeding of the Laurentian Hormone Conference*, Vol. IV. New York: Academic, 1949.

Plant, J. S. "Rating Scale for Conduct." *American Journal of Psychiatry*, 78, 547–572 (1922).

Postman, L. "Toward a General Theory of Cognition." In J. H. Rohrer and M. Sherif (Eds.) *Social Psychology at the Crossroads*. New York: Harper, 1951.

Potkin, S. G. et al. "Are Paranoid Schizophrenics Biologically Different from Other Schizophrenics?" *New England Journal of Medicine*, 298 (2), 61–66 (1978).

Premack, D. "A Functional Analysis of Language." *Journal of the Experimental Analysis of Behavior*, 14, 107–125, (1970). In *American Scientist*, 64, 674–683 (1976).

Pribram, K. H. and McGuinness, D. "Arousal, Activation, and Effort in the Control of Attention." *Psychological Review*, 82, 116–149 (1975).

Prince, M. "The Subconscious Settings of Ideas in Relation to the Pathology of the Psychoneurosis." *Journal of Abnormal Psychology*, 11, 1–18 (1917).

Quarton, G. C., Melnechuk, T., and Schmitt, F. O. (Eds.) *The Neurosciences*. New York: Rockefeller University Press, 1967.

Rakoff, V. M., Stancer, H. C., and Kedward, H. B. (Eds.) *Psychiatric Diagnosis*. New York: Brunner/Mazel, 1977.

Rapaport, D. "The Conceptual Model of Psychoanalysis." In M. M. Gill (Ed.), *The Collected Papers of David Rapaport*. New York: Basic Books, 1967, pp. 405–431.

Reik, T. *Listening with the Third Ear*. New York: Farrar, Straus & Co., 1952.

Rheingold, H. L. and Kip, E. S. "Effect of the Sex of the Examiner, of Changing Examiner, and of Repetition on the KR Association Test." Unpublished, 1938.

Richter, D. (Ed.) *Schizophrenia: Somatic Aspects*. New York: Macmillan, 1957.

Rickers-Ovsiankina, M. "Studies on the Personality Structure of Schizophrenic Individuals: I. The Accessibility of Schizophrenics to Environmental Influences." *Journal of General Psychology*, **16**, 153–178 (1937a).

Rickers-Ovsiankina, M. "Studies on the Personality Structure of Schizophrenic Individuals: II. Reaction to Interrupted Tasks." *Journal of General Psychology*, **16**, 179–196 (1937b.)

Rickers-Ovsiankina, M. "The Roschach Test as Applied to Normal and Schizophrenic Subjects." *British Journal of Medical Psychology*, **17**, 227–257 (1938).

Rieder, R. O. "Hospitals, Patients, and Politics." *Schizophrenia Bulletin*, Issue 11, 9–15 (Winter, 1974).

Rivers, W. H. R. *Instinct and the Unconscious*, 2nd ed. Cambridge at the University Press, 1922.

Rodnick, E. H. "The Response of Schizophrenic and Normal Subjects to Stimulation of the Autonomic Nervous System." *Psychological Bulletin*, 35, 646–647 (1938).

Rodnick, E. H. "The Effect of Metrazol Shock upon Habit Systems." *Journal of Abnormal and Social Psychology*, 37, 560–565 (1942).

Rodnick, E. H. and Shakow, D. "Set in the Schizophrenic as Measured By a Composite Reaction Time Index." *American Journal of Psychiatry*, **97**, 214–225 (1940).

Roe, A. and Shakow, D. "Intelligence in Mental Disorder." *Annals of the New York Academy of Sciences*, 42, 361–490 (1942).

Róheim, G. *"Spiegelzauber."* *Imago*, **5**, 63–126 (1917).

Róheim, G. *Magic and Schizophrenia*. New York: International Universities Press, 1955.

Romano, J. "The Central Core of Madness." In L. C. Wynne, R. L. Cromwell, and S. Matthysse (Eds.), *The Nature of Schizophrenia: New Approaches to Research and Treatment*. New York: Wiley, 1978, pp. 1–5.

Rosenthal, D. "The Spectrum Concept in Schizophrenia and Manic-depressive Disorders." In D. X. Freedman (Ed.), *Biology of the Major Psy-Res. Publ. Assoc. Res. Nerv. Ment. Dis.*, Vol 54. New York: Raven Press, 1975.

Rosenthal, D., Lawlor, W. G., Zahn, T. P. and Shakow, D. "The Relationship of Some Aspects of Mental Set to Degree of Schizophrenic Disorganization." *Journal of Personality*, **28**, 26–38 (1960).

Rosenthal, R. *Experimenter Effects in Behavioral Research*. New York: Appleton-Century-Crofts. 1966.

Rosenthal, R. and Rosnow, R. (Eds.) *Artifact in Behavioral Research*. New York: Academic, 1969.

Rosenzweig, S. "Further Comparative Data on Repetition-Choice After Success and Failure as Related to Frustration Tolerance." *Journal of Genetic Psychology*, **66**, 75–81 (1945).

Rosenzweig, S. and Shakow, D. "Play Technique in Schizophrenia and Other Psychoses. I.: Rationale." *American Journal of Orthopsychiatry*, **7**, 32–35 (1937).

Rosten, L. *The Joys of Yiddish*. New York: McGraw-Hill, 1968.

Salzinger, K. *Schizophrenia: Behavioral Aspects*. New York: Wiley, 1973.

Savage, E. S. and Rumbaugh, D. M. "Communication, Language, and Lana: A Perspective." In D. M. Rumbaugh (Ed.), *Language Learning by a Chimpanzee: The Lana Project*. New York: Academic, 1977.

Schiff, J. L. with Day, B. *All My Children*. Philadelphia: M. Evans & Co., 1970.

Schilder, P. *Medical Psychology*. New York: International Universities Press, 1953.

Schlesinger, H. J. "Cognitive Attitudes in Relation to Susceptibility to Interference." *Journal of Personality*, **22**, 354–374 (1954).

Schnack, G. F., Shakow, D. and Lively, M. "Studies in Insulin and Metrazol Therapy. I: The Differential Prognostic Value of Some Psychological Tests." *Journal of Personality*, **14**, 106–124 (1945a).

Schnack, G. F., Shakow, D. and Lively, M. "Studies in Insulin and Metrazol Therapy II: Differential Effects on Some Psychological Functions." *Journal of Personality*, **14**, 125–149 (1945b).

Schossberger, J. A. "Deanimation. A study of the communication of meaning by transient expressive configuration." *Psychoanalytic Quarterly*, **22**, 479–532 (1963).

Searles, H. F. *Collected Papers on Schizophrenia and Related Subjects*. New York: International Universities Press, 1965.

Sechehaye, M. *A New Psychotherapy in Schizophrenia*. New York: Grune and Stratton, 1956.

Sechehaye, M. *Autobiography of a Schizophrenic Girl*. New York: Signet Books, New American Library, 1970.

Semmes, J. "Hemispheric Specialization: A Possible Clue to Mechanism." *Neuropsychologica*, **6**, 11–26 (1968).

Semmes, J. "Protopathic and Epicritic Sensation: A Reappraisal." In A. I. Benton, Ed., *Contributions to Clinical Neuropsychology*. Chicago: Aldine, 1969, pp. 142–171.

Senf, R. Huston, P. E., and Cohen, B. "Thinking Deficit in Schizophrenia and Changes with Amytal." *The Journal of Abnormal and Social Psychology*, **50**, 383–387 (1955).

Senf, R., Huston, P. E., and Cohen, B. "The Use of Comic Cartoons for the Study of Social Comprehension in Schizophrenia." *American Journal of Psychiatry*, **113**, 45–51 (1956).

Shakow, D. "A Study of Certain Aspects of Motor Coordination in Schizophrenia with the Prodmeter." *Psychological Bulletin*, **29**, 661 (1932).

Shakow, D. "The Nature of Deterioration in Schizophrenic Conditions." *Nerv. Ment. Dis. Monogr.*, **70**, 1–88 (1946).

Shakow, D. "Some Psychological Features of Schizophrenia." In M. L. Reymert (Ed.), *Feelings and Emotions*. New York: McGraw-Hill, 1950, pp. 383–390.

Shakow, D. "The Psychological System." In R. R. Grinker (Ed.), *Toward a Unified Theory of Human Behavior*. New York: Basic Books, 1956, pp. 181–189.

Shakow, D. "Normalisierungstendenzen bei Chronisch Schizophrenen: Konsequenzen fur die Theorie der Schizophrenie." ('Normalization' Trends in Chronic Schizophrenic Patients: Some Implications for Schizophrenia Theory.) *Schweitz. A. Psychol. Anwend.*, **17**, 285–299 (1958).

Shakow, D. "Segmental Set: A Theory of the Formal Psychological Deficit in Schizophrenia." *Archives of General Psychiatry*, **6**, 1–17 (1962).

Shakow, D. "Psychological Deficit in Schizophrenia." *Behavioral Science*, **8**, 275–305 (1963).

Shakow, D. "Some Psychophysiological Aspects of Schizophrenia." In J. Romano (Ed.), *The Origins of Schizophrenia*. Amsterdam: Excerpta Medica Foundation, 1967.

Shakow, D. "Contributions from Schizophrenia to the Understanding of Normal Psychological Function." In M. Simmel (Ed.), *The Reach of Mind, Essays in Memory of Kurt Goldstein, 1878–1965*. New York: Springer, 1968.

Shakow, D. "On Doing Research in Schizophrenia." *Archives of General Psychiatry*, **20**, 618–642 (1969).

Shakow, D. "Discussion of Holzman and Silverman's Contributions on Perception in Schizophrenia." Unpublished, 1970.

Shakow, D. "The Worcester State Hospital Research on Schizophrenia (1927–1946)." *Journal of Abnormal Psychology*, **80**, 67–110 (1972).

Shakow, D. "Some Implications for Psychology of Recent Studies of Older Parts of the Brain." (Unpublished)

Shakow, D. and Huston, P. E. "Studies of Motor Function in Schizophrenia. II. Speed of Tapping." *Journal of General Psychology*, **15**, 63–106 (1936).

Shakow, D. and Jellinek, E. M. "Composite Index of the Kent-Rosanoff Free Association Test." *Journal of Abnormal Psychology*, **70**, 403–404 (1965).

Shakow, D. and McCormick, M. Y. "Mental Set in Schizophrenia Studied in a Discrimination Reaction Setting." *Journal of Personality and Social Psychology*, **1**, 88-95 (1965).

Shakow, D. and Rosenzweig, S. "Play Technique in Schizophrenia and Other Psychoses. II: An Experimental Study of Schizophrenic Constructions with Play Materials." *American Journal of Orthopsychiatry*, **7**, 36–47 (1937).

Shakow, D. and Rosenzweig, S. "The Use of the Tautophone ('Verbal Summator') as an Auditory Apperceptive Test for the Study of Personality." *Character and Personality*, **8**, 216–226 (1940).

Shakow, D., Rosenzweig, S. and Hollander, L. "Auditory Apperceptive Reactions to the Tautophone by Schizophrenic and Normal Subjects." *Journal of Nervous and Mental Disease*, **143**, 1–15 (1966).

Shands, H. C. "Novelty as Object: Precis for a General Psychological Theory." *Archives of General Psychiatry*, **17**, 1–4 (1967).

Shands, H. C. "Outline of a General Theory of Human Communication." In *Semiotic Approaches to Psychiatry*. The Hague, The Netherlands: Mouton, 1970a, pp. 305–349.

Shands, H. C. *Semiotic Approaches to Psychiatry*. The Hague, The Netherlands: Mouton, 1970b.

Shands, H. C. "Schizophrenia and the Once-Objective Universe." *Language Sciences*, **32**, 1–6 (1974).

Shimkunas, A. M. "Reciprocal Shifts in Schizophrenic Thought Processes." *Journal of Abnormal Psychology*, **76**, 423–426 (1970).

Shimkunas, A. M., Gynther, M. D., and Smith, K. "Schizophrenic Responses to the Proverbs Test: Abstract, Concrete, or Autistic?" *Journal of Abnormal and Social Psychology*, **72**, 128–133 (1967).

Simmel, M. L. "On Re-reading Lashley's 'The Thalamus and Emotion.'" Presented at the 4th Annual Meeting of the Psychonomic Society, 1963.

Simmel, M. L. "Mime and Reason: Notes on the Creation of the Perceptual Object." *Journal of Aesthetics and Art Criticism*, **31**, 193–200 (1972).

Slater, E. and Beard, A. W. "The Schizophrenia-like Psychoses of Epilepsy." *British Journal of Psychiatry*, **109**, 95–150 (1963).

Smythies, J. R. "Brain Mechanisms and Behavior." *Brain*, **90**, 697–706 (1967).

Southard, E. E. and Stearns, A. W. "The Margin of Error in Psychopathic Hospital Diagnosis." *Boston Medical and Surgical Journal*, **171**, 895–900 (1914).

Spearman, C. *The Abilities of Man*. New York: Macmillan, 1927.

Spitzer, R. L., Endicott, J., Cohen, J., and Fliess, J. L. "Constraints on the Validity of Computer Diagnosis." *Archives of General Psychiatry*, **31**, 197–203 (1974).

Spitzer, R. L., Endicott, J., and Robins, E. "Clinical Criteria for Psychiatric Diagnosis and DSM-III." *American Journal of Psychiatry*, **132**, 1187–1192 (1975).

Stanley, W. C. "Introduction of Maladaptive Behavior by Experimental

Manipulation of Feeding Experience in Infant Dogs." In J. F. Bosma (Ed.), *Third Symposium on Oral Sensation and Perception: The Mouth of the Infant.* Springfield, Ill.: Thomas, 1972, pp. 400–419.

Stanley, W. C. and Bacon, E. F. "Stimuli Controlling Maladaptive Consummatory Behavior in Infant Dogs." *Journal of Abnormal Psychology,* **84,** 151-158 (1975).

Steffy, R. A. and Cromwell, R. L. "Temporal and Task Factors in Schizophrenia Deficit." Unpublished.

Steiner, G. Review of *Caught in the Web of Words,* K. M. Elizabeth Murray (Yale, 1977), published in *The New Yorker,* November 21, 1977.

Steiner, G. "A Note on Language and Psychoanalysis." *International Review of Psycho-Analysis,* **3,** 253 (1976).

Steinhart, M. J. "The selling of Community Mental Health." *Psychiatric Quarterly,* **47,** 325-340 (1973).

Storch, A. "The Primitive Archaic Forms of Inner Experiences and Thought in Schizophrenia." *Nervous and Mental Disease Monograph,* (**36** (1924).

Strachey, J. (Ed.) *The Standard Edition of the Complete Psychological Works of Sigmund Freud,* Vol. 28 (1920–1922). London: Hogarth Press, 1955.

Strachey, J. (Ed.) *The Standard Edition of the Complete Psychological Works of Sigmund Freud,* Vol. 1. London: Hogarth Press, 1966.

Strauss, J. S. "A Comprehensive Approach to Psychiatric Diagnosis." *American Journal of Psychiatry,* **132,** 1193-1197 (1975).

Strauss, J. S., Carpenter, W. T., and Bartko, J. J. "A Review of Some Findings from the International Pilot Study of Schizophrenia." In R. Cancro (Ed.), *Annual Review of the Schizophrenic Syndrome (1974–1975).* New York: Brunner/Mazel, 1976, pp. 74–88.

Sullivan, H. S. *The Interpersonal Theory of Psychiatry.* New York: Norton, 1953.

Sullivan, H. S. *Schizophrenia as a Human Process.* New York: Norton, 1962.

Sullivan, H. S. "The Onset of Schizophrenia." In *Schizophrenia as a Human Process.* New York: Norton, 1962 [Reprinted from *American Journal of Psychiatry,* **84,** 105–134 (1928)] pp. 104–136.

Sullivan, H. S. *Personal Psychopathology.* New York: Norton, 1972.

Taine, H. A. *De l'Intelligence,* 1870.

Tanji, J. and Evarts, E. V. "Anticipatory Activity of Motor Cortex Neurons in Relation to the Direction of an Intended Movement." *Journal of Neurophysiology,* **39,** 1062–1068 (1976).

Test, M. A. and Stein, L. I. "Community Treatment of the Chronic Patient: Research Overview." *Schizophrenia Bulletin,* **4,** 350–364 (1978).

Tharp, L. H. *The Peabody Sisters of Salem.* Boston: Little, Brown, 1950.

Thompson, R. F. "The Search for the Engram." *American Psychologist,* **31,** 209–227 (1976).

Thurstone, L. L. "Current Misuse of the Factorial Methods." *Psychometrika*, **2**, 73–76 (1937).

Titchener, E. B. *Lectures on the Experimental Psychology of the Thought Processes*. New York: Macmillan, 1909.

Twain, M. "The Awful German Language." In *A Tramp Abroad*. Hartford, Connecticut: American Publishing Co., 1880.

Uznadze, D. N. *The Psychology of Set*. New York: Consultants Bureau, 1966.

Uznadze, D. N. and Bassin, R. V. "Consciousness and the Unconscious." In M. Cole and I. Maltzman (Eds.), *A Handbook of Contemporary Soviet Psychology*. New York: Basic Books, 1969.

Vaillant, G. E. *Adaptation to Life*. Boston: Little, Brown, 1977.

Van Ormer, F. B. "Retention after Intervals of Sleep and Waking." *Archives of Psychology*, **137**, 49 (1932).

Venables, P. H. and Tizard, J. "Performance of Functional Psychotics on a Repetitive Task." *Journal of Abnormal and Social Psychology*, **53**, 23–26 (1956).

Vonnegut, M. *The Eden Express*. New York: Praeger Publishers, 1975.

Walshe, F. M. R. "The Anatomy and Physiology of Cutaneous Sensibility." *Brain*, **65**, 48–112 (1942).

Washburn, S. L. "Human Behavior and the Behavior of Other Animals." *American Psychologist*, **33**, 405–418 (1978).

Warren H. C. *Dictionary of Psychology*. Boston: Houghton Mifflin, 1934.

Webster's New International Dictionary of the English Language 2nd ed. Springfield, Mass.: Merriam-Webster, 1944.

Weckowicz, T. E. and Sommer, R. "Body image and Self-concept in Schizophrenia." *The Journal of Mental Science*, **106**, 17–39 (1960).

Weiss, P. "Deformities as Cues to Understanding Development of Form." *Perspectives in Biology and Medicine*, **4**, 133–151 (1961).

Wegrocki, H. J. "Generalizing Ability in Schizophrenia. An Inquiry into the Disorders of Problem Thinking in Schizophrenia." *Archives of Psychology*, **254** (1940).

Werner, H. *Comparative Psychology of Mental Development* (rev. ed.). New York: Follett, 1948.

Werner, H. and Kaplan, B. *Symbol Formation: An Organismic-Developmental Approach to Language and the Expression of Thought*. New York: Wiley, 1963.

Wheeler, J. A. "The Universe as Home for Man." *American Scientist*, **62**, 683–691 (1974).

White, R. W. "Motivation Reconsidered: The Concept of Competence." *Psychological Review*, **66**, 297–333 (1959).

White, R. W. "Competence and the Psychosexual Stages of Development." *Nebraska Symposium on Motivation*. Lincoln, Nebraska: University of Nebraska Press, 1960.

White, R. W. "Ego and Reality in Psychoanalytic Theory." *Psychological Issues,* **3,** Monograph 11 (1963).

White, R. W. "The Experience of Efficacy in Schizophrenia." *Psychiatry,* **28,** 199–211 (1965).

Whitehead, A. N. *An Introduction to Mathematics.* New York: Oxford University Press, 1958.

Wilder, J. *Stimulus and Response: The Law of Initial Value.* Bristol: John Wright & Sons, 1967.

Wilson, E. B. and Deming, J. "Statistical Comparison of Psychiatric Diagnosis of Some Massachusetts State Hospitals during 1925 and 1926." *Quart. Bull. Mass. Dept. Ment. Dis.,* **11,** 1–15 (1927).

Wishner, J. "The Concept of Efficiency in Psychological Health and in Psychopathology." *Psychological Review,* **62,** 69–80 (1955).

Wishner, J. "Efficiency in Schizophrenia." *Bulletin de l'Association Internationale de Psychologie Appliquee,* **14,** (1–2), 30–46 (1965).

Wolters, A. W. "On Conceptual Thinking." *British Journal of General Psychology,* **24,** 133–143 (1933).

Wolters, A. W. "The Patterns of Experience." *British Association for Advancement of Sciences,* (1936), pp. 181–188.

Woodworth, R. S. *Psychology* (rev. ed.). New York: Holt, 1929.

Woodworth, R. S. *Experimental Psychology.* New York: Holt, 1938.

Wyatt, R. J. "Biochemistry and Schizophrenia. Part IV: The neuroleptics— Their Mechanism of Action: A review of the Biochemical Literature." *Psychopharmacology Bulletin,* **12,** 167–242 (1976).

Wynne, L. C., Cromwell, R. L., and Matthysse, S. *The Nature of Schizophrenia.* New York: Wiley, 1978.

Zahn, T. P. "Autonomic Reactivity and Behavior in Schizophrenia." *Psychiat. Res. Rep. Amer. Psychiat. Assn.,* **19,** 156–173 (1964).

Zahn, T. P. "Effects of Reduction in Uncertainty on Reaction Time in Schizophrenic and Normal Subjects." *Journal of Experimental Research in Personality,* **4,** 135–143 (1970).

Zahn, T. P. Comments on "Reaction time and attention in schizophrenia." *Schizophrenia Bulletin,* **3,** 452–456 (1977).

Zahn, T. P., Rosenthal, D., and Lawlor, W. G. "Electrodermal and Heart Rate Orienting Reactions in Chronic Schizophrenia." *Journal of Psychiatric Research,* **6,** 117–134 (1968).

Zahn, T. P., Rosenthal, D., and Shakow, D. "Reaction Time in Schizophrenic and Normal Subjects in Relation to the Sequence of Series of Regular Preparatory Intervals." *Journal of Abnormal and Social Psychology,* **63,** 161–168 (1961).

Zahn, T. P., Rosenthal, D., and Shakow, D. "Effects of Irregular Preparatory Intervals on Reaction Time in Schizophrenia." *Journal of Abnormal and Social Psychology,* **67,** 44–52 (1963).

REFERENCES IN APPENDIX C

Allport, F. H. *Theories of Perception and the Concept of Structure.* New York: Wiley, 1955.

Bartlett, F. C. *Remembering: A Study in Experimental and Social Psychology.* Cambridge at the University Press, 1932.

Boring, E. G. *A History of Experimental Psychology,* 2nd ed. New York: Appleton-Century-Crofts, 1950.

Brain, W. R. "The Concept of the Schema in Neurology and Psychiatry." In D. Richter (Ed.), *Perspectives in Neuropsychiatry.* London: Lewis, 1950.

Broadbent, D. E. *Perception and Communication.* New York: Pergamon Press, 1958.

Broadbent, D. E. *Decision and Stress.* London and New York: Academic, 1971.

Bruner, J. S. "One Kind of Perception: A Reply to Professor Luchins." *Psychological Review,* **58,** 306–312 (1951a).

Bruner, J. S. "Personality Dynamics and the Process of Perceiving." In R. R. Blake and G. V. Ramsey (Eds.), *Perception: An Approach to Personality.* New York: Ronald, 1951b.

Bruner, J. S. and Goodman, C. C. "Value and Need as Organizing Factors in Perception." *Journal of Abnormal and Social Psychology,* **42,** 33–44 (1947).

Bruner, J. S. and Krech, D. (Eds.) *Perception and Personality: A Symposium.* New York: Greenwood Press, 1968. [Reprinted from *Journal of Personality,* **18,** 1–2 (1949).]

Bruner, J. S. and Postman, L. "Tension and Tension Release as Organizing Factors in Perception." *Journal of Personality,* **15,** 300–308 (1947).

Bruner, J. S. and Postman, L. "Symbolic Value as an Organizing Factor in Perception." *Journal of Social Psychology,* **27,** 203–208 (1948).

Bruner, J. S. and Postman, L. "On the Perception of Incongruity: A Paradigm." *Journal of Personality,* **18,** 206–223 (1949a).

Bruner, J. S. and Postman, L. "Perception, Cognition, and Behavior." *Journal of Personality,* **18,** 14–31 (1949b).

Dashiell, J. F. *Fundamentals of Objective Psychology.* Boston: Houghton Mifflin, 1928.

Dashiell, J. F. *Fundamentals of General Psychology.* Boston: Houghton Mifflin, 1937.

Dashiell, J. F. "A Neglected Fourth Dimension to Psychological Research." *Psychological Review,* **47,** 289–305 (1940).

Davis, R. C. "The Relation of Certain Muscle Action Potentials to 'Mental Work.'" *Indiana University Publications: Science Series,* No. 5, 1937.

Davis, R. C. "The Relation of Muscle Action Potentials to Difficulty and Frustration." *Journal of Experimental Psychology*, 23, 141–158 (1938).

Davis, R. C. "Patterns of Muscular Activity during 'Mental Work' and their Constancy." *Journal of Experimental Psychology*, 24, 451–465 (1939).

Davis, R. C. "Set and Muscular Tension." *Indiana University Publications: Science Series*, No. 10, 1940.

Davis, R. C. "The Genetic Development of Patterns of Voluntary Activity." *Journal of Experimental Psychology*, 33, 471–486 (1943).

Davis, R. C. "The Psychophysiology of Set." In P. L. Harriman (Ed.), *Twentieth Century Psychology*. New York: Philosophical Library, 1946.

Freeman, G. L. "Mental Acitvity and the Muscular Processes." *Psychological Review*, 38, 428–449 (1931a).

Freeman, G. L. "The Spread of Neuro-Muscular Activity during Mental Work." *Journal of General Psychology*, 5, 479–493 (1931b).

Freeman, G. L. "The Facilitative and Inhibitory Effects of Muscular Tension upon Performance." *American Journal of Psychology*, 45, 17–52 (1933).

Freeman, G. L. "The Optimal Muscular Tensions for Various Performances." *American Journal of Psychology*, 51, 146–150 (1938a).

Freeman, G. L. "The Postural Substrate." *Psychological Review*, 45, 324–334 (1938b).

Freeman, G. L. "The Problem of Set." *American Journal of Psychology*, 52, 16–30 (1939).

Freeman, G. L. " 'Central' vs. 'Peripheral' Locus of Set; A Critique of the Mowrer, Rayman, and Bliss 'demonstration.' " *Journal of Experimental Psychology*, 26, 622–628 (1940a).

Freeman, G. L. "Concerning the 'Field' in 'Field' Psychology." *Psychological Review*, 47, 416–424 (1940b).

Freeman, G. L. *The Energetics of Human Behavior*. Ithaca, New York: Cornell University Press, 1948.

Freeman, G. L. and Kendall, W. E. "The Effect upon Reaction Time of Muscular Tension Induced at Various Preparatory Intervals." *Journal of Experimental Psychology*, 27, 136–148 (1940).

Gibson, J. J. "A Critical Review of the Concept of Set in Contemporary Experimental Psychology." *Psychological Bulletin*. 38, 781–817 (1941).

Haber, R. N. "Nature of the Effect of Set on Perception." *Psychological Review*, 73, 335–351 (1966).

Head, H. *Studies in Neurology* (2 volumes). London: Henry Frowde and Hodder & Stoughton (Oxford University Press), 1920.

Head, H. and Holmes, G. "Sensory Disturbances from Cerebral Lesions." In H. Head, *Studies in Neurology*, Vol. II. London: Henry Frowde and Hodder & Stoughton (Oxford University Press), 1920.

Hearnshaw, L. S. *A Short History of British Psychology 1840–1940*. London: Methuen, 1964.

James, W. *The Principles of Psychology* (2 volumes). New York: Holt, 1890.

Kahneman, D. *Attention and Effort*. Englewood Cliffs, New Jersey: Prentice-Hall, 1973.

Luchins, A. S. "An Evaluation of Some Current Criticisms of Gestalt Psychological Work on Perception." *Psychological Review*, **58**, 69–95 (1951).

Mowrer, O. H., Rayman, N. N., and Bliss, E. L. "Preparatory Set (expectancy)—an Experimental Demonstration of its 'Central' Locus." *Journal of Experimental Psychology*, **26**, 357–372 (1940).

Neisser, U. *Cognitive Psychology*. New York: Appleton-Century-Crofts, 1967.

Neisser, U. *Cognition and Reality: Principles and Implications of Cognitive Psychology*. San Francisco, Ca. W. H. Freeman, 1976.

Northway, M. L. "The Concept of the 'Schema.'" *British Journal of Psychology* (Gen), **30**, 316–325 (1940).

Oldfield, R. C. "Memory Mechanisms and the Theory of Schemata." *British Journal of Psychology*, **45**, 14–23 (1954).

Oldfield, R. C. and Zangwill, O. L. "Head's Concept of the Schema and its Application in Contemporary British Psychology." *British Journal of Psychology* (Gen):
Part I. Head's Concept of the Schema. 32, 267–286 (1942).
Part II. Critical analysis of Head's theory. 33, 58–64 (1943).
Part III. Bartlett's theory of memory. 33, 113–129 (1943).
Part IV. Wolters' theory of thinking. 33, 143–149 (1943).

Paul, I. H. "Studies in Remembering: The Reproduction of Connected and Extended Verbal Material." *Psychological Issues*, **1**, (2), Monograph 2 (1959).

Paul, I. H. "The Concept of Schema in Memory Theory." In R. R. Holt (Ed.), "Motives and Thought: Psychoanalytic Essays in Honor of David Rapaport." *Psychological Issues*, **5**, (2–3), Monograph 18/19 (1967).

Pillsbury, W. B. *The Essentials of Psychology* (rev. ed.). New York: Macmillan, 1920.

Postman, L. "Toward a General Theory of Cognition." In J. H. Rohrer and M. Sherif (Eds.), *Social Psychology at the Crossroads*. New York: Harper, 1951.

Postman, L. and Bruner, J. S. "Multiplicity of Set as a Determinant of Perceptual Behavior." *Journal of Experimental Psychology*, **39**, 369–377 (1949).

Postman, L., Bruner, J. S., and McGinnies, E. "Personal Values as Selective Factors in Perception." *Journal of Abnormal and Social Psychology*, **43**, 142–154 (1948).

Postman, L., Bruner, J. S., and Walk, R. D. "The Perception of Error." *British Journal of Psychology* (Gen), **42**, 1–10 (1951).

Postman, L. and Postman, D. L. "Change in Set as a Determinant of Retroactive Inhibition." *American Journal of Psychology*, **61**, 236–242 (1948).

Postman, L. and Schneider, B. H. "Personal Values, Visual Recognition, and Recall." *Psychological Review*, **58**, 271–284 (1951).

Postman, L. and Senders, V. L. "Incidental Learning and Generality of Set." *Journal of Experimental Psychology*, **36**, 153–165 (1946).

Steinfeld, G. J. "Concepts of Set and Availability and their Relation to the Reorganization of Ambiguous Pictorial Stimuli." *Psychological Review*, **74**, 505–522 (1967).

Vernon, M. D. *A Further Study of Visual Perception*. Cambridge at the University Press, 1952.

Vernon, M. D. "The Functions of Schemata in Perceiving." *Psychological Review*, **62**, 180–192 (1955).

Vernon, M. D. "Cognitive Inference in Perceptual Activity." *British Journal of Psychology*, **48**, 35–47 (1957).

Wapner, S. and Werner, H. *Perceptual Development: An Investigation within the Framework of Sensory-tonic Field Theory*. Worcester, Massachusetts: Clark University Press, 1957 (Clark University Monographs in Psychology and Related Disciplines, No. 2).

Werner, H. and Kaplan, B. *Symbol Formation: An Organismic-Developmental Approach to Language and the Expression of Thought*. New York: Wiley, 1963.

Werner, H. and Wapner, S. "Sensory-Tonic Field Theory of Perception." *Journal of Personality*, **18**, 88–107 (1949).

Werner, H. and Wapner, S. "Toward a General Theory of Perception." *Psychological Review*, **59**, 324–338 (1952).

Wolters, A. W. "On Conceptual Thinking." *British Journal of Psychology* (Gen), **24**, 133–143 (1933).

Wolters, A. W. "The Patterns of Experience." *Report of the British Association for the Advancement of Science*, 1936, pp. 181–188.

Wolters, A. W. "Some Biological Aspects of Thinking." *British Journal of Psychology*, (Gen), **33**, 176–183 (1943).

Woodworth, R. S. *Psychology* (rev. ed.). New York: Holt, 1929.

Woodworth, R. S. "Situation-and-goal set." *American Journal of Psychology*, **50**, 130–140 (1937).

Zangwill, O. L. "A Study of the Significance of Attitude in Recognition." *British Journal of Psychology* (Gen), **28**, 12–17 (1937).

Author Index

233

Hoskins, R. G., 44, 100, 101, 142, 144
Hovland, C. I., 109
Hritzuk, J., 10
Huebner, D. M., 85
Hurt, S. W., 52
Huston, P. E., 3, 35, 51, 64, 96, 102, 106, 107, 111, 112, 120, 180

Jackson, D. D., 150
Jackson, J. H., 91
James, H., 56
James, W., 1, 7, 8, 13, 37, 40-42, 45-49, 54, 56, 75, 78, 88, 96, 97, 119, 130, 185, 186, 206
Jelliffe, S. E., 163
Jellinek, E. M., 85, 100, 101, 111, 176, 177
Jenkins, J. C., 109

Kahneman, D., 6, 54, 192
Kant, I., 124, 186
Kaplan, B., 8, 12, 204, 207, 208
Kasanin, J. S., 110, 160, 161
Kaufman, B. N., 80, 127
Kedward, H. B., 4
Kempf, E. J., 160, 163
Kendall, W. E., 194
Kent, G. H., 1, 85
Kerr, J., 118
Kety, S., 100
Kip, E. S., 182
Kirk, S. A., 133
Klein, G. S., 52
Kohlber, L., 126
Konorski, J., 68
Kovach, J. K., 7
Kraepelin, E., 159, 163
Krech, D., 198
Kris, E., 130
Külpe, O., 35, 185

Laing, R. D., 124
Landau, S. G., 74
Lang, P. J., 65
Lange, N., 185
Langer, S., 151
Langfeld, H. S., 1
Lashley, K. S., 82, 108, 109
Lawlor, W. G., 43, 77, 104, 106
Lebeaux, T., 105
Leibnitz, G., 185

Levy, D. L., 52
Lewes, G. S., 7, 8, 40, 185
Lewin, K., 10, 43, 88
Lilly, A., 149
Lilly, J. C., 149
Limbar, J., 149
Linder, F. E., 101
Lively, M., 102
Livingston, R. B., 94
Looney, J. M., 101
Lowrey, L. G., 158
Luchins, A. S., 198
Luria, A. R., 10, 180

MacDonald, N., 42, 59
Malamud, N., 25
Maltzman, I., 9
Masten, A. S., 6, 8, 16, 183
Matthiessen, F. O., 56
Matthysse, S., 1, 13, 110
Maudsley, H., 185
May, J. V., 158
McCormick, M. Y., 106
McDougall, W., 21
McGeoch, J. A., 109
McGinnies, E., 199
McGuiness, D., 71
McWhirter, N., 11
McWhirter, R., 11
Melnechuk, T. J., 73
Meltzer, H. J., 147
Meltzer, H. Y., 52
Menninger, K., 52, 144
Meyer, A., 160
Milner, M., 144, 145, 151
Montaigne, M., 121
Moriarity, A. E., 137
Mowrer, O. H., 197
Mullahy, P., 68
Murchison, C., 2
Murphy, G., 7
Murphy, L. B., 137
Murray, K. M. E., 11

Nabokov, V., 87
Neisser, U., 6, 54, 68, 192, 197, 201ff, 203, 207, 208
Nietzsche, F. W., 124
Northway, M. L., 187, 189
Nuechterlein, K. H., 118

Subject Index